T0222227

Strategy, Planning and Organization
of Test Processes

Frank Witte

Strategy, Planning and Organization of Test Processes

Basis for Successful Project Execution in Software Testing

 Springer

Frank Witte
Landshut, Germany

ISBN 978-3-658-36980-4   ISBN 978-3-658-36981-1   (eBook)
https://doi.org/10.1007/978-3-658-36981-1

Foreword

With my first book *Softwaretest und Testmanagement* (*Software Test and Test Management*), I dealt with an overview of the entire testing process, and with my book *Metriken für das Testreporting* (*Metrics of Test Reporting*), I presented analyses and suitable procedures that are used during and at the end of the testing process for control and monitoring. With the present book, I would like to deal more with the beginning of the test process, I mainly describe a test phase where a test object does not necessarily exist yet and that evolves around test strategy, test conception, and planning. The organization and planning of projects basically extend over the entire project period, as it must be constantly adapted to new circumstances. However, one focus is on the concept phase at the beginning of the project.

Back in the day, there were still companies that seriously questioned the need for software system testing. After all, that has changed due to awareness across the board, whether it is a small business or a corporation. Every professional software developer learns in college how to test their software. Depending on whether it is a first release or an update, it is important to test the software as a whole or as part of regression testing as long as it makes sense. Not doing so is similar to a surgeon discussing whether disinfecting his hands before surgery is really necessary.

In project management, the rule is that 25–35% of the expected total project duration should be spent on planning. The clearer the objectives, framework conditions, and requirements are described, the easier and faster the project can be implemented later. Just as project planning is the main task of project management, well-thought-out and sound test planning is also key to a successful test project.

This book deals with strategy, planning, and organization of test processes.

Strategy was originally understood as the art of army command. Clausewitz further developed the military concept politically and economically. In business, the planned behaviors of companies to achieve their goals are understood as strategy. Consequently, a test strategy defines framework conditions and procedures but also necessary individual activities for a project, which are required for the successful implementation of the goal.

Planning is essential to shape the future and has to consider which means can be used to achieve which goal. For software testing, this means that goals, resources, and processes must be defined and documented. Thanks to planning, processes are constantly determined that are run in a structured manner in the operational environment. The results of planning are constantly implemented in the organization. This means that test processes must be continuously controlled, that is, the current test progress must be permanently compared with the planning, and corrective measures must be initiated if necessary.

A test concept is created for planning test activities in a software project. The test concept can be compared to a construction plan. The structure of the book is therefore based on the structure of a test concept according to the IEE829 standard. In addition, I provide guidance on test strategy, project and test planning, and methods for evaluation. New trends such as agile or cognitive testing also have an impact on the test organization.

The definition "IEEE 829 Standard for Software Test Documentation" is a standard published by the IEEE (Institute of Electrical and Electronic Engineers), which describes a set of eight basic documents for the documentation of software tests. The current version is IEEE 829-2008. The structure according to IEEE 829 can be adapted and extended, and not all parts are relevant to the same extent. However, it is useful to use it as a rough guideline and compass.

The test concept determines the delimitation, procedure, and means used and contains a schedule of the test activities. The test concept identifies the test objects, the features to be tested, and the test tasks. It forms the basis on which the test organization and the test infrastructure are provided, and the tests are performed.

In earlier times, testing activities usually started at a later stage of the project. This meant that the test department was faced with scheduling conflicts right from the start. Meanwhile, it has become widely accepted that the test manager should be involved in the project from the very beginning, that is, they should accompany the development process from the very beginning, and that the planning phase should therefore take place at the start of the project. Consequently, the test concept should also be created before or while the system development is in progress and the project phase of defining suitable test cases and the test execution phase have not yet begun.

The same applies to test planning as to the overall planning of projects: for efficient and effective project planning, a "rolling" approach is recommended. This means that at the beginning of the project, a rough plan is made for the entire project, which is then outlined in detail for each individual upcoming project phase. The advantages of this approach are that knowledge gained during the investigation can be incorporated into the planning and the planning effort remains reasonable [ORGH2019].

In the following, however, I would not only like to show the contents of the test concept like from a textbook but also point out the pitfalls and peculiarities in practice from experience. Already during the development of the test concept one can, with practiced observation, recognize risks arising during the project in advance and define possible countermeasures from the beginning. You can point out the weaknesses in the process and make the framework conditions transparent to be prepared from the outset if problems arise. The point is not to be a driven person in reaction mode as a test manager but to be able to act actively right from the start.

Every test project is embedded in a particular environment, and I recommend that every test manager first understand the context and the particular issues involved:

On the one hand, there is the issue of personnel: Are there enough testers available at all? Are the testers basically motivated? Are certain resources overloaded from experience? How is the workload over time? If an employee is planned with a capacity of 40 working days from 1 March to 30 April, but his work package has prerequisites that are not available until 15 March and the employee already has to deliver his test results on 15 April, he is massively overloaded at times, although the overall availability is correct. Are there (possibly from the past) personal differences in the team or coalitions? Are the employees exclusively available for the project, or do different projects access the individual testers? It is important to consider that each stakeholder makes communication more complicated: With only 10 stakeholders, there are 45 communication channels between all stakeholders, with 20 there are already 190. Especially, the "grapevine" can destroy a lot in larger organizational units.

Who will conduct the test, are the testers experienced or new to the project? Are they motivated or rather disillusioned, or do they perhaps even make a bad mood against the project? Are there personal differences within the stakeholders or alliances in the company, for example, developers versus testers?

What is the status of the project, is it politically desired, is it a high priority? Does the project have supporters in the company, or is it possible that it is being slowed down, blocked, or put on the back burner due to other priorities? Are there other projects with a higher priority, are a prerequisite for the upcoming project, or perhaps even contradict it?

Are there technical risks, innovations, or unknown side effects? A change of servers or data storage in the cloud is usually not directly related to the software under test, but in many cases, there are effects. A change in databases, for example, is similar. Are there other projects running in parallel that have a technical or business impact on your own project, or is the project under consideration even at their mercy? Which requirements have to be met to start certain activities at all or to be able to carry them out successfully? Do other projects depend on your own project?

How did projects work in the past? Are there company-specific or industry-specific problems? Are there "lessons learned protocols" for this?

A test manager who comes into a project from the outside (e.g., externally) often does not know enough about the technical and specialist features and the strengths and weaknesses of the individual employees. Someone who has been with the company for a long time may know all this, but again may be biased because of experiences from previous projects. What is the position of the test department in the company? Is it strong, or is testing rather considered as a necessary evil that ekes out a shadowy existence?

In the past, application testing was often seen as a necessary but not very useful appendage of classic software development projects. This view has changed, not least against the background that testing, considered over the lifecycle of an application, takes up between 25 and 50% of the total costs incurred. Software quality problems can also have serious consequences, such as a quality-related project delay, which often extends the time-to-market. Major commercial and material damage can occur if, for example, a booking platform fails for software-related reasons, important data is lost or falsified, or security gaps in the system lead to the theft of customer or credit card information. In addition, the ever-closer integration of business and IT increases the demands on time-to-market and quality, which increases the pressure on the test organizations to perform. At the same time, systems and IT landscapes are becoming increasingly complex, and software development and life cycles are becoming faster. In addition, regulatory and security requirements are becoming more stringent. In this respect, it is only logical that application testing has been one of the current focus topics of IT for several years [IODT2019].

From my point of view, unclear task definitions are a major concern in numerous test projects. Many of the communication problems are caused by the fact that the test object is not exactly defined from the start, how it is to be delimited, and what the expectations of the software test are. Experience has shown that requirements which are incomplete, interpretable, or contain contradictory content are unfortunately the rule rather than the exception. These problems then lead to defects during development and queries and bugs in the test process.

What expectations does management have of the project? Are these expectations realistic in terms of deadlines, costs, and quality? Where is the responsibility for costs located? Especially the test manager, who is supposed to ensure the quality of the software, has to warn against overly optimistic expectations right from the start.

Only when the corresponding statements are backed up with figures do they become concretely tangible.

For the evaluation, I recommend always converting the existing risks into real euros. A statement like "the risk is €750.000 due to insufficient test coverage" is much more forceful than a statement like "probably 5% of the planned test cases cannot be tested on time."

Many questions can be asked in advance and considered at a suitable point in the test concept. I will name typical problem cases in the following chapters. In some cases, it is recommended to create corresponding "help documents" for this purpose.

This book is intended to help bring the testing concept to life. Sometimes, the test concept is only created for reasons of audit security. Sometimes, it exists as a theoretical document, but does not reflect the actual state of the testing activities. This wastes the opportunity to individually design the test process with the necessary pragmatism and to document it in a well-founded manner. A test concept with an alibi function does not serve its purpose.

The released version is a plan that you start with. It is normal to gain new insights during testing activities and thus no longer be able to test strictly according to the predefined path. You have to be flexible enough to proceed pragmatically, and there can always be good reasons to deviate from the original plan. But, in this case, it is also necessary to adapt the test concept afterwards so that the actual test procedure emerges from it. If a wall is added to a new house on the construction site or a door is moved, the construction plan must also be changed. The same applies to the test concept.

The more the individual team members refer to the test concept when they have unresolved questions about software testing, the more they deal with it and make critical comments, and the sooner the entire test project can be steered in the right direction. The test manager in particular has the responsibility to make sure that the test concept is changed, if necessary, when current developments overtake the plan. Often, one learns rather incidentally that certain assumptions defined in the test concept are not applicable at all.

The test concept is not a product that is created at the green table. A test manager does not sit in a quiet room like a musical genius and creates his great work. A test concept is developed step by step in dialogue with experts and those who will be affected by the project in the future. For small projects, a few working days may be enough (to be fair, it should be mentioned here that a test concept requires an average of 5 to 20 PT of effort, for particularly extensive projects (e.g., multi-projects or large software packages)) even significantly more. To develop a test concept, a large number of necessary questions must be clarified with the right experts. Of course, individual details still need to be worked out afterwards, but the most important things should be outlined and thought through together. Alternatively, a test manager, test coordinator, or test responsible (or whatever you want to call them) can clarify the questions in individual interviews and collect everything bit by bit [PERF2017].

In agile teams, where work is iterative, not all questions have to be answered in advance. It is also sufficient to address them and to tackle their solutions in order of priority. For example, it is hard to see why a team has to define exactly which test artifacts (test cases, test protocols, reports, ...) it wants to keep from the beginning. But if an acceptance test by the business department is required for the next release, it is better to book the target group already now (and thus inevitably commit oneself). The above standard in the form of a task list can visualize the necessary clarifications well and ensure that you do not solve or decide anything too late during iterations. Increasing agilization and future trends lead to new environmental conditions to which the test concept must also adapt.

A central point applies to all elaborations and determinations: You need the unconditional agreement of those involved! Only if there is a consensus in the company, it is at all possible to achieve the goals of quality assurance which are implemented thanks to tests.

In this context, it is particularly important to subject the test concept to a review and to define the review process precisely. Review meetings with all participants are essential for this. Simply sending a test concept around and waiting for feedback is not effective. Not everyone involved can say a few words on all points in the test concept, but if you only ask for feedback, you run the risk that individual pages are not even looked at because an invited reviewer for certain chapters considers someone else to be responsible for assessing the content. Paper doesn't blush. Especially with reviews, I have often observed that people think they don't have time and therefore want to shorten or refrain from necessary activities. In the end, however, they use up even more time – according to the motto "we have time to do things wrong three times but not to do them right once."

A review cycle is therefore not used to find defects in the concept alone but, above all, to obtain approval. You have to actively seek this approval. Many people make the mistake of slapping a concept on the table and then assuming that everyone will (obligingly) observe it. Systemically, the responsibility lies with the developer of the test concept, and they will have to take care of everything themselves, which rarely makes sense [PERF2017].

Every project should have its own test concept, depending on the scope of the project.

A project is defined by the DIN 69901 standard as follows: It is a project that is essentially characterized by the uniqueness of the conditions in their entirety – there is a concrete target for the project, it is limited in time, it requires specific resources (e.g. financial and personnel), there is an independent process organization that is distinct from the standard organization of the company, non-routine tasks are handled, it consists of at least three participants, and has a minimum duration of 4 weeks.

A project has a beginning and an end, unlike a process, which is continuous. A project structure plan (PDF) is divided into work packages in which the individual activities, that is, steps to be carried out, are described. Often, a milestone is set at the end of a work package – a point in time at which the progress of the project is analyzed and, if necessary, presented to the clients in a meeting. The project manager is responsible for monitoring the process, and all members of the project team must work with the project manager and are responsible for the tasks assigned to them. Crisis management and the creation of documentation are also part of the management tasks [KARB2019].

The test manager is responsible for the project management of all test levels, and they coordinate and monitor the test activities. A good cooperation and close regular coordination with the project manager should therefore be given, otherwise it will be difficult or impossible to achieve good progress and results in the test process. Differences with the project manager should not arise in the first place or must be resolved immediately. If the project manager and the test manager do not pull in the same direction, other stakeholders will quickly notice this and the productivity of the project will suffer, or even the entire project will fail.

However, it is also possible to create a generic test concept for the entire company or the entire organizational unit under consideration, especially if recurring activities are involved.

The IEEE 829 serves as a guideline, but it is necessary to adapt the test concept to the operational conditions and individual characteristics. I have already created a number of test concepts, which are similar in the rough structure but differ in focus depending on the industry, company, and test object.

Experience shows that there are numerous questions that can be clarified during the creation of the test concept. The more stakeholders are involved in the planning phase, the more attention and trust are generated in advance, before the actual test implementation begins.

With official specifications and standards, one usually assumes an optimal working environment. This is often not the case. Instead, from the very beginning, one has general conditions that negatively influence the project, such as unclear tasks, delayed deadlines, and a lack of know-how in the test team: communication problems are usually responsible for this. The examples in many textbooks assume ideal environmental conditions that do not exist in practice. In the following, I will go into detail about how software testing can still be successful or how the worst can be prevented, especially under difficult boundary conditions. Many projects do not reach their goal in time and budget, often because planning was too optimistic from the beginning and/or too few parameters were considered. However, it is possible to use suitable methods to ensure that delays, cost overruns, or quality deficiencies are at least significantly minimized. To achieve this, one must walk along the royal path between a planned, structured procedure and the necessary flexibility. A pragmatic approach to existing realities is just as important as compliance with rules and standards.

The scope of a test concept certainly depends on the size of the project. But even for small projects, you need to have a plan for how to proceed with testing and document the crucial framework data.

If information already exists or is maintained elsewhere, redundant descriptions should be avoided. A stakeholder list with names, department designations, and telephone numbers must be updated in the event of an operational reorganization. However, describing only the role and name and referencing a document that is maintained for it anyway can be better, especially for large projects. This also applies to schedules. Redundant data maintenance always involves the risk that different, and therefore contradictory, information is kept, on which to build.

It is recommended to prepare a template for the test concept for an organizational unit, that is, to perform tests more frequently. If individual parts should not be relevant, this can then be noted in a suitable point in this template. This way, nothing will be forgotten, and you will already get hints on what to think about when creating the test concept.

You can orientate yourself on similar projects from the past and examine weak points that occurred at that time already at the beginning of the project: if you already know that the provision of the test environment was delayed several times in earlier releases or if you already suspect that there will be repeated defects during the integration of certain components, you can already plan sufficient buffers during the planning phase and point out corresponding risks already at the beginning of the project.

It should be borne in mind that a good test organization and a well-thought-out test concept require time. The estimates for the effort required for this should be based on experience, project scope, and the purpose of the application. Here, it is important for the test manager to stand behind his figures, to give these activities the necessary importance in the company, and to put the brakes on some excessive optimism.

Landshut, Germany   Frank Witte

References

[KARB2019]: https://karrierebibel.de/projektarbeit, accessed on 9 May 2020

[PERF2017]: https://www.informatik-aktuell.de/entwicklung/methoden/das-perfekte-testkonzept-in-6-schritten.html, accessed on 9 May 2020

[IODT2019]: https://www.iot-design.de/allgemein/transformation-von-testorganisationen/, accessed on 9 May 2020

[ORGH2019]: https://www.orghandbuch.de/OHB/DE/Organisationshandbuch/2_Vorgehensmodell/21_Projektvorbereitung/212_Projektplanung/projektplanung-node.html, accessed on 9 May 2020

Contents

1 Test Documents According to IEEE 829 1
  1.1   Standards 1
  1.2   Test Concept. 2
  1.3   Test Specification. 3
  1.4   Test Reporting 4
  1.5   Integrity level 6
  References. 8

2 Test Strategy 9
  2.1   Characteristics of the Test Strategy 9
  2.2   Integration Strategy 13
  2.3   Test Specifications 13
  2.4   Use of Tools 14
  2.5   Questions on the Implementation of the Test Strategy 15
  2.6   Balanced Scorecard 16
  References. 19

3 Test Objectives. 21
  3.1   Importance of Test Objectives 21
  3.2   Test Parameters 23
  3.3   Test Reporting 24
  References. 27

4 Test Planning. 29
  4.1   Contents of Test Planning 29
  4.2   Sub-plans for IT Projects. 30
  4.3   Test Requirements 32
  4.4   General Conditions of the Test Planning 33
  4.5   Test Tools. 34
  4.6   Test Efforts and Test Automation. 34
  References. 35

5   Designation of the Test Concept and Introduction 37
   5.1   Designation and Storage of the Test Concept 37
   5.2   Test Concepts for a Longer Period of Time...................... 38
   5.3   Formal Principles.. 39
   5.4   Introduction Test Concept 40
   5.5   Documents Referenced in the Test Concept 42
   5.6   Test Framework with Test Requirements, Defect Classes
         and Start Conditions..................................... 46
   References... 47

6   Test Organization 49
   6.1   Essential Criteria of the Test Organization 49
   6.2   Test Personnel and Tester Deployment Planning.................. 52
   6.3   Computing Time 53
   6.4   Data Provision 54
   6.5   Hardware Required 54
   6.6   Project Organization 54
   6.7   Stakeholders and Roles in the Project Organization 55
   6.8   Organizational Structure 55
   6.9   Project Steering Committee................................. 55
   References... 57

7   Process Description... 59
   7.1   Test process According to ISTQB 59
   7.2   Planning and Control..................................... 60
   7.3   Meetings at the Start of the Project 61
   7.4   Analysis and Design 63
   7.5   Realization and Implementation 63
   7.6   Evaluation and Report 64
   7.7   Test Completion.. 64
   7.8   Documents as a Prerequisite for Testing 65
   References... 66

8   Test Objects and Test Phases 67
   8.1   Test Objects 67
   8.2   Test Phases.. 68
   8.3   Factors Influencing the Determination of the Test Effort 70
   References... 72

9   Test Levels 73
   9.1   Classical Test Levels 73
   9.2   Exploratory Testing 76
   9.3   Test Levels in an Agile Project.............................. 77
   9.4   Integration of Testing Activities with Other Project Activities 81
   References... 82

10 Performance Characteristics to Be Tested 83
    10.1 Types of System Tests 83
    10.2 Special Test Procedures 86
    References 87

11 Features That Are Not Tested 89
    11.1 Test Coverage Through Test Procedures 89
    11.2 Prove by Other Methods 90
    References 91

12 Prioritization of Test Cases 93
    12.1 Test Scope 93
    12.2 Prioritization in System Tests and Acceptance Tests 94
    12.3 Prioritization in Module Testing and Integration Testing 94
    12.4 Prioritization According to Different Test Types 96
    12.5 Risk-Based Testing 98
    References 99

13 Permanent Test Organization 101
    13.1 Nature of the Permanent Test Organization 101
    13.2 Conditions for a Permanent Test Organization 103
    13.3 Critical Points for Permanent Test Organizations 104
    13.4 Test Guidelines 104
    Reference 105

14 Acceptance Criteria 107
    14.1 Characteristics of Acceptance Criteria 107
    14.2 Acceptance Criteria Catalog 108
    14.3 Organization of the Acceptance Test 110
    14.4 Definition of Suitable Acceptance Criteria 111
    14.5 Properties of Acceptance Tests 113
    References 114

15 Criteria for Test Discontinuation and Test Continuation 115
    15.1 Cases of Test Aborts 115
    15.2 Restart and Test Continuation After Test Discontinuation 116

16 Test Risks 119
    16.1 Project Success 119
    16.2 Assessment of Risks 120
    16.3 Possible Test Risks 121
    References 127

17 Test Data 129
    17.1 Test Data Management 129
    17.2 Approaches to Test Data Generation 131

17.3   Tools for Test Data Generation 133
17.4   Test Data Types 134
References... 134

18 Test Documentation 135
18.1   Test Documentation Objectives and Integrity Levels 135
18.2   Structure of the Test Documentation 137
18.3   Test Script 137
18.4   Test Case 138
18.5   Test Protocol 138
18.6   Summary of the Test Documentation........................ 139
18.7   Neglection of Test Documentation......................... 139
18.8   Test Completion Report................................... 141
18.9   Metrics... 141
18.10   Availability of the Test System 143
References... 145

19 Test Items.. 147
19.1   Types of Test Items 147
19.2   Role Descriptions....................................... 148
19.3   Standard IEC 62034..................................... 150
19.4   Problem-Solving Process.................................. 151
19.5   Test Tasks in Regression Testing 152
19.6   Test Tools... 153
19.7   Tasks for the Individual Stakeholders 154
References... 154

20 Test Environment 155
20.1   Need for Test Environments............................... 155
20.2   Adequacy of the Test Environment 156
20.3   Test Environment Management............................. 156
20.4   External Test Environments................................ 158
20.5   Test Environment in the Cloud 159
Reference 162

21 Responsibilities, Accountability and Communication................ 163
21.1   Determination of Areas of Responsibility 163
21.2   Communication in the Project.............................. 164
21.3   Definition of Responsibilities 165
21.4   Communication Matrix 166
21.5   Selection of Recipients Information 168
21.6   Definition of Communication Objectives 170
21.7   Determination of Information Content 170
21.8   Advantages of the Communication Matrix 171

21.9   Project Communication Requirements 171
21.10   RACI Method... 172
21.11   Common Sources of Defects 174
References.. 174

22   Personnel, Familiarization, Training.............................. 175
22.1   Test Personnel 175
22.2   Conflict Management.. 176

23   Schedule/Work Plan 179
23.1   Determination of the Test Duration 179
23.2   Detailed Work Planning...................................... 181
23.3   Cost Estimate... 182
23.4   Planning of the Individual Test Phases 182
23.5   Staff Utilization Plan 185
23.6   Detailed Test effort Planning 186
23.7   Estimation of Test productivity Using the COCOMO II Method 188
References.. 190

24   Planning Risks and Unforeseeable Events 191
24.1   Unforeseeable Risks... 191
24.2   Making the Target Contributions of the Alternative Courses of Action
        Visible 192
24.3   Methods and Tools as Decision-Making Techniques............... 192
24.4   Methods of Investment Appraisal 193
24.5   Balance of Arguments 193
24.6   SWOT Analysis 194
24.7   Consequence Table 195
24.8   Decision Tree... 196
24.9   Utility Analysis 197
24.10   Risk Analysis 199
24.11   Selecting and Using Decision-Making Methods and Tools.......... 199
24.12   Showing Decision Problems, Alternative Actions and Possible
        Consequences... 200

25   Approval and Release.. 203
25.1   Recommendation for Release 203
Reference 205

26   Project Organization.. 207
26.1   Staff Line Project Organization 207
26.2   Pure Project Organization 209
26.3   Matrix Organization... 210
26.4   Balanced Matrix Organization................................. 211

26.5   Powers and Responsibility for Objectives of the Project Manager 211
26.6   Formulas for Assessing the Progress of the Project. 212
References. 213

27   **Test Methods** 215
27.1   Use of Test Methods 215
27.2   Appropriate Test methods and Test Strategy 216
27.3   Testing Maturity Model (TMMi). 217
27.4   TMap (Test Management Approach). 219
27.5   Advantages of TMap 222
References. 222

28   **Maturity Level of Test Management According to TPI Next** 223
28.1   Determining the Maturity of the Test Process 223
28.2   Test Organization in the Maturing process According to TPI Next. 225
28.3   Classification of Maturity 226
28.4   Maturity Process for the Test Organization 226
28.5   Maturity Level "Initial" 227
28.6   Maturity Level "Controlled" 227
28.7   Maturity Level "Efficient" 228
28.8   Maturity Level "Optimizing". 229
28.9   Differences TMMi and TPI 230
References. 231

29   **Special Features of the Test Organization in Agile Projects** 233
29.1   Agile Projects. 233
29.2   Agile Methods 234
29.3   Organization and Goals of Agile Projects 236
29.4   Agile Projects and Traditional Organization 237
29.5   Necessary Requirements for Test organization in Agile Projects 237
29.6   Principles for Agile Testing 238
References. 239

30   **Artificial Intelligence and Cognitive Testing** 241
30.1   Artificial Intelligence. 241
30.2   Fields of Application of Artificial Intelligence 242
References. 243

Epilogue 245

Index 251

List of Figures

Fig. 1.1	Test documents and result types in the test	6
Fig. 2.1	Illustration of the project situation	19
Fig. 3.1	Project traffic light	26
Fig. 4.1	Sub-tasks in project planning	31
Fig. 5.1	Modular structure of the test concepts	38
Fig. 5.2	Defect detection curve	41
Fig. 5.3	Strategy processes in the classic and agile model	43
Fig. 5.4	Agile transition of the test manager	44
Fig. 5.5	Scrum and test management [AGIL2016]	45
Fig. 7.1	Test process [BAST2015]	60
Fig. 8.1	Test activities	69
Fig. 9.1	Example of a project and sprint test strategy	78
Fig. 12.1	Visualization of dependencies of modules/objects	95
Fig. 14.1	Acceptance tests	111
Fig. 16.1	Characteristics of project success [GPIM2015]	120
Fig. 17.1	Approaches to test data generation	131
Fig. 20.1	Sample process for setting up a test environment in AWS	161
Fig. 21.1	Communication matrix	167
Fig. 21.2	Communication matrix [PRMA2019]	169
Fig. 21.3	The RACI method	173
Fig. 23.1	Timeline of the test phases	182
Fig. 23.2	Bar chart	184
Fig. 23.3	Gantt chart with Excel [PROJ2019]	184
Fig. 23.4	Staff utilization plan	185
Fig. 23.5	Determining test productivity	189
Fig. 24.1	SWOT analysis	195
Fig. 24.2	Decision tree for software procurement	197

Fig. 26.1   Bar line project organization   208
Fig. 26.2   Autonomous project organization   209
Fig. 26.3   Matrix organization   210
Fig. 26.4   Balanced matrix organization   212
Fig. 29.1   Test quadrants as a model for testing activities in agile projects   235

List of Tables

Table 2.1	Advantages and disadvantages of a balanced scorecard [*PRBS2019*]	17
Table 2.2	Presentation of the project situation	18
Table 3.1	Test levels and test contents	27
Table 4.1	Subplans of the project plan	30
Table 4.2	Overview of stakeholders in the project	32
Table 6.1	Tester deployment planning per day in M/D	52
Table 6.2	Condensed tester deployment planning on an hourly basis	53
Table 6.3	Support of the project work by the corporate management	56
Table 7.1	Suitable meetings in the test process	61
Table 7.2	Tasks and powers of project members	62
Table 12.1	Exemplary evaluation of test types for a special application [*FRAN2007*]	97
Table 16.1	Calculation of project risks	120
Table 18.1	Example availability test system	144
Table 19.1	Example of an impact analysis	153
Table 23.1	Work plan	181
Table 23.2	Work plan per employee	186
Table 24.1	Consequence Table IT	196
Table 24.2	Utility analysis	198
Table 26.1	Advantages and disadvantages of the staff line project organization	208
Table 26.2	Advantages and disadvantages of the pure project organization	210
Table 26.3	Advantages and disadvantages of the matrix organization	211
Table 26.4	Powers and responsibility for objectives of the project manager	212
Table 26.5	Formulas for assessing the progress of the project	213
Table 27.1	The five levels of the maturity model	217

Abstract

IEEE 829 defines basic documents for software testing. The test concept describes the results of the test planning. Different types of test documents document the test contents, the test progress and the results of the test execution.

1.1 Standards

Standards help standardize business processes and procedures. A standard is a document that specifies requirements for products, services or processes. It thus creates clarity about their properties, facilitates the free movement of goods and promotes exports. It supports rationalization and quality assurance in business, technology, science and administration. Furthermore, it serves the safety of people and property as well as the improvement of quality in all areas of life [DIN2019].

The standardization process in software testing started much later than in other industries. For example, the certification process in the field of software testers was not started until the mid-1990s in Great Britain, which gave rise to the ISEB certification program in 1997 (ISEB = "Information System Examination Board").

In 1998, a first variant of IEEE 829 was described to establish certain test documents at all. This variant was expanded and updated in 2008.

The definition **IEEE 829 Standard for Software Test Documentation** is a standard published by the IEEE (Institute of Electrical and Electronics Engineers) that describes a

© Springer Fachmedien Wiesbaden GmbH, part of Springer Nature 2022
F. Witte, *Strategy, Planning and Organization of Test Processes*,
https://doi.org/10.1007/978-3-658-36981-1_1

set of eight basic documents for the documentation of software tests. The current version is IEEE 829–2008, which describes the form and content of each document. However, it does not prescribe which of the respective documents must be used.

This standard can be used for traditional, waterfall model software projects as well as for agile projects.

In September 2013, the first parts of the international standard **ISO/IEC/IEEE 29119** were published, replacing the IEEE 829 Standard for Software Test Documentation internationally.

The standard describes eight documents, which can be divided into three categories, as follows.

1.2   Test Concept

Test Plan: The test plan defines the scope, approach, means and schedule of the test activities. It determines the elements and product functions to be tested, the test tasks to be performed, the personnel responsible for each task, and the risk associated with the concept.

The test concept serves as a guideline for planning and organizing test activities.

The following shows a structure that has proved to be useful for creating test concepts.

1. Introduction
    1.1. Identification of the test concept
    1.2. Scope and coverage
    1.3. References
        1.3.1. External references
        1.3.2. Internal references
    1.4 System to be tested and test object
    1.5. Overview of the test items
        1.5.1. Organization
        1.5.2. Project test plan
        1.5.3. Integration stages
        1.5.4. Resource overview
        1.5.5. Responsibilities
        1.5.6. Tools, techniques, methods, metrics
2. Details
    2.1 Test process and test levels
    2.2. Documents
    2.3. Deviation and change management
    2.4. Reporting

3. General
   3.1. Glossary
   3.2. Change service and history [QYTE2019].

The test concept defines the scope, procedure, scheduling and required resources of the intended test activities. Test objects, features to be tested and the individual test tasks are identified.

Test tasks can also be assigned to individual employees. Sometimes, reference is made to a separate planning document for this purpose.

The test should take place independently of the development. Only if the test is a neutral, separate entity it will be able to guarantee this independence. The resulting organizational definition is also described in the test concept.

In addition, the test environment, the test design procedure and the procedures to be used for measuring the test activities and test results are described, and their selection is justified. The test concept includes a chapter on risks and possible countermeasures if these risks occur.

The test concept thus documents the results of the test planning process.

1.3   Test Specification

The test specification contains the documents, i.e., the test design specification, test case specification and test procedure specification.

The test design specification refines the description of the procedure for testing the software. It identifies features and functions that need to be covered by defined appropriately assigned logical test cases. It also describes the test cases and test procedures that are required for the test cases to be considered successfully completed. The criteria according to which tests are passed or failed are defined for each function [SETH2019].

The test case specification defines the input values to be used and the expected output values. In addition, the test case specification describes the necessary pre- and post-conditions, the objectives and test actions. The priority and duration of the test execution should also be documented, especially for test cases to be performed manually. If necessary, it should also be described how the system must be reset to an initial state after the test execution.

In the IEEE 829 standard, test cases are separated from the test design. This allows the test cases to be used in different designs and reused in other situations. In practice, the test design specification and test case specification are often stored together in one document and existing test cases are only copied for a new project. However, the modular structure in different documents leads to a higher quality, even if it is an additional effort at the beginning.

The test procedure specification is the description of all steps for the execution of the specified test cases and the implementation of the associated test design. For many test cases, the prerequisites must first be established (e.g., several booking steps) before the actual test case can even be started. Some tests consist of a series of steps. The test procedure specification is sometimes also called test procedure description, test script or test script. Mixed forms of test case specification and test procedure specification are also often used.

In many professional test management tools, the test procedure and the separation of test case and test procedure specification are mapped through different areas.

1.4   Test Reporting

The reporting system should summarize the results of all test runs of a version.

The test item transmittal report describes the transmission of test cases in case separate development and test teams are involved, or in case an official time for the start of a test execution is desired. In the test item transmittal report, a defined version is handed over to a test team, and the testable features are listed there.

The test log is used to chronologically record the events during a test execution. For each test execution, it must be defined which log files are required by the development to be able to reproduce misbehavior. This is especially important for automated tests that run overnight or on weekends. However, it should be noted that a high log level not only records a lot of information and therefore requires a lot of memory, but also that the increased logging can increase the response time and the system load to such an extent that defects occur that would not occur under normal operation.

The test incident report describes all events that occur during test execution and require further investigation. According to IEEE 108 (IEEE Standard for Software Unit Testing), a deviation is an event that occurs during testing and requires further investigation.

The test summary report summarizes the test activities related to one or more test design specifications. For example, when the system test or integration test of a defined software is complete, the test summary report is created to start the next test stage. If, for example, there is only a conditional release during the system test, the software can still be tested in the acceptance test, but certain restrictions must be observed. Sometimes, at the end of the test activities of a test level, defects have not yet been eliminated or successfully retested, so that the next higher test level can be carried out with these restrictions, but the product cannot yet be delivered in production as long as these bugs still exist. In practice, the test deviation report is often combined with the test deviation report in one document.

The test completion report is intended to document the bugs that occurred during the test with their current status, i.e., to make a statement about which defects were detected and corrected during the test phase. The test completion report is sometimes also referred to as a **test evaluation report.** This document also contains an evaluation of the test process and a field report.

In more extensive projects, individual test phases last for several weeks or months. It is therefore recommended creating a current **status report** at weekly intervals. As part of the test preparation, you should consider which statements you want to present and which metrics you want to use for this. It is recommended to define and agree on regular reporting in advance of the test phases. Ideally, metrics that only need to be configured for the current project are provided. If you have to answer questions about the test progress during the test execution phase, and then you are not prepared, in addition to stressful project phases you have the problem of presenting events in an appealing way and collecting and preparing the required information (not too much but also not too little).

In this context, the reporting rhythm should also be checked before the start of the project: How up-to-date are the events that flow into the test report? If the report for the previous week is only created on Wednesday and distributed throughout the company, or – even worse – a test report for the current month is only presented on the tenth of the following month, much of the information is long out-of-date. Reporting on progress, but also on problems, must always take place promptly, i.e., on a daily basis, and must therefore also be able to be created promptly.

With all reports, one should not underestimate the time needed to prepare and present the results. As a rule, it is difficult to summarize complex interrelationships on a few pages of reporting and to present them in a graphically appealing way. However, this is absolutely necessary for comprehensive reporting to management and, finally, for self-marketing as a test manager. Preparing facts for reporting can also become very time-consuming. In my experience, in many projects the reporting is not defined from the beginning in such a way that one can reasonably build on it with standardized reports that only need to be configured for the individual project. Clear reporting without embellishment, without scaremongering and without blame, but as a demonstration of the actual situation with a realistic assessment significantly improves communication in the project.

Figure 1.1 shows an overview of the interrelation between the individual documents

The input documents "Proj Doc" (**project documentation**) and "Item Doc" (**project product documentation**), as well as the "Test Item" (test object/software) are not the

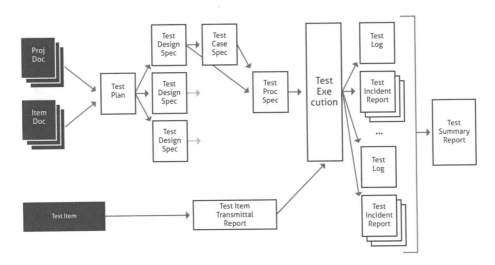

Fig. 1.1 Test documents and result types in the test

subject of the standard, but are defined and created by the adjacent processes in the previous chapter.

In addition, there are other typical documents which are not, however, stored in IEEE 829. These include, for example, the test progress **report**, the **test level description,** etc. In addition, there are other documents that are usually defined by the project management (e.g., profile of the test subproject, risk list, open points list, etc.) [PMQS2019].

Release notes should also be considered in this context. Release notes are documents that identify the test objects, their configuration, their current status and other information about the software used as part of the handover from development to testing at the start of test execution.

Care should be taken to ensure that all documents created are clearly identified, versioned and marked with the document status (e.g., "in progress", "in review", "completed", "accepted"). For this purpose, a flowchart of the respective document status should be used as the basis document for the test process.

1.5   Integrity level

IEEE 829 is intended to be suitable for an agile as well as for a conventional systematic approach and applies to systems as well as software. With IEEE 829, a documentation process (conforming to **ISO 12207, ISO 15288**) with input and output (task-oriented) has been created from the previously document-oriented principle "documents follow activities".

With IEEE 829, 4 **integrity levels,** depending on the fault tolerance of the system, are defined. Specific documents are proposed for each level:

4 – Catastrophic
Master Test Plan (static), Level Test Plan (dynamic and detailed), Level Test Design, Level Test Case, Level Test Protocol, Level Test Log, Anomaly Report, Level Integration Test Status Report, Level Test Report, Master Test Report

3 – Critical
Master Test Plan (static), Level Test Plan (dynamic and detailed), Level Test Design, Level Test Case, Level Test Protocol, Level Test Log, Anomaly Report, Level Integration Test Status Report, Level Test Report, Master Test Report

2 – Marginal
Level Test Plan (dynamic and detailed), Level Test Design, Level Test Case, Level Test Protocol, Level Test Log, Anomaly Report, Level Integration Test Status Report, Level Test Report

1 – Negligible
Level Test Plan (dynamic and detailed), Level Test Design, Level Test Case, Level Test Protocol, Level Test Log, Anomaly Report, Level Test Report

In accordance with the V-model, several stages are planned for the test. The documents Test Design, Test Case, Test Protocol, Test Log, Interim Test Status Report and Anomaly Report are therefore created for the Component, Component Integration, System and Acceptance Test stages as required.

To support the test manager, there is a template for a **Master Test Plan Metrics Report**, which includes metrics according to **ISO 9126.**

As with other standards, adaptation of the test documentation process to one's own organization (project or company) is expressly desired, as long as the requirements for comprehensible test documentation are met. The standard should serve as a guideline and orientation, the design and implementation are individually different. It is always important not to define rigid specifications, but to accommodate established processes and environmental requirements as far as possible without neglecting the justified basic requirements.

Beyond test documentation, the IEEE 829 standard also addresses the integration of testing into the organization. It defines and describes the following forms: (ISTQB compliant)

- Integrated: completely integrated in the development team
- Internal: tester in the development team
- Integrated: own team parallel to the developers in the same organizational unit

- Independent: own independent organizational unit within the company
- Independent: completely independent, outside the company, outsourced [ROBU2019].

Mixed forms are also encountered, such as when the integration test of a supplied component is outsourced to an external organization, but the system test and acceptance test are organized and performed by a specific department within the company.

References

1. https://www.din.de/de/ueber-normen-und-standards/basiswissen, accessed on 9 May 2020
2. https://www.qytera.de/blog/testkonzept-ieee-829-testmanagement, accessed on 9 May 2020
3. http://www.sebastianthiem.de/?page=Workshop/004_SoftwareTest.html, accessed on 9 May 2020
4. https://pmqs.de/index.php/testmanagement/prozesse-tm/32-04-ergebnistypen-im-test, accessed on 9 May 2020
5. http://robert.bullinger.over-blog.com/article-testdokumentation-nach-ieee-829-20510038.html, accessed on 9 May 2020

Test Strategy

2

Abstract

A test strategy is the prerequisite for planned action and the basis for defining the right test processes and determining the organization. A test strategy applies company-wide or to an organization within the company and not just to a single project. Deviations from the test strategy in one's own project must be justified. The test strategy must be considered in conjunction with the IT strategy. The use of balanced scorecards is recommended as an instrument for controlling the implementation of project strategies.

2.1 Characteristics of the Test Strategy

Developing strategies, making plans and implementing goals – that is the core business of management in companies. One prerequisite for this is strategic thinking. Thinking strategically does not necessarily mean making decisions with consequences for the entire organization or deciding how to allocate scarce budgets: It is enough to consider even the smallest decisions in the context of your organization's broader strategic goals. For example, it is highly strategic to nurture a relationship if it promises particular insights about a supplier, a customer or a competitor. So everyone has opportunities to be more strategic [HARV2014].

The **test strategy** is defined as documentation that describes the generic requirements for testing in one or more projects within an organization, including details about how testing should be performed. The test strategy is aligned with the **test policy.** Test policy

© Springer Fachmedien Wiesbaden GmbH, part of Springer Nature 2022
F. Witte, *Strategy, Planning and Organization of Test Processes*,
https://doi.org/10.1007/978-3-658-36981-1_2

refers to a document that summarizes, at a high level of abstraction, an organization's principles, approach, and key objectives related to testing [GLOS2019].

The test policy therefore usually applies to the entire company and not to an individual project. The template for test documents, such as a test concept, is also created on the basis of the test policy. However, if the company-wide test strategy is deviated from in a project for various reasons, this must be documented in the test concept of the corresponding project. In this case, for example, mark the parts that are intended as "not relevant" (this is better than removing them, because it documents that you definitely thought of these aspects during the conception phase and did not forget anything).

This is especially true for smaller projects where the integration effort is lower and therefore does not require a complete integration test or partial integration test. You can also keep the test concept small by referring to another project and only describing the deviations and special features in your own project. But even for small testing efforts of a few days, as is typical for numerous apps, for example, one should refer to the test guideline and a generic test concept and describe the project in the project-specific test concept and reference the requirements, define stakeholders, test stages and deadlines. A certain minimum scope must be given in any case.

When defining the test strategy, a key aspect is determining how intensively testing should be performed at which level. This depends on various factors, such as the available budget for testing, the risk, the complexity of the system to be developed, the number of teams, or even the knowledge about testing activities. The test manager must identify and consider as many of these factors as possible, often in close coordination with other roles such as a project manager or the **product owner** . One strategy may be that at the module level, each module must be developed using Test Driven Design before it is integrated and goes through integration testing, and subsequently at the system test level, all user stories must be run through manually. At each test level, the strategy can also be further refined. For example, at the system test level, each user story classified as critical can be tested both experientially and systematically by at least two testers, while for less critical user stories, only one of the two testers performs testing. Developer testing at the unit level can be both white-box and black-box based and is usually performed by the developers themselves. It is concerned not only with correct functionality for valid inputs, but also with correct interception of invalid input values. Each "smallest unit" is tested and checked as isolated as possible. In agile development lifecycles, the use of test-first or test-driven development has become established. Integration testing, on the other hand, tests the interfaces between units and thus tests the interaction of multiple units. Even if each unit works correctly on its own, the interaction of the components can still lead to faulty results. The integration test can be divided into several phases to cover everything from "small" integration steps to "large" integration steps. At this test level, regression testing plays a major role, especially in iterative development. The testing of non-functional aspects such as performance or security can already be started in the integration test. The system test, on the other hand, is performed on a black-box basis and includes testing of the complete system, usually from the user interface. The aim is to test whether the user's goals can be achieved with the application on the basis of the input. Non-functional testing also takes place at this test level. All these test levels take place in the development environment. Only the acceptance test takes place in the environment of the future users and repeats test cases that have already been run through in the system test. Module testing is performed daily as part of the agile approach, and integration testing is performed at the end of the sprint. System testing is started after a few sprints, testing complex test scenarios. The last sprint before the release is then used again explicitly for quality assurance, and acceptance tests are performed.

As part of the follow-up and evaluation, it is continuously checked whether the initial test strategy makes sense and must be adjusted if necessary. If, for example, it becomes apparent during development that a component that was not previously assessed as high-risk is high-risk, test efforts should be additionally concentrated here, for example through additional module or integration tests. Defects found during testing at the various stages should be documented and analyzed in detail (e.g., in a bug tracking tool) in order to further optimize future quality assurance and, if necessary, to decide whether bugs can be found earlier or avoided entirely [PQ4A2015].

The better the test strategy is polished, the more you can do without describing all the considerations again in the individual small project. A modular structure of the test concept is therefore recommended in any case.

In the long term, strategies must adapt to new trends, new behaviors, new technologies, and a changed business environment. This is also true for test strategy. Strategies, like blinkers for horses, are designed to help you move in a straight line and pursue a specific goal, but they prevent you from using your peripheral vision. By focusing the efforts and attention of all parts of an organization, the organization runs the risk of not changing its strategy when it should. As a result, large companies in particular cling to rigid outdated structures even though the technological and social environment has long since changed. This delays and prevents necessary innovations. It is often better to move forward slowly, a little at a time, not looking too far ahead – but very alert! – so that behaviour can be changed within a very short time [BUSW2019].

The test strategy concerns several test levels. Depending on the task, software-specific topics for integration testing (especially in embedded systems of software and hardware), component testing and system testing are also considered.

The test strategy considers different aspects of testing:

- Customers and internal company quality specifications place requirements on the test and influence the type and scope of the tests. Ideally, measurable goals are defined for this.
- Before developing the test cases, the test requirements must be clarified, the test planning must be carried out, the integration strategy must be defined and the test scope must be precisely determined. The structure and content of the test specifications and test protocols are determined in the process.
- The test environment for the test object and the test tools are defined. A test procedure is defined to ensure reliable and error-free functionality.
- Test execution also includes individual test preparations and criteria for the end or termination of testing, checking the test results and releasing the software.

When testing embedded software, special aspects have to be tested in addition to purely software-based applications:

- Hardware dependencies,
- Real-time boundary conditions,
- Limitations of the test environment:
  - Functionality,
  - Availability,
- Interference:
  - Bit errors in digital signals,
  - Interruption of signals.

Frequently, requirements already defined by the customer are placed on the software. This is often the case with embedded software that is built into capital goods or mass-produced items. In this case, the customer is also interested in saving his own testing efforts by expecting his suppliers, who deliver systems or components to him, to meet specified quality targets. There are often contractually stipulated requirements to deliver test protocols as part of the product documentation.

In many cases, the verification measures and test processes are also determined by the customer. The process specifications are usually based on norms and standards, e.g. the safety standards **IEC 61508, ISO 26262** or **EN 50128, SPICE** and **CMMI** . If these process specifications are only poorly implemented in the organizational unit under consideration, there is a project risk because test results may not be accepted by the customer at the end. If certification according to a standard is part of the project and certain weaknesses in the organization are already known at the concept phase, which lead to additional effort in order to pass this certification at all, this point should also be listed as a risk in the test concept of the project.

Qualitative specifications for the test concern the creation of test documentation and the procedure for test case implementation. A certain test coverage and an expected scope of regression tests are also specified [EISE2012].

It may be necessary to deviate from the test strategy defined for the entire company or organization for certain reasons, such as when additional integration stages are required or certain roles need to be redefined. Should this be the case, these deviations must be justified in the test concept for the affected project and the effects evaluated.

2.2   Integration Strategy

An integration strategy is part of the test strategy, because the software is usually composed of several modules.

As a model, the individual software modules are first tested individually, then integrated into subsystems and finally into a complete system. In the process, it must be checked whether the individual modules work together correctly. However, it is often the case that individual modules are not yet finished and only placeholders (mocks, stubs) can be used. As a rule, the project deadlines are also too tight to be able to completely finish the individual module tests before moving on to the next test stage.

It should also be borne in mind that the **testing effort required** for the individual modules varies. For example, a higher testing effort is required for safety-critical modules compared to non-safety-relevant software. In some cases, additional test tools must also be used to demonstrate test coverage. For software components supplied by other companies, integration tests must also be provided. Hardware-related software must usually be tested on the target system in a meaningful way.

The integration strategy determines the order in which the individual modules are integrated into a complete system. It is recommended to integrate the most important modules for processing at the beginning and to integrate the input modules before the output modules. A parallelization of integration steps (e.g. application software and hardware-related basic functions) is usually required anyway due to tight project schedules.

2.3   Test Specifications

Part of the test strategy is to plan for the creation of test specifications. The test specifications should be essentially completed and reviewed at the start of the test execution. Although the test specification must also be reviewed and detailed during test execution and supplemented with test cases that come to the tester's attention during exploratory testing, the structure and framework should be in place at an early stage of the test activities and the description should be available in principle.

2.4   Use of Tools

The test strategy defines which tool is used and how the individual test cases are structured. It is important to agree on a defined tool throughout the entire company and not to use several tools next to each other. Otherwise, the effort for comparison and benchmarking of the individual areas increases enormously and there is a risk for the test manager to be comprehensively informative.

The following information should be available in the tool in any case:

1. **Test case ID**: Unique identification number so that the test case can be found again at any time and is archived.
2. **Test object**: The application to be tested is described. A short description should already emerge from the heading.
3. **Test configuration/test requirements/test data**: What hardware and software configuration and test environment must be in place? What are the environment parameters? Do other steps need to be performed before starting the actual test case? If necessary, you can reference a precisely designated test environment described in a configuration management document.
4. **Test description**: Exact description of the test case and the test procedures. The steps that are performed in sequence during execution must be documented.
5. **References**: Reference to the requirements specification or to other test cases. It is highly recommended to use a matrix in which requirements from the requirements specification and the assigned test case are compared. In this way, it is always possible to find out which requirement can be verified with which test case, and – in another direction – why a particular test case is required. This is also a prerequisite for successful certification, e.g. according to SPICE.
6. **Priority**: Is the test case absolutely necessary or rather subordinate? Especially for regression tests, the test case can then be omitted or even for deliveries arriving at short notice one after the other. However, even low priority test cases should be tested at least once for a successful acceptance with the final version. If test cases cannot be tested due to time constraints, this should be documented as a risk during acceptance.
7. **Detail fields or comment fields** for additions and special notes are to be provided.
8. **Target result or expected result**: What result is to be expected and should be achieved according to the specification? Care must be taken to ensure that the goal is formulated in a measurable way. The description must therefore be so detailed that it leaves no room for interpretation.
9. **Actual result**: Description of the actual result.

10. **Evaluation of the result**: Was the test successful, i.e. "OK" or "NOK".
11. **Reference to the bug**: If there occurred a bug during test execution, the number should be noted here. It should also be listed in which phase the error arose (rough design, fine design/design, implementation, test) in order to draw conclusions for the entire development and test process.
12. **Comments and remarks on** the results (free text) are to be included.
13. **Tester** who performed the test or, in the case of automatic scripts, a reference to the program run must be recorded.
14. The **date and time the** test was performed should be noted.
15. **Test duration**: The test duration is to be collected above all for manual test execution, in order to define the tests to be carried out as far as possible, especially when time and resources are limited.

Depending on the specifics of the test environment and the operational environment, further specifications may be required. Professional test tools generally offer a selection of possible fields that can be individually configured when used in the company or project.

2.5   Questions on the Implementation of the Test Strategy

In connection with the test strategy, it is advisable to answer some questions that also apply to the IT strategy:

- What is the project for, what is the test supposed to do?
- What is measured and how is it controlled? (Object of consideration – product/process/ resource/framework condition)
- What aspects need to be considered? (Reference variables/properties/metrics)
- What measure is used for the measurement? (Unit of measurement/measurement for measuring the expression)
- Which target values are being pursued? (Selected target values)
- How is it measured? (Measuring method)
- When is the measurement performed? (Time and period of the measurement)
- Where will be measured? (Place/Site)
- Who carries out the measurement? (Person/device)
- How are the measurement results documented? (Quality data)
- How are measurement results evaluated? (Comparison against target values)
- What measures, if any, are taken to sustainably reduce the deviation or dispersion and who controls their effect?
- What preventive measures, if any, are taken?

In the early 1990s, Robert S. Kaplan and David P. Norton conducted a study of twelve large American companies. The aim was to determine how these companies measure their performance and what deficits the methods used in each case have. It was about the important topic of performance measurement. The study found, among other things, that there are the following central problems in performance measurement:

- The measurement systems are incredibly complicated and differentiated. The essential information gets lost in front of all the measurement figures and complex calculation systems.
- There is a lot of measurement in the operational area without manageable, central and strategic information.
- Most key figures used for performance measurement only depict the past. They are not very suitable for estimating developments in the future.
- Most ratios are focused exclusively on financial aspects, they ultimately map the flow of money. Other factors that are not directly related to money are not considered. This means that crucial elements of the corporate strategy are not reflected in key figures at all [BUSW2020].

2.6   Balanced Scorecard

Therefore, **balanced scorecards** (BSC) were developed from the findings of the study and have since established themselves as a proven instrument for controlling the implementation of strategies. The focus on strategic goals requires a concentration on approximately 20 goals. In order to be able to plan and track the achievement of objectives, the individual objectives are described with monetary and non-monetary metrics and their target values are described. Strategic actions for the individual goals ensure goal achievement. Each strategic action is given a deadline and budget as well as a person responsible. Due to this stringency, the subtitle "From Strategy to Action" was added to the BSC. The BSC approach is characterized by the fact that the strategic goals are each assigned to a specific point of view – the so-called perspective. This assignment prevents one-sided thinking. Through the principle of taking into account all perspectives – including non-monetary ones – that are important for the strategic positioning of the company and of linking all perspectives, the BSC makes complex interrelationships transparent.

The linkage takes place with the help of cause-effect chains. The top-down approach is used in planning and the bottom-up approach in implementation. Four perspectives are distinguished within the framework of the BSC:

- **Financial perspective**: What objectives are derived from the financial considerations of the investors?
- **Customer perspective**: What are the objectives to be set in terms of structure and requirements of our customers in order to achieve the financial objectives?
- **Process perspective**: What are the objectives to be set in terms of our process quality in order to achieve the objectives of the financial and customer perspective?
- **Potential perspective**: What goals need to be set with regard to our potentials in order to be able to meet current and future challenges?

The balanced scorecard can be used in the line organisation, in (large) projects and in multi-project management for the following purposes:

- Planning, development and implementation of strategies,
- Target and performance agreements with managers,
- Monitoring strategy implementation,
- Presentation of the strategy to stakeholders.

The following table (Table 2.1) shows the strengths and weaknesses of the balanced Scorecard:

In addition to balanced scorecards, project scorecards are also used, which are a good way of presenting the current **project situation** (Table 2.2).

A suitable graphical representation of the project situation is shown in Fig. 2.1.

When using a project scorecard, it is important to ensure that

- a special information culture is required, which must first be learned and then lived;
- it can be flexibly changed at any time;

Table 2.1 Advantages and disadvantages of a balanced scorecard [PRBS2019]

Strengths	Weaknesses
The balanced scorecard focuses on the key control variables and thus helps to align the critical success factors with the strategy.	The balanced scorecard is not an instrument for strategy development, but merely supplements it with the aspect of key performance indicators.
It provides a quick overview, as it presents the most important key figures for strategy implementation on one page.	It does not replace cost and activity accounting. It is too imprecise for that and does not reflect tax or commercial law aspects.
	It does not reflect all key figures that are relevant for controlling the company or the project. Further key figures may be required for subareas of the company.
It is easy to understand and can therefore be used well for communication.	It can be misused for corporate political purposes.
It can be flexibly adapted to all business requirements.	

Table 2.2 Presentation of the project situation

Objectives		Achievement of objectives	
		1st quarter	2nd quarter
Finances			
	Profitability		
	Increase in sales		
	Total		
Clients			
	New customers		
	Customer satisfaction		
	Total		
Processes			
	Punctuality		
	Quality		
	Total		
Colleagues			
	Employee satisfaction		
	Absenteeism		
	Fluctuation		
	Total		
Overall			

- it is updated at regular intervals;
- it's limited to the essentials;
- it is an instrument with which one works on a daily basis; new proposals must always be discussed and evaluated with regard to their target effect.

For the special needs of test projects, it makes sense to modify the project scorecard accordingly and to include new criteria for it.

For example, criteria such as test coverage, degree of automation or number of defects can be defined as measurable target values.

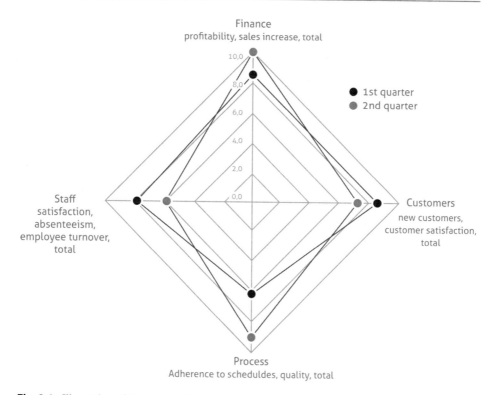

Fig. 2.1 Illustration of the project situation

References

1. http://glossar.german-testing-board.info/v3.21/#t, accessed on 9 May 2020
2. Thomas Eißenlöffel, Embedded-Software entwickeln, dpunkt Verlag Heidelberg 2012, https://bilder.buecher.de/zusatz/34/34536/34536969_lese_1.pdf, accessed on 9 May 2020
3. https://www.business-wissen.de/hb/was-strategisches-denken-bedeutet/, accessed on 9 May 2020
4. https://www.projektmagazin.de/methoden/balanced-scorecard-mit-kennzahlen-erstellen-beispiel, accessed on 9 May 2020
5. http://www.pq4agile.de/PQ4WP/wp-content/uploads/2015/02/PQ4Agile-AP-2.2-Teststrategie-festlegen-und-Teststufen-aufeinander-abstimmen-V.11.pdf , accessed on 9 May 2020
6. https://www.harvardbusinessmanager.de/blogs/management-strategisches-denken-verbessern-a-950400.html, accessed on 9 May 2020
7. https://www.business-wissen.de/hb/balanced-scorecard-einfach-und-verstaendlich-erklaert/, accessed on 26 May 2020

Test Objectives

3

Abstract

Test objectives are a subset of the project objectives and are to be measured using appropriate methods. Suitable metrics should be defined to evaluate the test objectives. For this purpose, a project traffic lights should be used as suitable evaluation scales with which test results can be summarized and presented pictorially during reporting.

3.1 Importance of Test Objectives

A **test objective** is defined as a target relevant to testing for the customer, often expressed in terms of IT-based business processes, realized user requirements or use cases, critical success factors, proposed changes, or risks being covered. Test objectives are a project-related subset of project objectives. In this context, **project objectives** are the establishment of requirements, quantified as far as possible, that must be fulfilled in order for a project to be considered successfully completed. To formulate test objectives, you must therefore ask yourself what results you want to achieve with the software testing activities.

Since software testing consists of numerous individual measures that are usually executed over several test levels and on different test objects, each test case has an individual test objective. The individual test stages also have different test objectives, such as the test of a computing function, the successful verification of commissioning, or the fulfillment of defined performance objectives in a load test. The expected result of the individual test case documents these test objectives. Therefore, a test objective can also be described as a defined set of software properties that are set as measurable quality objectives in the specification and design phase. In testing, these test objectives must be named. They must be described in such a way that their achievement can be realistically measured [ENZY2019].

© Springer Fachmedien Wiesbaden GmbH, part of Springer Nature 2022
F. Witte, *Strategy, Planning and Organization of Test Processes*,
https://doi.org/10.1007/978-3-658-36981-1_3

Conversely, this means that test objectives must be achievable and measurable in the first place. Although this sounds obvious, the test objectives are often formulated too vaguely in operational practice and are therefore open to interpretation.

With suitable tests during the realization or implementation, the number of defects should be kept as low as possible. In addition, it should be ensured that the developers can already learn from detected bugs during the project. Testing is therefore much more than a tedious task that can be delegated to a quality manager. In the development cycle of an IT solution, quality assurance must be embedded in the project flow and must not be limited to a test phase at the end of the project.

With the acceptance, the client confirms that his requirements are fulfilled, which are described in the project order or specifications or customer specification. Acceptance is a prerequisite for project completion. It also has legal effects, e.g., for invoicing or warranty. The basis for acceptance is the acceptance test, which checks whether all acceptance criteria have been met. It is important that the acceptance criteria are defined at an early stage and are known to all participants.

In IT projects, testing thus links the value-adding project processes (i.e., creation) and the project management processes, e.g., of quality management and acceptance. On the one hand, the **testing processes** must therefore be integrated into the plan of the respective project, and on the other hand, a testing organization must be established that aligns testing and management processes [PRMA2019].

In addition, there are global test objectives: what do I want to achieve with the test, how far should my evidence go? This also includes a clear delimitation of what the test can and cannot do. What quality standard should the test meet? When is the test considered passed or successful? And what metrics and parameters can be used to prove and document this?

The test objectives differ depending on the test level: in the **component test,** the test objective is the input and output behavior of the test object. Therefore, the component is subjected to several test cases, where each test case covers a specific input and output combination. In **integration testing**, on the other hand, the test objective is to detect interface defects. Therefore, dynamic tests are usually performed here to detect error conditions in the data exchange or communication between the components. In **system testing,** the test objective is to verify whether and how well the finished system meets the specified functional and non-functional requirements. Here, the goal is to uncover incorrect, incompletely implemented, or inconsistently defined requirements from the user's perspective. Undocumented or forgotten requirements are also documented [SPIL2007].

3.2   Test Parameters

The use of test objectives leads to an objectification of the test process and an operationally manageable result control. **Test parameters** are defined for this purpose:

A **test coverage parameters (TAK)** is an activity-oriented test parameters that results from reviewing system elements and considering them in the test.

Examples of test coverage parameters for specifying test objectives are

TAK1 = Number of branches executed/Number of existing branches and
TAK2 = Number of modules executed/Number of modules present.

A concrete value can be defined as a measurable test objective for the module test, e.g., TAK1 = 90%, TAK2 = 100%.

A **test result characteristic (TEK)** refers to a result-oriented test characteristic that is derived from the results of test activities.

Examples of test result indices are the meantime between detected defects, the required execution time for a test, the required computation time for a test/number of found bugs, the cost of a test or the cost of a test/number of detected bugs [WALL2011]. Thus, index values are formed that allow comparability between different algorithms, applications or projects. Different parameters can be weighted accordingly.

It is often the case that too little data is available on the decisive questions: How many function points do the applications have? How high will the defect rate be? How many test cases are required? In addition, many of these parameters can only be collected during the project. The data is usually also distributed throughout the company, and a considerable amount of effort is required to compile it, which is not worthwhile for the individual project, but can only be presented as a higher-level quality assurance task. Considerable deficits can often be seen in this process. Information is hidden and not made transparent, and thus cannot address problems adequately. In many companies, one experiences busy actionism rather than goal-oriented action based on such data. However, it is precisely in this area that there is considerable potential for optimization in the medium to long term.

For this purpose, it is necessary to collect suitable metrics to be able to measure the test coverage and the test result. The following list does not claim to be complete, but is merely intended to express the minimum metrics to be used:

- Number of requirements,
- Number of documented test cases,
- Distribution of test cases according to priority,

- Number of tested test cases,
- Number of successful or incorrectly tested test cases,
- Number of defects,
- Duration of troubleshooting,
- Defects per test level,
- Breakdown of defects by impact or priority.

The individual values are to be set relating to each other. For example, as follows: There are 200 test cases documented, 100 of which are tested, 90 of which are OK and 10 of which lead to bugs. 5 of the 10 defects have low, 3 medium and 2 high impact.

It is recommended to use further parameters for a detailed evaluation, which, however, is not carried out at regular intervals, but rather as required, to evaluate the project. Particularly when recurring problems are identified in a comparison of several projects, e.g., that the error rate is too high throughout the company, this example could be used to check whether the quality of the requirements is sufficient, whether special test levels are particularly affected, whether the training of developers should be increased, whether certain components exhibit an accumulation of bugs, or whether there are external influencing factors. There are numerous suitable parameters for this.

The regular reporting should be illustrated and supported thanks to graphics and charts. A picture is worth a thousand words.

3.3 Test Reporting

Defining the test objectives includes thinking about the assessment scale and what statements will be made. Basic requirements for **test reporting** should be considered from the outset. This is especially true if different groups are involved in the test, which otherwise evaluate their test progress and quality according to different criteria.

It should be clarified in advance how extensive the reporting should be. This depends above all on the criticality and size of the project. The information can no longer be processed meaningfully in management at too fine a granularity, especially since management is presented with several projects. However, a purely subjective summary without reference to determined values and parameters for the achievement of objectives is also insufficient. It is necessary to find a suitable compromise, already in the phase of test preparation. An experienced test manager usually already recognizes at the start of a project how time-critical, complex and challenging it is likely to be.

A "**project traffic light**" with the colors red, yellow and green is usually used to summarize the assessment. The traffic light colors make the result values and key figures (= indicators) easier to interpret in reporting.

Green means that everything is "in the green". The defined indicators do not show any deviations from the plan, all decision points have been reached according to plan or better. In short, there is no need for a decision or action by the higher authority. However, if you rate your projects as green too often, this can also be interpreted as having planned too pessimistically from the start and having applied for and used too many resources for the project. In the worst case, resources may even be deducted from the project.

Yellow means attention and urges caution. The indicators show deviations from the plan, there is a need for action. New and/or additional measures must be taken to achieve a decision point according to plan. In this case, a list of the required measures with their justifications must also be submitted. A need for decision or action on the part of the superordinate instance is announced with yellow, and becomes necessary if the measures taken are not effective. Yellow leads to a certain awareness, but also means that the project manager and the test manager are in control of the existing problems. Experience shows that most projects in the company are shown in yellow in the project traffic light.

Red means stop! The defined indicators show clear deviations from the plan. The measures to achieve the decision point according to plan were not effective or not possible. A need for decision or action by the higher authority is mandatory and usually urgent in this case. Management support is required, but it can be construed that even as a test manager, one was not capable of handling the problems. Therefore, one will often try to avoid red and rather show a "deep dark orange" still as yellow.

Gray means that the traffic light is off or broken. It means that the indicator value could not be determined. For example, the quality assessment cannot be carried out at all if the test execution has not been started yet, although it was originally planned for the corresponding time period. In most cases, the substitute rules intended for this case apply.

A more detailed form of the project traffic light (see Fig. 3.1) uses 9 levels, i.e., 1–3 for red, 4–6 for yellow and 7–9 for green. In my experience, these 9 levels are necessary because the subdivision into red – yellow – green is not fine granular enough.

It should be documented in a generally valid manner for all projects of the organizational unit which criteria in detail lead to a traffic light being red, yellow or green. Otherwise, the interpretations diverge too much within the company.

Test progress and **quality** are to be evaluated regularly. The costs are usually determined by a budget from the outset. The test budget in turn affects the test objectives: if it is clear from the outset that only very limited test coverage is possible with the planned costs and that certain test activities will therefore be dispensed with, this must be described in the test concept.

For this purpose, trend curves (upwards, downwards, constant) are documented in reporting, which express the course of progress or quality. A rising trend line is thus not possible at level 9 and a falling curve at level 1.

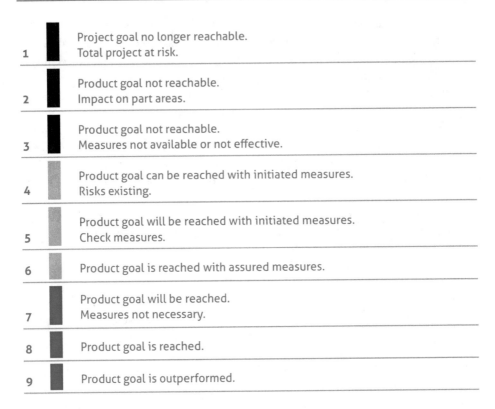

Fig. 3.1 Project traffic light

This reporting should be done on a weekly basis. A daily assessment is too extensive and shows too many distortions, a monthly evaluation of the test status allows too much time to elapse to be able to counteract problems in time. In some cases, steering committees are scheduled at monthly intervals, at which the reporting on a week that has just passed should be presented. Presentations to a larger committee also have to be prepared well in advance, so that only the current figures have to be inserted if necessary. Otherwise, at a time when the project is already in a work-intensive phase, one must additionally consider how to present one's results in a meaningful way.

The evaluation scheme should apply throughout the company and should only be referenced in the test concept of an individual project or only described if it is deviated from for specific reasons.

With the test objectives, care must also be taken to precisely define the responsibilities for test execution and the **quality objectives.** This applies especially in the case that individual components are supplied by other suppliers: Does the supplier provide a test report? What quality level has been agreed? How extensive were the supplier's tests? Is the individual component executable in itself? Which defects are known at the supplier? To be

Table 3.1 Test levels and test contents

Subject	Test level	Test
Response time	Load test	Load of the system with 500,000 requests within one hour
Database access	Integration test	Test of the integration of components A and B with database D
Settlement data set	System test	Checking the correct data set and fields
Print layout	System test	Control of the layout of the output documents: Logo arrangement Header Text (spelling, line breaks, arrangement) Page breaks

able to carry out this evaluation, it is recommended to also provide the supplier with corresponding index values to be able to carry out an evaluation that is as neutral as possible. Unfortunately, contractual agreements with suppliers usually contain no clear or insufficient specifications regarding quality level and test scope.

It is recommended to document the topics and test types in a table in the chapter on test objectives, for example, as in Table 3.1.

Reference should be made to the test specification or the tool in which it is recorded. The individual topics covered in the test concept must be found there.

References

1. https://www.enzyklo.de/, accessed on 9 May 2020
2. https://www.projektmagazin.de/artikel/testmanagement-it-projekten-teil-1_7180, accessed on 9 May 2020
3. Andreas Spillner, Tilo Linz, Basiswissen Softwaretest, 2007 dpunkt Verlag Heidelberg
4. Ernest Wallmüller, Software Quality Engineering, 2011 Carl Hanser Verlag Munich

Test Planning

4

Abstract

Test planning determines which work packages are to be completed by whom and in what order, plans the test resources and shows dependencies. Professional tools should be used for test planning. Suitable test methods and a realistic test effort estimate, the observance of time and cost restrictions and an evaluation of the test tasks are to be provided by the test manager within the framework of test planning.

4.1 Contents of Test Planning

Test planning is a subarea of project planning. Within software-developing organizations, software is predominantly developed in the form of projects. Since test planning and test effort determination are also tasks within the scope of project implementation, the project proves to be a relevant level of consideration for this work. Projects are characterized by the uniqueness of the conditions under which the set task is solved, and have the following features according to the **DIN 69901 standard**:

- Defined goal
- Time limit
- Relative novelty and complexity
- Risk liability and
- Interdisciplinary task [DOWI2009].

4.2   Sub-plans for IT Projects

The following sub-plans are usually prepared for IT projects (Table 4.1).

This overview basically also applies to subprojects for testing and quality assurance. The individual criteria must be considered in the test concept.

Table 4.1 Subplans of the project plan

Planning object/results	Questions that can be answered by the sub-plans
Project structure: **Work breakdown structure (WBS)**	What activities are necessary to achieve the project targets? (What needs to be done in detail?) What is the relationship between the project tasks? (form hierarchy of subtasks) How can objects and activities for the project be divided into work packages?
Project **schedule**: **Project schedule**	What are the phases of the project? In what order are the activities to be completed? Where are their logical dependencies? Which work packages can be executed in parallel?
Project dates (times): **Schedule**	How much time is estimated to be spent on each activity? By when is which activity to be completed? Are there certain milestones to be observed?
Resource demand, resource capacity, resource use: **Resource plans**	How many employees are needed for the individual work packages? What material resources are required? Which capacity limitations regarding resources have to be considered (capacity plan)? When is the availability of resources necessary (resource deployment plan)?
Costs and project finances: **Cost and financial plan**	Which costs (types of costs) are incurred for which work packages? How high are the total costs for the respective work package? What will the project cost in total and approximately? Can the total be determined by adding the work package costs (so-called direct costs) and the overhead costs? How high are the personnel costs incurred? How are the funds released? (timing, conditions)
Quality: **Quality assurance plan (QA plan)**	Which results should be processed in which quality/form? What quality assurance measures are to be taken during the project? (project-internal guidelines, QA training measures, reviews, tests)
Risk management: **Risk plan**	Which project risks are conceivable, and what is the probability of their occurrence? What are the possible effects in the event of risk? What preventive measures can be taken to minimize risks (priority plan of risks)?

(continued)

Table 4.1 (continued)

Planning object/results	Questions that can be answered by the sub-plans
Project organization: **Organizational plan,** **reporting plan**	What are the roles in the project? Which tasks, competencies and powers are to be assigned to each role, and how is the interaction between the project roles regulated? How is the communication between team, client and other stakeholders planned? How should the reporting system be organized? How is the project documented?

Fig. 4.1 Sub-tasks in project planning

The relationship between the subtasks in the planning of IT projects can be illustrated by Fig. 4.1:

The rough test planning should be done with a professional planning tool (a project management software such as Microsoft Project). Unfortunately, a paid license for such tools is saved in many projects. This kind of austerity usually increases the project costs ("we save, whatever it will cost"). If you do not consistently keep an eye on the deadlines and dependencies in test management and immediately take countermeasures in case of delays, you will quickly overlook problems and recognize warning signals too late.

Table 4.2 Overview of stakeholders in the project

Responsibility	Department	Employees	Phone number
Project management	XX1	Müller	11
		Rep: Meier	12
System test component A	XX2	Schmidt	15
		Rep: Huber	16
System test component B	XX2	Huber	16
		Rep: Schmidt	15
Integration test	XX3	Farmer	21
		Rep: Lehmann	22
…	…	…	…

It is still possible to manage smaller projects using Excel; however, this approach is clearly only possible to a very limited extent. The unavailability of professional planning tools alone is one of the unfavorable conditions that should be mentioned in the test concept. However, it should also be noted that the tool should be used consistently. If only the framework data is recorded once in the planning tool and the tool is only used for documentation purposes (unfortunately, this also happens again and again in practice), the purpose of the tool is reduced to absurdity.

For an overview of the individual test phases for the stakeholders, it is recommended to use a presentation as shown in Table 4.2.

4.3   Test Requirements

Systematic test planning requires certain information without which precise planning is not possible. If you want to plan the individual test activities precisely, you must know which and how many test cases are to be tested. This information can be derived from the requirements for new systems and from the system documentation or code analysis for existing systems. Therefore, requirements analysis is an absolute prerequisite for test planning and must take place before test planning. In practice, however, requirements analysis is unfortunately treated far too often shabbily: The documents for the offer are only at the sales department, the developer gets them maybe two days to be viewed but often only has the time to skim them and does not even check in detail what is coming to the programming. Often it is done "on the side" because the current project is not yet finished, and the future one is not yet pressing for time. During the project, this creates additional time and effort, so that again not enough time is planned for the requirements analysis of the subsequent project. Because many projects end late, resources are tied up and one does not get to the next project but one and so on and so forth. Unfortunately, a workshop with the customer and the development department is often dispensed due to "lack of time". In practice, the motto is often "We don't have the time to do things right once, but we have the time to do them wrong three times".

In component testing, it is necessary to analyze the source code of the component first. To define the test objectives. Before the integration test, the system architecture must first be analyzed. In system testing, it is the concept or the requirements specification that must be analyzed first to define the scope of the system test.

In agile process models, planning and execution are executed in short iterations. An **agile project** is by definition a non-deterministic process. The scope and content can still change during development, and no one can say at the beginning exactly where development will end, how long it will take, and how much it will cost. If, on the other hand, the requirements have been worked out and modeled in detail in classic projects, the information will be sufficient for systematic planning.

To define the test objectives – the reason – size measures of the system, e.g., the size of **function points, object points, test points** or statements and the failure rate of past or similar projects are needed. For new systems, the size measures must be obtained from the requirements analysis. For existing systems that are to be replaced, refurbished, migrated, or integrated, it is necessary (if no description is available) to first reverse engineer the old system to subsequently document it and then obtain the size measures from the post-documentation. This is a time-consuming and defect-prone process. The bug rate of previous projects can be determined from an analysis of the defect database. Without these measurements, it is hardly possible to define measurable test targets.

4.4   General Conditions of the Test Planning

The determination of the test dates depends on the delivery dates. The delivery dates are generally determined in the test plan. Consequently, test planning presupposes general project planning, and the test plan builds on the project plan.

The definition of the test location requires knowledge of the availability. At the time of test planning, the test manager must already know which hardware equipment will be used for testing and when this equipment will be available. The decision to distribute or centralize the test depends, among other things, on the availability of computer resources.

Choosing the right **test method** requires that the test manager knows the type of the application. He must know what is important, where the risks lie and where the most defects can occur. Only with this knowledge is he able to select the appropriate approach and in turn adapt it to the project. In addition, the test planner must be familiar with the common system test methods. Otherwise, he will not know which approaches are even available for selection.

4.5   Test Tools

For the targeted use of **test tools**, one must know which tools are available and for which task these tools are suitable (e.g., evaluation tools for measuring test coverage, test case generators). This is because, in contrast to the design of a new system, where one tool is usually sufficient, test execution requires a separate tool for each type of test activity. Test planning therefore requires information about the functionality and quality of the tools in question and the time needed to train them. To distribute the test work to the right employees, one must know the testers and test tasks exactly to be able to optimally distribute the available employees to the test tasks. The test itself also requires different focuses, e.g., in areas of script programming, methodology of expertise. Good coordination of the test manager can significantly increase productivity in this area.

4.6   Test Efforts and Test Automation

For the **test effort estimation,** mostly data oriented toward past project is required. This involves the defect rate (number of bugs found in previous projects) and the defect density as the number of defects per 1000 or 100 size units, which can be transferred to the new system as a measure. The units of size can be lines of code, statements, function points, or even test cases. This measure must be put into perspective by the degree of test coverage. It is therefore not sufficient to know only the number of absolute defects, but one must also consider the size of the affected software and the degree of test coverage in addition.

Testers need to develop as many effective **test cases** as possible to track down possible causes of defects. The extent to which they succeed in doing so depends on their productivity. In system testing, productivity is a measure of the number of test cases that a tester is capable of performing per unit of time. This number varies from project to project and depends strongly on the degree of test automation as well as on the experience and creativity of the testers. Nevertheless, future efforts can only be predicted based on previous productivity. For this purpose, corresponding empirical values are required for test planning, from which the ratio of tester days performed to the number of test cases executed is derived [SNEE2012].

To evaluate **test automation,** it is necessary to define in advance how high the degree of automation is for test case creation, test execution and test reporting. Often, only the test execution is considered unilaterally – however, the preparation and planning of the test runs and the evaluation of the test results require an effort that is often underestimated, even with automated tests.

References

1. Sneed, Baumgartner, Seidl: Der Systemtest, Carl Hanser Verlag Munich 2012
2. Ulrike Dowie, Testaufwandsschätzung in der Softwareentwicklung, Josef-Eul-Verlag Cologne 2009

Designation of the Test Concept and Introduction

5

Abstract

For test concepts, whether they are created generically for the entire company or project-related, some general specifications and the correct versioning of the document must be observed. In the introduction to project-related test concepts, the necessity of the corresponding project must be addressed. Relevant project documents must be referenced in the test concept. Agile projects have some special features that must be taken into account already in the concept creation phase. The test concept must be elaborated at the beginning of the test phase.

5.1 Designation and Storage of the Test Concept

Each test concept must have a unique designation (ideally an ID) so that it can be found again even after the test activities have been completed. Versioning must also be carried out. If the test concept was created using a template, there must be a cover sheet that has been completed in full.

It should also be examined where the test concept is stored, e.g. whether all stakeholders have access to the corresponding drive. The testers should get used to consulting the test concept first for open questions.

© Springer Fachmedien Wiesbaden GmbH, part of Springer Nature 2022
F. Witte, *Strategy, Planning and Organization of Test Processes*,
https://doi.org/10.1007/978-3-658-36981-1_5

5.2   Test Concepts for a Longer Period of Time

Sometimes a project drags on over a longer period of time. In this case, it may make sense to create individual test concepts for different releases or versions. In general, a modular structure should be chosen when creating test concepts (Fig. 5.1):

The test concept describes the environment, activities and procedures for the tests of the project described. It concretizes the processes and guidelines described in the document that was created for the overall test strategy of the entire company. Any deviations are described and justified here.

The test concept builds on information from other areas that work together. The modular structure (Fig. 5.1) avoids redundancies and the reading effort corresponds to the respective information requirement.

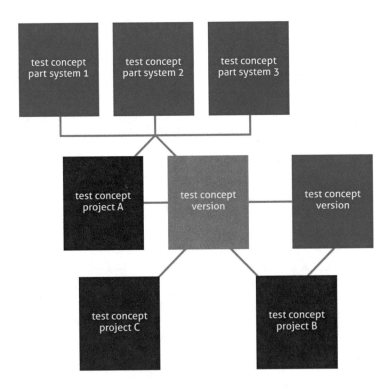

Fig. 5.1 Modular structure of the test concepts

5.3   Formal Principles

The **review** of the test concept should ideally take place before the start of the test phases. It should be provided with a version (e.g. version 2.1 from May 6, 2020).

This **versioning** means that a defined version is available at the start of the test activities.

One must be able to define at any time (e.g. in the context of an audit) which version of the test concept was valid at a defined test phase or at a certain point in time.

Example:

Version 1.0: 10.03.

Version 2.0: 03.04.

Version 2.1: 06.05.

Testing of Release 1.0 took place from 20.04. to 30.04., so Version 2.0 from 03.04. is the test concept to be followed for this release.

The name already defines the subject and the object of the test. Any naming conventions that apply in the company for the designation must be observed. In any case, the name must be unique and correspond to the name of the project. Attention must be paid to details: If the project to be tested is called "Introduction 3-D Secure", the test concept must not be called "Test Concept Introduction 3D-Secure", but rather "Test Concept Introduction 3-D Secure". Otherwise, such details can lead to serious problems during assessments or audits. How can a test manager be believed to ensure quality if his statements are not 100% accurate?

When creating the test concept, it should be considered to ensure a clear structure and good, concise outline. The test concept should contain tables and graphics and be easily understandable for all stakeholders of the project. The test concept should contain a table of contents, abbreviations, definitions and sources. It should be considered that the table of contents is consistent with the outline of the document. All terms and abbreviations that are not commonly known must be defined or explained within the text. The pages of the test concept should be numbered and clearly identifiable as belonging to the document version. The document must be complete, i.e. no pages, text passages or illustrations may be missing, cross-references must be unambiguous and reference documents must be listed. When using images and graphical representations, it will be necessary that they complement the text in a meaningful way, that they are clear and not overloaded, that they are comprehensible with regard to the symbols used and that they are clearly assigned to the relevant chapters or passages in the text. General company-internal or project-specific guidelines for the preparation of documents must be observed. Methods, tools and standards must be taken into account. Confidentiality levels and copyrights must be identified and observed.

5.4   Introduction Test Concept

The introduction to the test concept should describe the project: What is the test item at issue? What features does the product contain, and which of them should be tested and which should not be tested? Which individual **test objects** are included?

For this purpose, it is advisable to include a summary of the technical description, i.e. a brief presentation of the corresponding project. The presentation of the project background helps the stakeholders to better understand the content of the test concept. This presentation should clearly show the background for the task and the benefits, so that all stakeholders can identify with the project in the best possible way.

What is the reason for the necessity of carrying out the project, a new technology, an improvement of the workflow, legal requirements? The name already defines the topic and the object of the test. It should also define why the project should be carried out. Reasons for the necessity of carrying out the project can be:

- contractual obligations (e.g. from tenders, contracts),
- legal regulations (e.g. EU directives, requirements of supervisory authorities),
- consequences of corporate decisions or corporate strategy (e.g. group strategies, customer quality offensive, cost reduction measures, sales plans),
- technological necessity (e.g. necessary replacement of legacy systems),
- dependencies on previous projects (e.g. project builds on expertise provided by a preliminary project),
- Project is a prerequisite for follow-up projects (e.g. project creates expertise on which an already planned/parallel/later project is based, the project serves as an "enabler" for further projects).

In addition, this chapter should describe when the test is finished or when it is terminated. As a rule, the end of testing is limited by costs and deadline restrictions anyway; you cannot continue testing indefinitely in order to possibly still find errors.

The **defect detection curve** normally follows approximately the following course (Fig. 5.2):

You can see that at a certain point the productivity of the test team decreases and hardly any new defects are found. An experienced test manager can roughly estimate this point, and experience values from previous projects can also be used. However, it is also possible to carry out detailed planning, which makes the test progress dependent on the test depth and the implementation of the requirements (acquired "**test points**"). However, this is a more involved procedure. In practice, the time available for testing is limited by the project plan anyway, so the question of the sensible end of testing activities is rather academic.

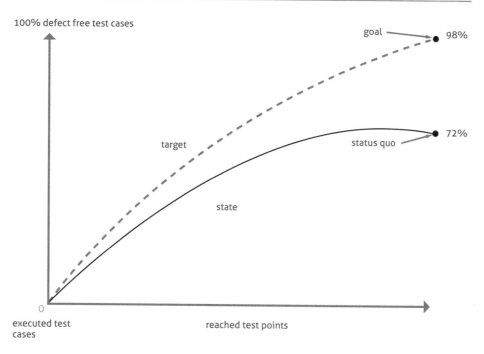

Fig. 5.2 Defect detection curve

In the introduction to the test concept, the test objective should be discussed: What is to be achieved with the test? Which risks should be avoided? What is the quality standard of the project or the organization? This also determines the depth to which the test must be carried out. Which standards and guidelines are to be observed during the test? Is the test objective to pass a certification according to a certain standard or guideline?

In the test concept, criteria for **test interruption** and **test restart** should also be documented in an introductory chapter. If the application contains serious errors, e.g. a response time that is considerably too long or important basic functions are not available, it may make more sense to interrupt the test and only restart it after the error has been corrected. The conditions for this (e.g. errors with priority "critical" or errors that prevent testing, e.g. if the application under test cannot be started at all) must also be defined in the introduction to the test concept. A test interruption, however, can lead to the fact that one must give up one's resources intended for one's own project to another project. If the software is ready for testing again after some time and the interruption is over, you may not be able to get the testers back because they will then be tied up in the other project, and you will have to allow for further delays in the project. It is therefore better to use the time of the test interruption for test-related project work such as improving the level of test automation.

5.5   Documents Referenced in the Test Concept

At this point in the test concept, reference should also be made to the **documents** relevant to the test:

- Specifications, rough concept, detailed concept,
- Technical design, design documents,
- User manuals, operating manuals, operating instructions as well as.
- Installation notes.

Here it is advisable for the test manager to at least roughly sift through the available documents and check their quality. First of all, it should be checked whether the documents already exist or whether they are still in the process of being created. Furthermore, the level of detail of the specifications and concepts and the clarity of the **requirements** are decisive for the success of the test.

If you already notice at this point that requirements are missing, contradictory or unclear (which experience shows is unfortunately the case in most projects), you can already formulate a considerable test risk here. The test can only be as good as the requirements and framework allow it to be. If you already notice that there is a considerable need for action in this regard when creating the introduction to the test concept, you can proactively propose measures here to prevent the project from failing. If one has not started all testing activities too late (this also still happens far too often!), one can at least still warn in time which problems are to be expected in the near future.

It can also be seen time and again that development is started too quickly. There is a good reason for this, because you want to be able to present presentable results as quickly as possible. This is particularly the case when an existing pre-product is technologically expanded or modified. People like to invest in the demonstration of a prototype because this gives them a vivid idea of the final product and customers or clients a better impression of the target state. In most cases, investment in testing activities is only made later in the course of the project, because it is noticed that there are many errors in the product that need to be improved. Then, however, the task definition and concepts are still incomplete, and this is gradually noticed during testing. It can also often be observed that development has long since overtaken the design phase and the system architecture subsequently documents what was developed anyway, but does not lay down the basis from the outset as it should be implemented in classic models according to the V-model. The agile approach in turn has the problem that development is supposed to start even faster and the individual project phases are supposed to be accelerated, but often too little attention is paid to the correct definition of requirements.

Classic / Waterfall

Agile / Repetitive

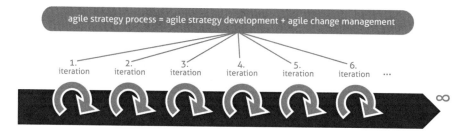

Fig. 5.3 Strategy processes in the classic and agile model

This is not a problem of the **agile process model** itself, but of a wrong implementation of the agile model, which can be observed in many organizations. People write "agile" on their banner without having sufficiently considered the meaning and consequences, and are basically engaging in label fraud. One of the tenets of agile principles is that the best architectures, requirements, and designs emerge from self-organized teams. But nowhere does it say that this can be dispensed with.

Test management is also crucial for agile projects; the role of the tester is changing, but by no means dissolving. Agile testing requires good plannability, traceability and verifiability of the test activities, a high level of systematic test design and, as a result, high and reproducible test coverage.

The following sketch (Fig. 5.3) shows the difference between the **strategy processes** in classical and agile approaches:

In **release planning**, a complete release is planned. However, the test concept is still required for the individual project. Several projects are usually implemented in one release. The transition from the classic to the agile model is shown in the following figure (Fig. 5.4).

The test concept is still required. Each task of the role "Test Manager" can be assigned Scrum artifacts (Fig. 5.5).

In the case of a cross-departmental or cross-project test concept, strategic objectives for quality assurance, basic organizational specifications and the necessity of a general, overarching test concept should be explained. In this case, the overarching planning, management and control of all test activities of the company or a department in the company is described, which applies generically to all projects, unless specific specifications are made

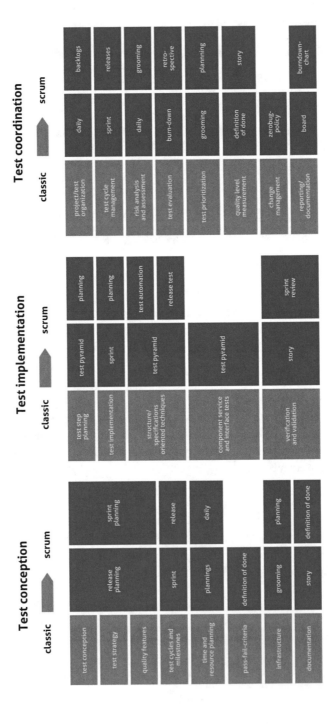

Fig. 5.4 Agile transition of the test manager

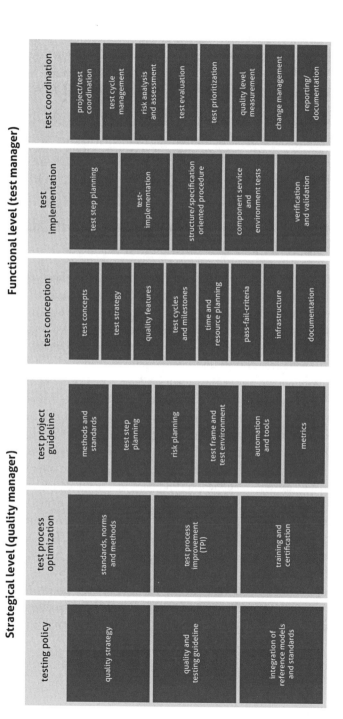

Fig. 5.5   Scrum and test management [AGIL2016]

in the individual project. In practice, it is often the case that this concept is either not known at all, is outdated, or is so general that it is of no help in the daily process. As a consequence, the department responsible for quality assurance or the quality manager of the project stands as a separate instance next to the projects and is not sufficiently perceived by the development projects. However, it is an essential task for a quality department to implement general guidelines for quality assurance and to adapt them to the operational processes. Particular difficulties and discrepancies between theory and practice thus become evident and can be optimized in a targeted manner.

The test concept should allow a software development project to be tested in a comprehensible and traceable manner at any time and a release decision to be made.

5.6   Test Framework with Test Requirements, Defect Classes and Start Conditions

The introduction to the test concept should also describe the rough time frame and the **test requirements.** The conditions for starting the test should also be clearly stated.

During a software test in a corresponding test level according to ISTQB (component test, integration test, system test, acceptance test), many errors are detected. So that the developer knows which problems he must solve with high, medium and low priority, it has proven useful to define **defect classes.** In the acceptance test, the defect class is still linked to corresponding regulations between the client and the contractor. For example, a **contractual penalty** can be stipulated for each defect in defect class 1. It is also conceivable that the client can withdraw from the contract after a certain number of defects. This can be freely arranged in the contract between the parties.

In general, the errors are divided into 3 **error classes.** Error class 1 (serious bugs) are bugs that lead to the software not being usable. These include bugs in central functions that lead to the abortion of the entire application and bugs that preclude the testing of further subareas. For bugs of error class 2 (medium bugs) are bugs in the application that do not lead to termination, but are nevertheless so significant that a live transition is not reasonable and cannot be circumvented by organizational means (tricks to circumvent the bugs = workaround). Minor bugs (error class 3) are all bugs that cannot be assigned to error class 1 or 2 [BLMS2012].

The test concept should be created at the beginning of the **test phase**. If the test object is software that has only been developed in a new version, but was introduced in a first version some time ago (e.g., if the new version represents a significant expansion of functionality), you can build on an existing test concept. However, it is usually better to create a new document. However, this also depends heavily on the scope of the changes or enhancements.

References

1. https://2016.agileworld.de/sites/agileworld/files/agiletestmanagement.pdf, zugegriffen am 09.05.2020
2. https://blog.milsystems.de/2012/04/fehlerklassengenerator-zur-klassifikation-von-softwarefehlern/, zugegriffen am 09.05.2020

Test Organization

6

Abstract

Successful projects require professional organization. In this context, among other things, detailed test planning, the organization of test resources, regular status meetings and coordination during the project must be considered. The test organization forms a subarea of the project organization and must consider the structures of the project and the organizational unit.

6.1 Essential Criteria of the Test Organization

The professionalization of testing goes hand in hand with a transformation of today's organization. New service concepts, often in the form of so-called **test factory models**, are applied. Precisely defined areas are cut out of the customer organization's test portfolio and then implemented in the form of an industrialized "**managed service model**". The design of the **test factory services** is varied depending on the individual customer requirements: the scope of the test procedures, scalability of the test volumes, flexible test content and billing models on a test case basis characterize these solution models. In addition, service level agreements tailored to customer requirements are among the important components of a test factory implementation [IODT2019].

The chosen form of **test organization** should be dealt with in a separate chapter of the test concept. The individual stakeholders and their roles should be defined and their responsibilities shown. The individual employees should be identified with their exact area of responsibility, telephone number/address data and, if applicable, department name. If necessary, the telephone list of the organizational unit should be referenced to avoid multiple data maintenance.

© Springer Fachmedien Wiesbaden GmbH, part of Springer Nature 2022   49
F. Witte, *Strategy, Planning and Organization of Test Processes*,
https://doi.org/10.1007/978-3-658-36981-1_6

For a test manager, it is absolutely necessary to know about the status of the test activities and possible problems at any time. This can be achieved with daily or, at most, weekly short coordination meetings. The individual meetings may be short, it is often just a matter of a "water-level report", but the intervals between the reconciliations should not be too long, so experience shows that one week apart is the maximum.

The **test progress report thanks to** used tools shows the test progress and quality in a standardized way. This test progress report should also be created weekly in every project from the beginning for the following reasons:

- Information of all stakeholders and management about assessment of progress and quality and significant activities, problems, changes of the current period.
- Outlook on planned next measures.
- Identification of the strategy and any necessary changes to the strategy during the life of the project.
- Identification of risks and measures to reduce these risks.
- Commonly known assessment of progress and quality.
- Serious defects that jeopardize the achievement of objectives or prevent testing activities.
- Securing of one's own position and self-marketing for the importance of test management.

It is recommended that the test status report is prepared on Friday and presented on Monday at the latest. This is because if there are any changes based on the current status or if management recommends other countermeasures, it is possible to instruct changes relatively quickly. If a status report from the previous week is not presented until the middle of the current week, many statements are already outdated because the dynamics in projects are generally too high for this. In many projects, it is common to send the test status report only by mail. From my experience, this is not sufficient. At least once a month, a project review is recommended to be able to point out certain problems directly or to emphasize certain aspects. A project review meeting has the advantage that all participants deal intensively with the topic at the same time, whereas a written report is sometimes only skimmed over and filed away, unless the content looks like serious difficulties.

Experience shows that it becomes challenging when part of the test team is located offshore. This can already be difficult if the team is distributed across different locations within a few kilometers (I speak from my own experience as well), and with a test team abroad there are also language problems, cultural differences and possibly different time zones. It is therefore invaluable to regularly check in with offshore teams on the other side of the world at least every few months and to discuss open problems on site. In such a case, regular conference calls are needed anyway, but they generally reduce productivity and efficiency in the team considerably. Even today, video technology is usually not yet professional enough for a virtual conference to even come close to a face-to-face exchange.

Unfavorable framework conditions that a test manager recognizes right from the start should be quantified. For example, in the case of a distinct offshore organization or organizations that are distributed across several locations, planning values for the test effort can be set at a flat rate of 10–20% higher than for a team that constantly works together on site. Single days of working from home, on the other hand, are possible with a well-established team without significantly reducing productivity. However, these assumptions should always be converted into hours and, consequently, into money because only in this way can the risk assessment be sufficiently transparent and evaluated and not just dismissed as general whining by the test manager. One can have different opinions about certain assessment factors, but it is crucial that they are applied and documented from the outset. Working from home is well suited for delimited, defined work packages, such as defining test cases or coding a piece of software. The possibilities for distributed work have improved considerably in recent years due to technical progress, but personal exchange must still be guaranteed.

To speed up communication in the test team, it makes sense to set up a **chat** between the test manager and the test team. In a chat, communication can be accelerated, but sometimes it develops a momentum of its own that can hardly be captured. If you are a test manager and use chat to inform your team because some facts have come as a surprise or decisions have to be communicated to all members immediately, it can be difficult to catch the communication again. I was once in the situation of having to communicate a certain piece of information that affected the entire team to the staff via chat, and then had to recapture the communication with 5 testers who disagreed with the decision, complained about it, and were goading each other. The communication quickly takes on a life of its own; suddenly people are chatting about topics that are only indirectly related to the original problem. This is a phenomenon that exists in social media and forums in general. In this case, I had to call a meeting to calm things down and in the end, I lost an entire day for the whole team.

It is also urgently necessary to establish clear rules for the chat from the beginning, when and how it is used, what may and may not be the subject of the chat. You can often talk more informally in a chat than in an email, but it should not get out of hand because otherwise essential information could be lost.

However, from my point of view, it is still better to set up a chat and increase the dynamics than to let rumors arise and spread them via "office grapevine". In this case, the dynamics in communication are even more difficult to capture. It can be very problematic if the project is talked *about* in a company unit and not *with* the responsible test managers and project managers.

The test organization includes the organization of the **test resources**. These can be test personnel, computing time, data provision and hardware required for the test.

6.2   Test Personnel and Tester Deployment Planning

Regarding the test personnel, it must be checked which employees are available for the test and to what extent. Is the employee needed for other activities or other projects that may have a higher priority than the own project? Furthermore, it must be considered when which tester is needed for which work package in the project process.

Example of **tester scheduling** (in hours):

Tester scheduling should be broken down to the individual workday and then condensed to weeks and months.

The specialties of the individual testers must be considered: If one tester is primarily responsible for describing the test cases and another is more likely to perform the automated scripts, their deployment plan must provide for this in the corresponding phases. The tester scheduling can be done in PT (as in Table 6.1) or on an hourly basis (as in Table 6.2).

After you have created the tester deployment planning based on individual working days, you can condense it to a weekly or monthly basis.

However, there are often shifts within the project: in the above plan, tester B was scheduled for March for 140 hours. If it is about the test execution, but the software is not ready on time in March, his effort is partially shifted to April. Now, however, he may be on vacation for 2 weeks scheduled in April, so he may start later and be on the "**critical path**" with his effort. So, you have to reschedule and check if a substitute can be used and if the postponement of the delivery may have an impact on the planned end date. Therefore, the use of a professional planning tool is recommended for resource planning. Especially when testers are tied up in different projects, it may happen that they are not utilized at all or underutilized in certain periods, but over-scheduled in other periods. When planning the test effort, always include time that has been set aside for general internal coordination or

Table 6.1 Tester deployment planning per day in M/D

Tester	Monday 15 Feb.	Tuesday 16 Feb.	Wednesday 17 Feb	Thursday 18 Feb.
A	1	1	1	1
B	0.5	1	1	0.5
C	0	0	1	1

Table 6.2 Condensed tester deployment planning on an hourly basis

Tester	January	February	March	April
A	60	80	80	40
B	40	80	140	80
C	0	60	80	100

further training. There should therefore be regular communication between the line organization and the project or test management about deployment areas and availabilities. In
my experience, this relatively trivial point in particular is not given sufficient attention in
many companies. I have often had testers scheduled for certain tasks and then suddenly
heard from the line organization at short notice that they are otherwise scheduled or absent
during this period. In this case, a lot of flexibility and spontaneity is required from the test
manager and the entire department.

Especially when test automation is not yet sufficiently advanced, it may be necessary to
repeat test cases manually for a transitional period. You do not necessarily need trained test
analysts for this, but can perhaps also recruit temporary staff (e.g., via a temporary employ-
ment agency) or students to carry out the tests. For this to happen, however, the test cases
must be precisely described, and the analysis must be clear. In most cases, this means that
working with temporary staff comes up against very narrow limits. In this case, it must
also be possible to react quickly at short notice. A certain amount of time and effort for
training and general organization must be planned. However, the general goal must always
be to automate test cases as much as possible. But it must also be borne in mind that test
automation requires a certain lead time and does not go live with the first test cycles, but
rather pays off in the medium term.

6.3   Computing Time

In the 1970s or 1980s, computing times for the mainframe were often allocated to individual projects. In the meantime, computing time is irrelevant for most projects, since the
computing capacity of the hardware used has long ceased to be a limitation, but is usually
only utilized to an incredibly small fraction, and consequently no restrictions need to be
observed here. Only in the case of very computationally intensive projects, for example in
astronomy, space travel or meteorology, or the evaluation of very large data volumes, is the
computing time still a relevant factor limiting the test.

6.4   Data Provision

Each tester needs his own data, so that the data of other users are not changed during the test execution. However, the data is not always kept separate. It still happens that the disk storage capacity is not sufficient, or the database system only allows one copy. However, this problem has also diminished significantly in most organizations in recent years.

6.5   Hardware Required

If special machines or additional equipment are required for the test environment, it may be necessary to book them. This may also involve the need for special test workstations to be available in a laboratory for specific projects. This includes, for example, the scheduling of test vehicles for test drives. In the case of test drives abroad lasting several days, in addition to configuring the test vehicles with the appropriate hardware and software, regulations regarding driving and rest times must also be observed. Particularly for tests in the field, the hardware also includes equipping the testers with mobile phones and sufficient backup media. Copying hard drives alone can be a logistical feat.

6.6   Project Organization

Every company or organization has a certain structure. For example, there is the company management, departments and the employees working in them. This structure is called the master organization (or line organization).

However, since projects are complex and demanding "special projects", project teams and organizational structures are formed (temporarily) to ensure better implementation, which separates them from the "normal" organizational structure.

Thus, in addition to the core organization, a project organization is formed that describes the composition of the roles, authorities and interfaces of a project. And thus, the project organization is of central importance for the success of the project.

Because only if all persons involved know which tasks, responsibilities and authorities they have within a project (and how these relate to the parent organization), they can also behave accordingly (correctly).

6.7   Stakeholders and Roles in the Project Organization

Each project has its own composition of project participants. Therefore, the composition of a project organization can also vary greatly from case to case. However, the following parties should always be considered (and only excluded with a good justification):

- The **client** is the person or organization (unit) that has given the order for the implementation of the project, and must therefore also be represented in the project organization.
- The **steering committee** is a decision-making body superior to the project manager and has the following tasks, among others: Formulating the project mission, allocating resources, approving budgets and project phases, etc. It can make sense to form a steering committee for a project; however, it is not mandatory.
- The **project manager** (or **project lead**) is responsible for planning, monitoring and controlling a project and must therefore be represented in the project organization in any case.
- And finally: the **project team members** who are to implement the tasks [ERFO2016].

6.8   Organizational Structure

It is absolutely essential that the company management or the client of the project take care to create the necessary organizational structure (values and guidelines of the company) and the structural prerequisites for holistic-situational project work. If they do not do justice to this task, the project can be doomed to failure before it has even begun.

Table 6.3 shows the necessary requirements.

6.9   Project Steering Committee

The establishment of steering committees is particularly useful for larger projects. As a decision-making, coordination and controlling body, the establishment of a **project steering committee** (PLA) at the overall organizational level is frequently encountered. This committee is sometimes also referred to as a decision committee, decision commission, steering group, steering board, steering committee, steering committee or control board. It forms the interface between

- Project, project management and project team on the one side and.

Table 6.3 Support of the project work by the corporate management

General conditions	Guidelines (project management culture)
Sufficient freedom for the project team is guaranteed	At least one member of the corporate management is involved in terms of content (as a "sponsor").
The conditions for an optimal information basis of the team members are created.	No one in the company should see project work as a threat, but as an opportunity to innovate and make improvements.
A positive working atmosphere for the cooperation of project team and specialist departments is ensured.	Competent employees are to be released or made available for the project work upon request. Ongoing training for the advancement of project team members shall be provided.
Sufficient administrative support will be provided to the project management and the project team.	There should be no rivalry between project management in the company and the other managers, but a willingness to learn from and support each other.

- Management and external stakeholders on the other side.

This committee surveys the project from inception to implementation. It represents the highest committee for the planning and control of all projects that are realized in an organization. This is where the decisive course is ultimately set for further project progress. Thus, the project steering committee can usually decide whether the project should be stopped or even aborted if it becomes apparent that the project goals will not be achieved at all or that other higher-level goals will even be jeopardized by the project.

Regarding the composition, it has proven successful to delegate high-ranking executives to this committee. Since decisions of considerable importance are made in each committee, a member of the management and the IT management should always be represented in the project steering committee. The project management can sometimes also participate in the meetings (with different voting rights).

It has proven to be useful for the members of the steering committee to meet at regular intervals (e.g., monthly), and also on an unscheduled basis if necessary. Regarding the decision-making rules, the "unanimity principle" applies to achieve extensive coordination between the areas involved and for subsequent implementation.

In the project management method **PRINCE 2** (projects in controlled environments), the composition of the members of the project steering committee depends on the project phases so that they always meet regularly at the end of each project phase to sign off the completed project phase and approve the following phase. The project steering committee can also be convened outside the regular meetings as needed to decide on so-called exception reports or urgent change requests.

References

1. https://www.iot-design.de/allgemein/transformation-von-testorganisationen/, accessed on 9 May 2020
2. https://erfolgreich-projekte-leiten.de/projektorganisation/, accessed on 9 May 2020

Process Description

7

Abstract

The test process consists of several phases and is to be accompanied by regular defined coordination meetings. The project members in the test team have certain tasks and contribute to the success of the test through active action and targeted communication. Test requirements necessary for the success of the project must be observed and organized.

7.1   Test process According to ISTQB

The **test process** defined according to the ISTQB standard consists of five activities (Fig. 7.1):

- Planning and control,
- Analysis and design,
- Realization and implementation,
- Evaluation and report and.
- Test completion.

The individual steps do not have to be executed exactly one after the other, but can also run in parallel. Feedback can also occur, for example if it is noticed during test execution that the test design must be changed for a particular test case.

© Springer Fachmedien Wiesbaden GmbH, part of Springer Nature 2022   59
F. Witte, *Strategy, Planning and Organization of Test Processes*,
https://doi.org/10.1007/978-3-658-36981-1_7

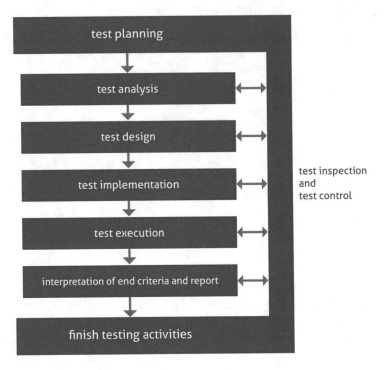

Fig. 7.1 Test process [BAST2015]

7.2   Planning and Control

The test process must be handled in a structured manner. Therefore, the availability of the required test resources must be planned exactly. A schedule for the individual test activities is a necessary component of a test concept.

Test control includes the ongoing monitoring of all activities within the scope of tests, developments and corrections, but also the on-time and correct test reporting.

Appropriate **meetings** (Table 7.1) are scheduled for test control during the project period.

If necessary, defect meetings can also be convened spontaneously, for example on a specific defect, to discuss further activities and necessary steps. Regular defect boards or change control boards are used to evaluate the scope and consequences of defects and to initiate the necessary measures.

During test execution, requirements are often changed, or additional requirements are added. This is especially the case in agile projects. A change process must be introduced for this.

Changes must be documented, their effects on the overall system and on the test must be evaluated, and the costs must be calculated. The changes must be checked and released

Table 7.1 Suitable meetings in the test process

Meeting	Purpose	Participant	Rhythm
Status meeting	Informing management about test activities and defining possible control measures	Project manager Test manager Quality manager	Weekly
Defect meeting	Status and necessary activities for troubleshooting	Test manager Release manager Integrator Developer	Weekly
Test phase completion	Acceptance meeting and decision on continuation of test activities into next test phase	Project manager Test manager SW integrator	After each test phase
Review meeting	Document review	Test phase Tester	As needed
Acceptance meeting	Decision on going live after the acceptance phase	Steering committee Project manager Customer Test manager Integrator Release manager	Unique
Release meeting	Information about the activities in the release and definition of possible control measures	Test manager Release manager	Weekly

by defined bodies. The rules and processes for assessing changes and the competencies must be clearly described in advance [EPHE2016].

7.3   Meetings at the Start of the Project

Especially at the beginning of a project, motivation, awareness of the project and agreement on forms of cooperation for the members of the project team are of particular importance. In addition, all those who will be affected by the project results in the future, as well as those who are to be involved in the project work, must be adequately informed in advance. It has proven useful to hold two types of **launch events:**

- a **start-up workshop** with the project team, and,
- an information event for all those concerned (= **kick-off meeting**).

With a well-prepared project-related start-up workshop, the first foundations for a successful project are laid. In particular, the start-up workshop can help to ensure that

- The members of the project team get to know each other better (personal experiences and goals may also be addressed),
- A common identity develops in the project team,
- An initial casting of roles in the project is made, and
- Potential risks and conflicts for the project work are already identified in the start-up phase.

The kick-off meeting is usually prepared by the test manager or test project manager and differs from the start-up workshop on the one hand in terms of the group of participants. In addition to the project management and the project team should participate:

- Representative of the client (for external projects representative of the client),
- Management of the implementing institution (such as a corporate sponsor) and
- Key project stakeholders and persons affected by the projects (stakeholders).

Stakeholders in IT, whether software developers or testers, each speak a specific language and view the project from entirely different perspectives. The team is highly interdisciplinary, so project management and test management must enable people with different ways of thinking to work together.

The project team is ultimately responsible for the execution of the various subtasks in the project, whereby each team member must make his or her appropriate contribution.

Table 7.2 shows the typical tasks of the project staff and their existing powers.

Table 7.2 Tasks and powers of project members

Typical tasks	Powers/responsibility
Independent and responsible processing of work packages	Participation in ensuring that the project objectives are achieved
Objectively qualified completion of the tasks taken on within the agreed time frame	Completion of work orders on time and within budget
Regular status reports on the status of the work packages taken over	Co-determination in decisions and agreements on project work
Immediate notification of the project manager in the event of factual or time-related deviations from the plan	Active participation in team meetings and dynamic communication
Support of the project management by participation in the project planning	Timely request of personnel, material resources (capacities) and finances from the project management
Preparation of decision papers	
Preparation of reports necessary for project control (activity reports, work orders and work order completion)	

7.4   Analysis and Design

The analysis is carried out in the test concept creation phase. The first step is to check whether the relevant processes are known and the test objectives can be clearly defined. The requested test coverage must also be described.

Furthermore, it must be calculated whether the required scope of testing can be performed at all with the existing resources. If it is not possible to acquire additional testers at short notice, a risk analysis must be carried out to determine which test cases can be dispensed with.

In this phase, it must also be assessed to what extent the system is testable at all. If only partial functionalities are available at the beginning of the test, it must be checked to what extent a statement about the testability of the entire system can be derived from this.

The definition of the test cases is usually started somewhat later than the creation of the test concept. The definition of the test requirements, test data and references to preceding tests are also part of the test design. Deviations and special features compared to standard processes must also be planned in this phase. The conception for test automation in the project should also start parallel to the test case definition. Each test case that is to be executed automatically must have been tested manually at least once in a basic version.

7.5   Realization and Implementation

This phase begins with a smoke test, which checks the basic availability of the test system. This can determine whether problems already exist with main functions or basic features.

Especially during manual test execution, test cases should be processed in a prioritized manner. The functionality of essential functions of the test object must be in the foreground to be able to make statements about the software quality relatively quickly. This is especially true if resource bottlenecks or delays in the provision of the test object have already occurred.

In complex test scenarios, in which one step builds on the other, if a function fails at the beginning of the chain, the entire test process should not be aborted immediately, but the defect should be noted and, if necessary, tested further with a workaround solution. Then it is still possible to deliver meaningful results over the period. However, there is a risk that subsequent defects will occur, which will also no longer occur if the first bug is corrected. This requires a lot of experience and system knowledge on the part of the tester. Very complex test scenarios with many dependencies of the individual steps within the procedure therefore always bear the risk of delays and unsuccessful test results.

Such constellations can also occur with automated test cases. In these cases, the statistics show a considerable decrease in quality. It is therefore critical to allow sufficient time for a target-oriented analysis of the results, even with automated tests.

Regression tests (test repetitions) should always be carried out completely. In practice, it often happens that when a defect is corrected, new bugs occur as a side effect of the correction, or a defect was masked by another defect and can only be found after the defect has been corrected. If complete repetitions are dispensed with for reasons of time, a risk assessment must always be carried out by the test manager and the risk documented and evaluated in the final report.

The specifications for implementation and execution should generally be made in the overall test concept.

7.6   Evaluation and Report

Metrics should already be defined in advance, which will be collected and reported on a weekly basis as part of the test implementation (Chaps. 1, 6, 3).

The ongoing evaluation allows the test manager to ensure that the schedule is adhered to and to record the time of acceptance.

In the event of particular problems or urgent need for clarification, escalation should also take place outside reporting cycles.

7.7   Test Completion

At the end of the test process, an **acceptance test is** to be performed to demonstrate the correct functioning of the test system using selected test cases.

For this purpose, a special date is agreed with the customer. The test cases to be demonstrated should be defined in advance and should have already been presented to the customer.

As a rule, one restricts oneself to the essential functions and features of the system, not to exotic special cases. Selected test scenarios are defined for this purpose. The acceptance test is demonstrated on an environment that exactly mirrors the production environment (if necessary, also on the production environment if there are no problems in production). This is important, as otherwise the results of the acceptance test cannot be transferred with certainty.

Experience has shown that all stakeholders and other projects that use the acceptance environment should be informed of this in advance. I have experienced a customer acceptance that had to be repeated because the environment was not configured as agreed on the same day. This is extremely embarrassing when several representatives of the customer were specially invited and have to travel from another location on that day.

Special care and sufficient time must therefore be planned for the preparation of the acceptance test. The acceptance should be carried out one day before the customer's visit as a "general rehearsal" exactly as on the day itself to minimize the risk of a failed acceptance. Otherwise, it is better (if possible) to postpone the date from the outset instead of having to carry out a repeated acceptance.

7.8   Documents as a Prerequisite for Testing

The test concept should define what information the tester needs from the development department in addition to the software.

The following documents are recommended:

- **Release notes**: Release notes are documents that are distributed with software products, sometimes when the product is still in development or testing status. For products that have already been used by customers, the release note is sent to the customer when an update is released.
- **Feature list:** The feature list provides an overview of all features. If the software offers different scopes in the differently licensed versions (e.g., "Gold" – "Silver" – "Bronze"), the possible features per version are marked. In the case of a handover during the development project, the feature list can be used to document the features that have not yet been completed.
- **Documentation of limitations**: This describes whether there are any known bugs or limitations in the software delivery that can only be fixed in a subsequent version.
- **Requirements:** This documents which requirements have already been implemented in the software and for which requirements the realization is still open. A **traceability matrix** describes which requirement is covered by which test cases and which test case refers to which requirement. This document is important for the traceability and evaluation of new requirements, and not least for audits of the test process.

- **Architecture sketch:** For users and developers of the software project, a well-constructed software architecture easily gives a basic understanding of the system. Important factors that influence the aptitude of software architecture are project planning, risk analysis, organization, development process, workflow, hardware, quality assurance and requirements. This software architecture is captured pictorially in a diagram. In the case of a web application, for example, an architecture description includes the structure of the system from databases, web/application servers, e-mail and cache systems. It must be checked which information is required to be able to carry out a test.

References

1. https://ephesos.fhsg.ch/documents/10328/103271/13983558_Fiorelli+Roger_Masterarbeit.pdf/ 17786419-b168-415f-b7fb-1258cb73024f, accessed on 10 May 2020
2. Bucsics, Baumgartner, Seidl, Gwihs: Basiswissen Testautomatisierung, dpunkt Verlag Heidelberg 2015

Test Objects and Test Phases

8

Abstract

Test cases are linked to test objects. Test objects determine the content of the test activities. Test activities within the individual test levels take place in several phases. Different influencing factors are responsible for determining the test effort.

8.1 Test Objects

The **test objects** are all objects affected by a test case. A test case is associated with one or more requirements and thus indirectly with a use case. A use case runs through the methods of several objects.

Example: The test case is "If the article quantity in stock falls below the minimum quantity, it must be automatically reordered".

In this case, the following objects are affected:

- Order management.
- Customer base.
- Ordering.
- Article master.
- Delivery item.

In this context, one also speaks of the **impact domain of** the test case in the **object model**. It is usually a subset of the impact domain of the use case because in the use case "sales order processing" not all test cases will reach the article object, and only this test case will create a delivery order.

The individual test objects or components must be clearly described, including version numbers, transfer medium and specifications.

The test objects define the test content and thus determine what is tested. The system to be tested is described in the test objects. The test objects must be precisely delimited from each other. Objects that are not tested during the test, but are taken as given, must also be described here. However, objects can only be taken as given if they do not change for other reasons during the project phase. If, in the above example, the item master does not change due to the requirement and therefore does not need to be explicitly tested, this only applies as long as other applications do not make changes to it. Therefore, a requirement system that recognizes which requirement influences which system and thus indirectly which test case is of particular importance. This is the only way to know that the system behavior may change during test execution and that the test case may have to be adapted. The information in the test concept must be sufficient to derive test cases.

In this context, the states of the affected objects before the execution of the test case are called **test case pre-states** and the states after the execution of the test case are called **test case post-states** [SNEE2012].

8.2   Test Phases

Within the individual test levels, certain activities and phases are always run through (Fig. 8.1):

Based on empirical studies, it can be assumed that just under 50% of the total effort of the test activities is accounted for by test execution and just under 20% each by test preparation and test evaluation. If test automation is well advanced, the share for test execution drops, but does not become zero. In this context, we should warn against unrealistic expectations of automated tests, which unfortunately can be found again and again in many companies. As important as it is to advance test automation, it is unrealistic to assume that all automated tests will work "at the push of a button" and that there will be no more testing effort.

Depending on the quality of the software, the repetition of the test execution must be carried out with varying frequency. Sufficient time must always be planned for regression tests. One can orientate oneself on various parameters, for example the lines of code, and then form index values such as "expected defects per 1000 lines of code" to forecast the number and effort required for defect correction and thus the necessary regression tests.

On the one hand, constructive **quality assurance measures** that are used for preventive quality design are to be distinguished from the testing effort. They address the process

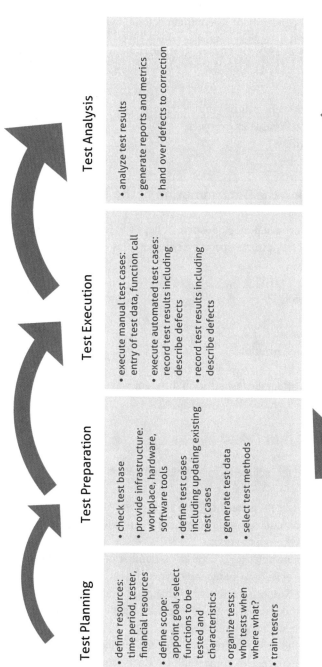

Fig. 8.1 Test activities

quality and thus indirectly contribute to improving the software product quality. On the other hand, testing excludes activities of static analytical quality assurance, through which the test object is analyzed independently of its environment, i.e., without executing code.

Accordingly, the test effort is defined as follows:

- The working time.
- All those involved in testing.
- For the preparation, execution and evaluation.
- All automated and manual test cases in a project.
- Without test planning activities.

8.3   Factors Influencing the Determination of the Test Effort

When determining the test effort in a project, positive or negative general conditions must be considered appropriately. The project-specific characteristics that influence the test effort are grouped as follows:

- Characteristics of the product.
- Characteristics of the team.
- Characteristics of the resources.
- Characteristics of the test organization.

These **influencing factors** affect the test effort in different ways and several times.

8.3.1   Characteristics of the Product

The characteristics of the product include factors explained below:

- Market importance: sales targets, strategic goals (e.g., diversification, market entry) pursued with the test object, number of customers of the previous release, number of expected customers, planned product price;
- Novelty: New development or redesign of a product, number of pre-releases, familiarity and experience with the development technology used;
- Dynamics of requirements: Number and timing of changes during the life of the project;
- Degree of customer individuality: variability of the use of the customer product, individual adaptation of the product to different needs;
- Customer expectations of the product: importance of the product from the customer's point of view (criticality), existence of comparable products from the customer's point of view, number of complaints from customers of the direct pre-release;

- Scope of the software product (scope of the requirements);
- Complexity of the software product: Development technologies used, number of external interfaces, number of internal interfaces between product components in the project or between subprojects;
- Intended quality of the software product: Intended functionality, reliability, usability and efficiency;
- Documentation of the requirements and the design: Quality of specification and design documentation.

8.3.2   Characteristics of the Team

The characteristics of the team can be broken down into the following factors:

- Experience: Developers' experience with the subject area, developers' experience with their tasks, testers' experience with the product (in a broader sense industry knowledge), testers' experience with their tasks;
- Motivation and attitude towards quality: Commitment of testers, commitment of developers, attitude of project management towards quality;
- Team size (number of project team members);
- Cooperation: Continuity of the team, pursuit of a common goal, working atmosphere;
- Communication: Number of different mother tongues in the team, number of locations of project staff;
- Role assignment: Test case creation and test execution by tester or developer.

8.3.3   Characteristics of the Resources

The characteristics of the resources consist of the following factors:

- Personnel restrictions: Availability of team members, dependence on subcontractors;
- Customer participation in testing: Number of customers and contacts participating in the test;
- Existing test cases and data: Quality of existing test cases, reusability of test data;
- Test infrastructure: Availability and stability of the test system, degree of test automation;
- Time for project implementation (in total at the beginning of the project).

8.3.4   Characteristics of the Test Organization

The characteristics of the test organization include the selection of test cases and the time distribution of the test effort.

8.3.5   Other Factors of Other Models

The testability of the software is often attributed a strong influence on the testing effort. Not only the code, but also other artifacts such as design and documentation contribute to this.

The test effort is further influenced by the ability of the developers because, depending on the extent of their skills, the developers identify or avoid more or fewer possible bugs in advance during requirements analysis, system design, drafting and coding, and as a result, the developed product has more or fewer defects from the outset. In this context, it is important for the management to know the strengths and weaknesses of the developers and to deploy the individual employees where their strengths are most effective and their weaknesses can do the least harm.

The test methods used also have an influence on the test effort. A **test method** is a planned procedure based on a set of rules for deriving and selecting test cases. In this context, a basic distinction is made between function-oriented and structure-oriented procedures, for which the terms **black-box** and **white-box procedures** are used. In testing, different procedures must be used to find different types of defects. It is not sufficient to test only the correct user behavior, but it is also necessary to think of creative defect cases to test how the system reacts in unplanned situations, i.e., whether understandable bug messages are issued or whether system crashes occur. Due to the varying effectiveness and efficiency of the test methods with the defects to be detected and their varying effort in the application, the test effort is influenced [DOWI2009].

References

1. Sneed, Bauimgartner, Seidl: Der Systemtest, Carl Hanser Verlag Munich 2012
2. Ulrike Dowie, Testaufwandsschätzung in der Softwareentwicklung, Josef-Eul-Verlag Cologne 2009

Test Levels

9

Abstract

The test process takes place in several test levels. The test concept defines the contents of the individual test levels and delimits them from one another. A good test strategy ensures efficient test execution, prevents duplicate activities in different test levels and ensures the highest possible test coverage. Special test strategies apply to agile projects.

9.1 Classical Test Levels

The test **levels** and their contents must be defined in the test concept.#.

Each function should be tested at the earliest possible test level to prevent defects from propagating to higher test levels.

In general, there are the following test levels:

- **Component test:**
  Individual software components are tested isolated from other software components of the overall system. Any defects found are assigned to the tested component. The test environment is the development environment, the mode of operation very close to development. The task of the component test is the correct and complete realization of the input and output behavior of the test object. To check correctness and completeness of the implementation, the component is subjected to a series of test cases, where each test case covers a specific input/output combination (partial functionality). In addition to functionality and robustness, the component test should also check all those component properties that can no longer be tested in higher test levels or can only be tested

© Springer Fachmedien Wiesbaden GmbH, part of Springer Nature 2022
F. Witte, *Strategy, Planning and Organization of Test Processes*,
https://doi.org/10.1007/978-3-658-36981-1_9

with considerably more effort. This applies, for example, to the non-functional properties of efficiency and maintainability.

In component testing, the tester usually has access to the source code, making component testing a typical **white-box test**. The term white-box test refers to a method of software testing in which the tests are developed with knowledge of the inner workings of the system under test. So, unlike a **black-box test**, this test is allowed to look into the source code, i.e., testing is done on the code. The component test is performed by the developer.

- **Integration test:**
The integration test checks the interaction of the individual components with each other. The integration test procedure is divided into two different strategies: The **test goal-oriented strategy** only requires the system components necessary for testing. There, the test cases are created and executed according to defined test objectives. The **procedure-oriented strategy** depends on the integration sequence from the system architecture.

Another distinction is the way the components are integrated: The **"incremental integration"** adds the modules together step by step. For this, missing modules must be simulated. **"Non-incremental integration"** assembles all components simultaneously and integrates them into the system under test. For this, all modules must already exist before the integration test ("big bang"). This variant has proven to be unsuitable in practice. If you put too many components together at once, bugs are much harder to localize. In addition, masking of bugs can occur (one bug causes another bug not to occur at all and therefore cannot be detected during the test, a "hidden defect" occurs), which results in an increased effort for defect correction.

For each dependency between two components of a system, a **test scenario** is defined which can prove that both components and the data exchange via the common interfaces function according to specifications after merging. At this point, the functional tests prove that the correct component was used. Interface tests are used to check the data that is exchanged between the components.

Integration testing requires test drivers that supply test objects with test data and receive and log results. As a rule, test drivers already available from the component test are used for this purpose. The **test objective** of the integration test is to detect interface defects. Typical defects in data exchange include the transfer of syntactically incorrect data, different interpretations of transferred data, timing problems (data is transferred correctly) but at the wrong or delayed time, and throughput, load, or capacity problems (data is transferred at short intervals).

- **System test:**

    In the system test, the system is viewed as a whole in a test environment that corresponds as closely as possible to the later productive environment. Instead of test drivers and placeholders, the hardware or software products that will actually be used later should be installed and configured in the test environment at all levels (hardware equipment, system software, driver software, network, external systems, etc.). The test objective is to verify and validate the functional and non-functional requirements. Defects and deficiencies due to incorrectly, incompletely or inconsistently implemented requirements in the system should be detected and previously undocumented or forgotten requirements should be identified.

- **Acceptance test**

    The acceptance test is performed as a final test together with the customer or user before the software is put into operation. Selected test cases are presented and demonstrated. This documents the fulfillment of the contractually agreed functional scope. Acceptance tests can also occur as part of lower test levels or distributed over several test levels.

The test concept should determine which system aspects must be tested how intensively and at which test level this should be done [SPIL2007].

The individual test levels should be defined in terms of dates and clearly differentiated from each other. The transfer between individual test levels should also be defined. It is quite possible that test levels are run in parallel. If a function is only developed at a later point while other functions are already in the integration test, it can happen that it is only integrated at a later point into a product that is then partially integrated.

The individual test levels are carried out by different stakeholders: The component test is carried out by the developer, while the integration and system test are handled by a separate test instance and, in the case of the acceptance test, the client/customer is also involved in the test execution. The individual persons responsible should be named, and the activities described in the test concept. In addition, regular meetings should be organized from the beginning to track the test progress and to be able to initiate necessary activities in a timely manner.

Especially when individual components are supplied, it must be defined which test coverage is required for quality assurance. In this case, the supplier is responsible for the partial product, which is integrated and tested together with other components in the test levels starting with the integration test. This requires precise specifications so that some functions are not tested several times and others not at all.

The dates of the individual test levels usually result from the release planning.

9.2   Exploratory Testing

In this context, the scope for **exploratory testing** must also be defined: in addition to methodological approaches, test cases must be determined intuitively. This is necessary because in practice the requirements are never complete, but there are always incomplete definitions that can usually only be uncovered during test execution. The intuitive ability and experience to select test cases according to expected defect states and effects is the basis of explorative testing, where methodical procedures reach their limits rapidly. Experience of which functions have been particularly prone to defects in the past and guessing where bugs are likely to recur in the future are necessary for this and mean that experienced testers are needed in the project. This type of test case generation is also referred to as **defect guessing** [SPIL2007].

Exploratory testing is defined as a form of software testing that emphasizes the personal freedom and responsibility of the individual tester to optimize the quality of his or her work by treating test design, test execution, test interpretation, and test-related learning as mutually supportive activities while continuing throughout the life of the project. The emphasis here is that while individual testers enjoy personal freedom in planning their work, this freedom also comes with responsibility for their work. Responsibility in this context means that the tester also ensures that his work results can be replicated, for example by having notes on his test activities.

In exploratory testing, therefore, the three individual parts of testing are, by definition, interconnected. Exploratory testing is simultaneous learning, test design and test execution in one. This means that exploratory testing does not completely separate the three parts of traditional testing.

One structure in exploratory testing is to look at the application from different aspects. The **FCC CUT VIDS touring heuristic** was introduced for this purpose. The letters stand for features, complexity, claims, configuration, user, testability, scenario, variability, interoperability, data and structure. These stand for individual tours that can be taken through the application as a tester. They thus give structure to the test activity – individual parts that come together to form a whole.

Another structure for exploratory testing is the **HICCUPPS** mnemonic by James Bach and Michael Bolton. HICCUPPS stands for history, image, comparable products, user expectations, product, purpose and standards and statutes. Behind this are various **oracles** – a principle or mechanism by which we can determine whether software is working in the spirit of a particular user. Oracles help identify inconsistencies in a product. For example, if the user interface changes completely from the 2003 product version to the

2007 product version of Microsoft Office, then it is inconsistent with the way users are used to working, the history in the list above.

The fact that the change in Microsoft Office was – hopefully – made on purpose illustrates another aspect of oracles: they are heuristics and can sometimes be wrong. This means that the tester still has to use his brain thanks to heuristics. After all, an automated test cannot decide on its own whether a change is intentional or unintentional; you need human interpretation of the results, as unfortunately far too many teams are shocked to discover time and time again. One erroneous configuration can cause thousands of automated test cases to become erroneous all at once (and, if defect capture is automated, thousands of tickets to be captured as a result). An experienced tester, on the other hand, will quickly realize that the bug in the configuration will most likely affect other test cases and will not even continue to run those tests before fixing the configuration error.

Heuristics, oracles, and touring models are different structures that we use in exploratory testing. In this context, test automation can support exploratory testing, just as exploratory testing can inform test automation about new test cases. Both approaches form a symbiosis, especially in agile software development, as they strongly support each other. For example, thanks to test automation, one can start testing around the tested values. For example, if you have an automated test for the values 5 and 10, you can quickly run a test with the values 1, 11, 42, and MAXINT.

Exploratory testing is considered a testing approach that can be combined with other techniques. Every form of testing is explorative to a certain degree and at the same time predetermined or created as a script. Repetitive test activities are better left to automation and the human factor is used specifically where it can make a significant contribution: in learning and in the creative design of test cases based on test cases that have already been executed. This is precisely what the human brain is designed for [EXPL2019].

9.3 Test Levels in an Agile Project

The following sketch (Fig. 9.1) illustrates a best practice for the test levels in an agile project:

This defines the focus of the individual test levels in the test process and how these test levels interact to avoid duplicate testing. In a test strategy that is created for the project, as well as detailed planning for each sprint, the procedure should be defined early on to ensure efficient test execution.

The test levels should be selected and refined (e.g., an integration test can be split into a module test and a system integration test), and the requirements for the system to be tested should be clear. In addition, the specific development process must be known to be

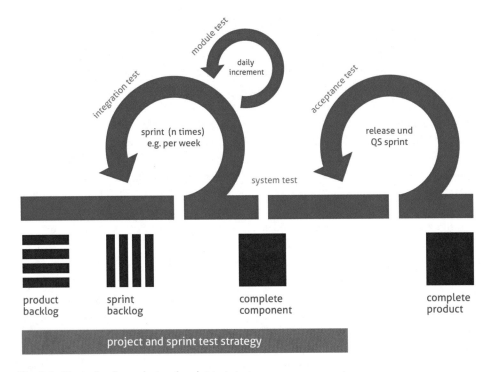

Fig. 9.1 Example of a project and sprint test strategy

able to assign the strategy and the specific test activities to be performed to the respective test levels.

Especially for larger projects, it is advisable to create stage test concepts for each test level, including a description of the test methods, tools and test criteria to be used. In this case, the test concept has sections that apply to all test levels in addition to sections that are only relevant for a specific test level.

The first step in the staged approach is to define the test strategy for the individual test levels. An essential aspect of this is a determination of how intensively testing should be carried out at which level.

This depends on several influencing variables:

- Available test budget.
- Risk.
- Complexity of the system to be developed.
- Number of teams.
- Know-how about testing activities.

The test manager is responsible for identifying and considering as many of these factors as possible, often in close coordination with other roles such as a project manager or the product owner. The **product** owner is one of the six roles in the **Scrum process**. The product owner is one of the central players in the process, along with the Scrum Master and the development team. This person is responsible for adding value to the product in the development process and leads the team. A strategy can be that on the module level each module has to be developed with **test-driven development** before it is integrated and runs through the integration test and on the system test level all user stories have to be run through manually.

Test-driven development means that tests are used to drive software development. The process of this programming is cyclical:

- A test is written that initially fails.
- Exactly enough productive code is implemented to pass the test.
- Test and productive code are refactored.

The tests are typically, but not necessarily, implemented with the XUnit framework in the same language as the productive code. Tests that pass successfully are represented by a green bar, unsuccessful ones by a red bar. This is therefore referred to as the "red-green refactor cycle".

Test-driven development proceeds incrementally. Each TDD cycle enriches the software with new capabilities – and does it so meticulously because each cycle section should take no longer than a few minutes.

Writing the tests before the components that you actually want to test is very distinctive of TDD. This is called test-first and that is why TDD is not a testing strategy but a design strategy. Because if the test is written first, the interface of the component under test is used before it actually exists. The developer gets feedback as early as possible whether the design will be usable.

The implementation of the productive code only takes place when a test is available that requires this. Exactly enough code should then be written for the test to run successfully. If too much productive code is written for a test, untested areas are created that can cause problems during refactoring.

During **refactoring,** the tests and the productive code are cleaned up in equal measure. The goal here is to make the software simple, non-redundant, and understandable. This phase of the TDD cycle immediately precedes the beginning of the cycle: To write a particular test, it may be necessary to first perform refactoring on the other tests or the productive code.

The cycle is non-overlapping, each activity in test-driven development can be assigned to a section. No tests should be written in phases 2 and 3 and no productive code in phases

1 and 3. When refactoring, the behavior of the code is not changed, i.e., nothing is functionally changed either in the tests (phase 1) or in the productive code (phase 2).

Principles that TDD unites are continuous design improvement, simple design, and test-first. TDD itself is a core technique of **Extreme Programming** and thus part of agile software development. It promises quality software and a significant upgrade of the software architecture thanks to evolutionary design.

Advantages of test-driven design are:

- Maintainable quality software (no untested code, clean and testable architecture through test-driven design as design strategy, no or little redundancies through timely refactoring).
- Effective and efficient creation of the software (no unnecessary code as a reserve, focus on the essentials) [ITAG2020].

At each test level, this strategy can be further refined. For example, at the system test level, each user story classified as critical can be tested both experientially and systematically by at least two testers, while for less critical user stories only one tester performs tests. Developer testing at the unit level can be on both a white-box and black-box basis and should be performed by developers. This is not only about correct functionality for valid inputs, but also about correct interception of invalid input values. Each "smallest unit" ("unit") is tested and checked as isolated as possible.

In agile development life cycles, the use of test-first or test-driven development has become established. Integration testing, on the other hand, tests the interfaces between units and thus tests the interaction of several units. Even if each unit works correctly on its own, the interaction can still lead to erroneous results. The integration test can be divided into several phases to cover everything from "small" to "large" integration steps. At this test level, regression testing plays a major role, especially in iterative development. The testing of non-functional aspects such as performance or security can already be started in the integration test.

System testing, in turn, is performed on a black-box basis and involves testing the complete system, usually from the user interface. The aim is to test whether the user's goals can be achieved with the application based on the inputs. Non-functional tests also take place at this test level.

All these test levels take place in the development environment. Only the acceptance test takes place in the environment of the future users and repeats test cases that have already been run in the system test. Figure 9.1 shows an example of an agile approach and names the test levels – the module test is performed daily here, the integration test at the end of the one-week sprint. System testing is started after a few sprints and initial test cases are run. The last sprint before release is explicitly used for quality assurance. Acceptance tests are also performed in this sprint.

With this procedure, it is continuously checked whether the initial test strategy makes sense and adjusted if necessary. If, for example, it becomes apparent during development that a component that was not previously assessed as high-risk is high-risk, test efforts should be additionally concentrated here, for example through additional module or integration tests. Bugs found during testing at the various stages should be documented (e.g., in a bug tracking tool) and analyzed to further optimize future quality assurance and, if necessary, to decide whether bugs can be found earlier or avoided altogether.

9.4   Integration of Testing Activities with Other Project Activities

Testing activities are part of the overall project. Test activities depend on test objects being available for test execution, and rollout plans are only possible once the software has been accepted and released for productive rollout. Therefore, the **test plan** should be seen as part of the overall project plan.

Risks and consequences resulting from these interdependencies must be examined and evaluated from the very beginning. In the process chain, the weakest link determines the speed and ultimately the quality of the end product. Therefore, the evaluation of the test environment is of particular importance.

The effects and the risk should be quantified thanks to suitable parameters. The **cyclomatic complexity** according to McCabe or the **complexity measure according to Rechenberg** are suitable values for this.

The structural complexity of a program code thanks to the paths is drawn on the control flow graph. McCabe assumed that all program branches triggered by conditional statements (e.g., if statements) or loop blocks increase the complexity of a program. The set of individual paths in the control flow graph reflect the number of test cases required for complete path coverage. Many possible paths mean a high level of complexity. High complexity usually makes it under to understand and test source codes. As a result, there is a risk of serious defects creeping into the code at development time.

In the Rechenberg complexity measure, readability, comprehensibility and changeability depend on the statement structure, expression structure and data flow of a program. The complexity of nestings is derived from the individual complexities, which are weighted with suitable factors.

References

1. Basiswissen Softwaretest, dpunkt Verlag Heidelberg, 3. Edition 2005 corrected reprint 2007
2. https://www.it-agile.de/wissen/agiles-engineering/exploratives-testen-mit-struktur/, accessed on 10 May 2020
3. https://www.it-agile.de/wissen/agiles-engineering/testgetriebene-entwicklung-tdd/, accessed on May 2020

Performance Characteristics to Be Tested

10

Abstract

The test objects are described in the test concept. In the process, functional tests, load tests and stress tests must be planned and defined in more detail for the performance features to be tested. For testing the user interface, A/B tests and multivariate tests are used for Internet applications.

10.1 Types of System Tests

The test concept describes the **performance characteristics** of the DUT. It therefore describes what or which functions and features must be tested, it names the test objects, but not how the test is to be carried out in detail.

The test concept therefore does not contain the individual test specifications and test cases, but references their storage location. This can be a special drive or a defined tool.

However, the essential functions (i.e., the headings to chapters of the test specifications or **test clusters**) should be described in the test concept, especially for extensive projects. In this context, it must be clarified how long the test cases must be kept. In the event of errors that only occur in the life cycle of the tested product, it may still be necessary to be able to fall back on them.

In general, you should define the following types of system tests:

1. **Functional test**
   The functional test checks the correct implementation of the functional system requirements, i.e., whether the behavior of the software or the system corresponds to the requirements in the functional specification. Functional tests are used for system tests and acceptance tests (also called acceptance tests, procedure tests or user acceptance

tests). These types of tests are black-box tests, since "only" the external behavior is tested, without taking the internal structure or code into account.

To know the functional requirements in the first place, efficient **requirements management** is required in the project. This involves the following activities:

- **Establish an attribution of the requirements**: Evaluation, prioritization, source of requirements are possible attributes that are documented and tracked.
- **Change management**: Dealing with changes of requirements so that their impact can be tracked and the consequences of the change can be shown and thus evaluated accordingly.
- **Assessment and prioritization of requirements**: Analyze the criticality of the requirement and assign requirements to versions to meet time and cost constraints.
- **Traceability of requirements**: Establishing dependencies between requirements, proving the implementation of a requirement (Which requirement was tested with which test cases? To which requirements does a particular test case refer?). This includes the definition of the processes for traceability.
- Version **management**: Versioning of current work statuses, prerequisite for configuration management in the project.
- **Variant management**: When a product line is developed, different variants are defined. The requirements manager must take this variability into account for the process to be developed or used [BLHO2015].

In practice, it happens again and again that requirements management is not present or only rudimentary. Often it is also reduced or omitted when the project was started too late or planned too optimistically (sometimes also out of supposed savings, which later turns out to be a fatal mistake). In this case, a clear test risk must be declared in the test concept. The quality of the test management and the development itself is strongly influenced by the requirements management, since it is at the beginning of the development project and other processes can only build on it. In the end, the test can only be as good as the requirements management because it represents the basis.

In any case, test tasks for all central functions must be defined in the test concept right from the start. Test tasks must also be defined for checking the quality characteristics. One must also keep in mind that any further development of products becomes problematic if the first version was developed without a sufficient basis.

It should also be noted that some requirements are formulated too generally to be demonstrated in a test, or that they refer to other requirements (in another document). In this context, it is necessary to break down these requirements in sufficient detail and define them in such a finely granular manner that a test or other suitable form of proof is possible.

In the context of requirements, special care must be taken to ensure that requirements are not contradictory and are complete. When creating test cases, it is regularly noticed that there are open questions due to the underlying documentation of the requirements. If these open questions are not sufficiently clarified, this also represents a test risk, since in this case, the functional test is not documented adequately enough. This can be performed, but the expected behavior remains questionable.

2. **Test of the load behavior (load test)**

The load test checks how the system behaves in the event of a permanently high number of accesses. The load test generates a very high load on the system to be tested to bring it to the limit of its performance and examines its behavior. The objectives of the load test are:

- Detecting errors not found in the functionally oriented system test/integration test;
- Proving the fulfillment of non-functional requirements, such as required response times as well as volume processing or numerous simultaneous accesses to a database, for productive operation;Checking the dimensioning of the hardware equipment.

A tool is required for a load test, since it is important to execute several thousand transactions consecutively and side by side within a short time, i.e., several test scripts are executed in a loop at different workstations at the same time. The workstations can also be simulated by a program. It is important to ensure that the same data is accessed from test sequences running in parallel, so that queues are created in front of the databases. In this way, the occurrence of **dead-lock situations** is provoked. The time for each transaction between pressing the Enter key or the start signal and the return of the response is measured. At the end, a mean response time for all transactions as well as a total time for the processing of transactions is obtained. Furthermore, it is determined whether the system can handle such a load at all without aborting or reacting incorrectly. Therefore, the results of the load test must also be corrected for correctness. Considering the amount of data, this check must be automated [SNEE2012].

3. **Stress test**

When the system is deliberately pushed to its limits beyond the defined load limit or sudden load peaks are simulated, this is called a stress test. While the load test is about a high but constant load, the stress test is about outliers.

The load (number of virtual users) will be increased step by step until it exceeds the defined load limit.

Thus, the following questions are investigated:

- How does the response time behavior change depending on the load?
- Can the system still be operated acceptably under high load?
- Does the system show undefined behavior (e.g., crash)?
- Does data inconsistency occur?
- Does the system go back to normal after the overload decreases?

Tools specifically suited for stress testing should be used.

4. **Testing the user interface**

What is the human-machine interface, the look and feel of the application? Especially for web applications, there are the possibilities of user surveys in the lab, also through eye tracking. In this case, it is also about compliance with design criteria.

User interface tests have also been increasingly automated for several years. In the case of JUnit tests, it is possible to connect the test execution to continuous integration systems (CI systems) such as Jenkins.

For web applications, a test in a special laboratory can also be recommended. Specialized service providers offer solutions for this, where the look and feel of an interface can be tested using eye tracking, for example.

Especially for internet applications, A/B tests or multivariate tests are also used for this purpose.

10.2   Special Test Procedures

The **A/B test** (also "split test") is a test method for evaluating two variants of a system, in which the original version is tested against a slightly modified version. This method is mainly used in software and web design with the aim of increasing a certain user action or reactions. Over the years, it has become one of the most important testing methods in online marketing. However, A/B testing is also used to compare prices, designs, and advertising efforts. In A/B testing, the target group (e.g., visitors to a website or recipients of a newsletter) is divided into two subgroups: Group A and Group B. This division must be random. According to the division of the target group, the test object, such as a landing page or an advertisement, is also produced in two parts: the original variant and a modified variant. Both variants should only vary in one component because only in this way can differences in the reactions be clearly attributed to the change. The original version is then used for group A and the modified version for group B, and the reactions are compared. A/B tests thus form a simple method for evaluating a page design and are useful in a variety of situations.

Multivariate testing uses the same basic mechanisms as A/B testing, but compares a larger number of variables and provides additional information about how those variables affect each other. As with A/B testing, website traffic is split between different design variations of a page. The purpose of multivariate testing is to measure the effectiveness of different element combinations in achieving the actual goal. If a site has enough traffic to run such a test, the data from each variation can be used not only to determine which is the most successful design, but also possibly to determine which elements have a particularly positive or negative effect on visitor behavior.

When testing each performance characteristic, appropriate metrics must be collected from the outset.

For example, the number of requirements can be determined, an index value can be formed of how many requirements are covered by test cases, or the number of test cases already defined through suitable test procedures can be surveyed (Chap. 3).

This creates transparency in the test project and makes it meaningful. In the test concept, you should already define which parameters you want to evaluate and which metrics you want to set up for this.

References

1. http://blog.hood-group.com/blog/2015/03/31/der-requirements-manager-als-vorarbeiter-fuer-den-requirements-engineer/, accessed on 9 May 2020
2. Sneed, Baumgartner, Seidl: Der Systemtest, Carl Hanser Verlag Munich 2012

Features That Are Not Tested

11

Abstract

The test concept should also set out which criteria are not demonstrated and clearly delineate the test activities so that no unrealistic expectations of the test are created. In this context, the importance of reviews should be emphasized.

11.1 Test Coverage Through Test Procedures

In addition to the performance characteristics to be tested, the test concept must also consider which criteria will not be demonstrated. This is therefore a matter of delimiting the work and clearly communicating the expectations of the test. By excluding these features, the test team evades responsibility for the functionality of these features and forces a definition elsewhere of who should be responsible for the quality assurance of the functions [SNEE2012].

In the test concept, you must describe whether suppliers are responsible for certain tests and whether an already tested component is included as a defined product within the test object. In this case, the test of these components is omitted.

Unfortunately, it is often the case that the contractual regulations with the suppliers only insufficiently address the need for a preliminary inspection. However, it is important to work towards a common understanding throughout the entire delivery process. Even at the tendering stage of a project, a test manager should ideally be called in and defined tests should be demanded from the supplier to be able to meet the required quality standard towards the company's own customers. This also involves delimiting the test activities between the client and the supplier so that certain functions are not tested twice, while others are not tested at all.

© Springer Fachmedien Wiesbaden GmbH, part of Springer Nature 2022
F. Witte, *Strategy, Planning and Organization of Test Processes*,
https://doi.org/10.1007/978-3-658-36981-1_11

Reasons to forego certain tests, resulting in lower **test coverage**, include:

- Lack of resources,
- Scheduling restrictions,
- Budget constraint or.
- Technical requirements.

However, it must also be made clear in the test concept which consequences and risks result from the deliberately chosen lower test coverage. It is advisable to convert these risks into euros because forecast figures can be used to present this risk much more transparently.

11.2   Prove by Other Methods

However, it is also a question of documenting evidence that is to be met in another way, i.e., not through a software test but, for example, through a document review.

A **review** is a formally organized meeting of people to review the content or form of a product part or product. The review is carried out according to predefined test criteria and checklists.

A review can only lead to good results if the review documents are available in good time and if the persons involved have the necessary competence. A systematic approach is achieved if checklists are provided for the review. In addition, subsequent monitoring is important to ensure that any deficiencies found are also rectified.

However, reviews with their special forms of inspections and walkthroughs are not only used to manually check documents. Test results, which are also not formal, or source code can be reviewed in addition to other types of testing. The inspection of programs as a special form of review is known as **code inspection.**

The main field of application of reviews is the verification of documents.

Examples are

- System documentation:
  - Requirements specifications (requirements),
  - Feasibility studies,
  - Systems analysis documents,
  - Draft documents,
  - Program descriptions,
  - Test designs and
  - Operating instructions;

- Instructions for the system administrator.

The objectives pursued by reviews are:

- The detection of defects and thus the avoidance of consequential costs,
- The documentation of the project progress,
- The dissemination of know-how within the project team, and
- Consensus building within the project team.

No solutions are discussed during the review [GOLL2011].

Another special case, in which proof in the test environment is deliberately dispensed with, exists when the use of the software is only partially possible in the rollout under real conditions.

Especially in logistics or industrial manufacturing, e.g., if a machine control of productive systems is affected by the test, the provision of an own test environment is too costly. The costs for the additionally required hardware would be too high in this case. In this case, a system is evaluated at one location, for example, which is rolled out to other locations at a later date. In this case, the test activities are carried out at the pilot site in production, for example at only one of several sorting systems or in production at one of several production lines. It is important to highlight the risks and consider the lower productivity of the pilot site during the test phase. This approach is also only possible if the pilot site and the planned deployment are intensively supported on site. Precise deployment plans and milestones must also be developed for this purpose. It must also be examined to what extent the test may hinder production and what risks this entails.

In this case, the selected reference plant must represent real-time operation as well as possible. If there are local peculiarities at other locations, the test operation must also be carried out at these other locations. However, official acceptance processes and software releases are just as essential as if the test had been carried out in a test environment.

References

1. Sneed, Baumgartner, Seidl: Der Systemtest, Carl Hanser Verlag Munich 2012
2. Joachim Goll: Methoden und Architekturen der Softwaretechnik, Vieweg+Teubner Verlag Wiesbaden 2011

Prioritization of Test Cases

12

Abstract

The reasonable scope of the test activities must be determined during test planning. In the context of prioritizing test cases, test cases that exhibit high risks in the case of faulty functionality and test cases for the verification of frequently occurring business processes are to be preferred.

12.1 Test Scope

Within the framework of the test concept, one has to consider how high the reasonable **test scope of** the project under consideration is.

The following example shows that a complete "testing" of a program is almost impossible:

- There are exactly x ways to run a program, and if all x ways are tested in the test, the program is fully tested.
- Suppose a procedure expects 2 integer values as input data.
- With 32-bit length, there are already $2^{32} \times 2^{32}$ combinations of input values (approximately 1.8×10^{19})
- Even if an automatic test driver can execute a test case in 1 ms, the complete test of all input values takes about 570 million years.

So, if you were to test all combinations of the software, you would have to handle at least hundreds and thousands of test cases. With test automation, manual repetitive activities can be avoided, but the effort of automation, maintenance, updating, one-time creation of the scripts and the targeted evaluation of the results remains. Test automation is also not

© Springer Fachmedien Wiesbaden GmbH, part of Springer Nature 2022
F. Witte, *Strategy, Planning and Organization of Test Processes*,
https://doi.org/10.1007/978-3-658-36981-1_12

something that runs automatically, but requires a high organizational and administrative effort.

A software test is not a mathematical proof. The purpose of a test is to prove functionality to the effect that business transactions in practice meet expectations, and in doing so, one should certainly also test combinations that rarely occur in daily operation. Optimal test coverage, however, does not mean finding every conceivable defect that may occur once in many years, but perhaps would have never been discovered in production operation anyway. A software project always has restrictions due to deadlines and costs, so in my experience, the case of having tested too many test cases and having too much test coverage in the end hardly ever happens in business practice. In most cases, too few tests are carried out at the end of the project, and it regularly happens that at least a few bugs are not noticed until after the introduction of production.

In some cases, incremental software deliveries are planned, especially in the agile environment. Therefore, it is often not possible to test the entire intended scope of testing with each delivery, but only once, for example, shortly before product delivery.

Because of these limitations, it is necessary to prioritize test cases.

12.2   Prioritization in System Tests and Acceptance Tests

The prioritization of the test cases for the system test is to be carried out in detail during the design of the test cases. In the test concept, however, it should be pointed out what the core functions are, on which areas in the test a special focus should be directed.

Occasionally, test cases that exist in theory but hardly ever occur in practice are tested in great detail and one gets lost in academic discussions, but other business cases that exist far more frequently are neglected. This circumstance should be addressed in advance. Therefore, it is also recommended, especially for applications that are also used in one's own company, to involve a user from the field from the very beginning, who knows the operational processes exactly and focuses on the crucial business processes. This also helps to achieve greater acceptance right from the start when piloting and introducing the new software.

During the acceptance test, only selected test cases are demonstrated to the customer anyway, or some test cases already performed in the test environment are repeated in a production environment. The acceptance test is usually limited to a few working days at the most, which results in a concentration on selected frequently performed business cases.

12.3   Prioritization in Module Testing and Integration Testing

Especially in module testing and integration testing, additional software is usually required to test newly developed software. Therefore, the order of testing is partly given from the beginning. However, if you are free to decide in which order to test, you should start with the module that has the fewest dependencies. A module is understood to be additional methods in a method test, additional classes in a class test, and additional components in an integration test.

Figure 12.1 shows a corresponding initial situation, in which different modules are represented as boxes with their dependencies. The dependencies are not sketched in the case that is to be achieved as far as possible, i.e., that they are not cyclic, e.g. A is not dependent on B on further ways or D is not dependent on B, so that one could get back to A by following the arrows.

If you have a free choice, you should start with the test of module G in the example, since it does not depend on any other modules. Afterwards, only test modules that depend exclusively on modules that have already been tested. There may well be different possibilities for the sequence, such as F-D-A-H-E-C-B or F-H-D-E-A-C-B. In this case, the selection of the appropriate sequence depends on the order of completion of the individual modules.

The general rule for testing is to focus exclusively on the functionality under test and assume the rest of the functionality to be correct. For example, after testing component G, one assumes that G is correct when creating test cases for component F and does not write any further test cases to check this correctness again. This is similar to taking the correctness of classes from a Java library as given. Only if one considers it likely that a previously tested module does contain defects, one can develop further tests for this module. This applies analogously to the testing of interfaces, where one concentrates exclusively on these interfaces in themselves, but not on the modules whose functionality has already been checked without the interfaces anyway.

However, it is often the case in practice that the sensible approach presented is not usable for various reasons. This is the case, for example, when the creation of G turns out to be more complex or the resource that was supposed to create G simply did not finish (due to other priorities, failures...), but the developer of D absolutely needs a way to test to

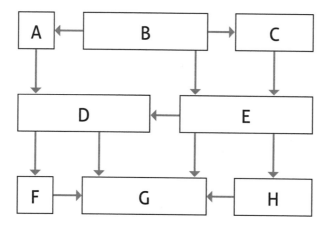

Fig. 12.1 Visualization of dependencies of modules/objects

complete the delivery of his component. It gets even a notch more complex when component D is also urgently needed as part of another project, so the priority is to complete it and G has been pushed back in time to do so. In these cases, mocks or stubs need to be developed, which is an additional effort.

But, it is often the case with complex systems that certain modules can only be tested at great expense, since they are databases or web servers, for example. In our example, the modules A, B and C could, for example, stand for a web interface that is connected to a server on which the domain-oriented logic is implemented in modules D and E. The domain-oriented logic then uses the modules F, G and E. The web interface is connected to a server on which the domain-oriented logic is implemented. The business logic then uses modules F, G and H for efficient data management. Again, the approach of testing the layers separately first and later assuming that the previously tested core functionality is correct when linking the individual layers must be tried. Indeed, the very approach of testing all functionality over the interface, if possible, often fails for a variety of reasons. Often, not all functionality can simply be addressed via the interface, and it is often technically very costly to provide the required hardware and software for each tester for all tests. In this case, too, it can make sense to resort to **mock objects,** which then simulate the required parts of the modules used. Mock objects implement the interfaces through which the object under test accesses its environment. They ensure that the expected method calls are executed completely, with the correct parameters, and in the expected order. The mock object does not return real data, but values that have been defined in advance to match the test case. The mock object can thus be used to mimic a specific behavior. Therefore, especially databases, network connections or connected, possibly expensive external software are interesting candidates for an implementation as mocks to make the testing of software more efficient.

This raises the question whether all testers in module testing need to be experts in frameworks. This is typically not the case in larger projects, as the mock or framework usage is completed by the other testers in such a way that they only need to have the knowledge of what is to be tested. The abstraction of the concrete test frameworks is also called **test architecture.** In addition to the much more efficient test development made possible by the abstraction, the chance that one only has to change one or a few places for minor changes in the environment of the software to be tested or the framework used and thus most tests and testers are not affected by the changes also plays an important role [KLEU2018].

12.4   Prioritization According to Different Test Types

When prioritizing the different types of tests, it is also possible to determine which test types should be used with which priority. The tests must be planned and executed depending on the test objectives, the quality requirements of the web application and the technical environment in which it is to be operated.

For example, for a website that mainly provides information, a findability test is more important than a reliability test. If an application is operated in an intranet where all users use the same browser anyway, a browser test across all existing browsers is not necessary. However, if the user base consists of the worldwide web community, browser and accessibility testing have a higher priority.

In Table 12.1, the individual test types in the web test are evaluated for an exemplary test object.

The example is based on a financing calculator that calculates the monthly installments for a car financing and is operated in a web portal.

Table 12.1 Exemplary evaluation of test types for a special application [FRAN2007]

Test type	Rating	Justification
Document test	High	Requirements specifications contain business-critical functional descriptions
Functionality tests		
Class test	Low	Intensive component testing by the test team
Component test	High	Business-critical functions
Integration test	High	Integration of business-critical subsystems
Functional system test	High	Business-critical functions
Link test	Low	No external links provided
Cookie test	High	Business-critical functions use cookies
Plugin test	Low	Plugins are only needed to read PDF documents
Safety test	High	Processing of sensitive data, execution of business-critical transactions
Usability tests		
Content test	High	Business-critical web presence
Surface test	High	Corporate standards must be complied with
Browser test	Medium	Users of the company portal usually only use one specific browser
Usability test	High	Customer satisfaction is a critical success factor
Accessibility test	Medium	Accessibility not explicitly required
Findability test	Low	Users come via the well-visited company portal
Tests for changeability and transferability		
Code analysis	Medium	Only random code inspections necessary
Installation test	Not relevant	Application is operated in-house, no client installations necessary
Efficiency and reliability tests		
Performance/load test	High	Processing of business-critical transactions, performance is therefore a critical success factor
Fail-safe test	Low	Security measures to the existing company portal are established and tested
Availability test	High	24-hour availability required

12.5   Risk-Based Testing

Exhaustive testing of software systems is hardly possible in reality due to complex inter-faces and environmental conditions. In addition, the available test budget limits the num-ber of test cases that can be executed and evaluated. Therefore, a selection of appropriate test cases and their prioritization for the order of test execution is necessary. A promising approach for prioritizing test cases is risk-based testing. A risk-based test plan ensures that parts of a software are tested more intensively, the higher the risk that these parts will lead to non-negligible damage when the software is used. Thus, in risk-based testing, the test cases are weighted particularly regarding the extent of damage in case of malfunction. The higher the weighting of the process under test and thus the extent of possible damage, the higher the priority of the test case [INNO2014]. Typically, test cases of "high" priority must be successfully executed in all test cycles and those of "medium" priority in at least one test cycle. Test cases of "low" priority are "nice to have".

However, a direct prioritization of test cases based on this risk is costly for complex software systems and each update of the risk assessment requires a new prioritization of the entire set of test cases [FRAU2008].

It still happens in many projects that the test cases are specified, but the time to execute all specified test cases is not available. This is especially common when the test team was available at the beginning of the project as planned, but the development team has delays in development (due to resource constraints or complex requirements), so that a testable version is only available late in the project period. Often there is no time to automate these test cases because the effort of test automation is rather reflected in the medium to long term and not for the current project, whose time budget is already tight. Then a sensible selection of test cases must be made to ensure that as many critical defect effects as pos-sible are still found despite the limited number of test cases to be performed. Prioritization must therefore be carried out in such a way that, if the tests are terminated (prematurely) at any point, the best possible result up to that point is achieved.

Prioritization also has the advantage that the most important test cases are executed first, and that severe bugs effects can be detected and corrected at an early stage. It is gen-erally recommended to record the duration of the average defect rectification – i.e., the duration from recording to successful retesting of a defect. From my own experience, management is often surprised that average values of 3–4 weeks per defect are usually collected. One always underestimates the idle times during process execution.

An equal distribution according to the sprinkling effect to all test objects of the project makes little sense, since with such a procedure, critical and non-critical program parts are tested with the same intensity. In this case, insufficient testing has been performed on the critical parts, while resources have been uselessly wasted on the non-critical program parts [SPIL2007].

References

1. Stephan Kleuker, Qualitätssicherung durch Softwaretests, Springer-Vieweg, Wiesbaden 2018
2. Klaus Franz, Handbuch zum Testen von Web-Applikationen, Springer-Verlag, Berlin Heidelberg 2007
3. Basiswissen Softwaretest, dpunkt Verlag Heidelberg, 3. Edition 2005 – Corrected Reprint 2007
4. http://publica.fraunhofer.de/dokumente/N-76418.html, accessed on 10 May 2020
5. https://www.innobis.de/uploads/tx_news/2014_12_Banken_Sparkassen_26f.pdf, accessed on 10 May 2020

Permanent Test Organization

13

Abstract

A permanent test organization takes over defined test services for several organizational units. The goal of the permanent test organization is to accelerate processes while reducing costs and increasing quality. The division of tasks between the permanent test organization and project-related test activities is defined in test guidelines,

13.1 Nature of the Permanent Test Organization

Organizations may decide to establish a **permanent testing organization** that provides a variety of test services. Unlike project-oriented testing, a permanent testing organization sets up a specific element of a testing process across projects, but this does not mean that testing is not performed within projects.

Which activities are performed by a permanent test organization differs depending on the organization? For example, the preparation and execution of tests can be assigned to the permanent test organization, but also the setup and maintenance of the test environment or test tools. As a result, each process related to a specific test part (test execution, test environment, test tools, etc.) is carried out with a fixed method and with reusable tools. The permanent test organization provides these elements for projects as so-called **test services**. The process will have the same quality, regardless of the project.

It depends on the client how the individual elements of the test process are elaborated by the permanent test organization and which test services are provided. For example, the client may be a tester who needs an environment to automate manual test scripts or the owner of an application who needs certain regression tests.

Apart from the client, the objective of a permanent testing organization may also determine the testing services. For example, the organization may have received a mandate from outside ("Ensure that all test environments are efficiently set up and maintained" or "Provide a solution for all issues related to test automation"). However, an organization may also set a goal for itself ("We will perform regression testing"). An organization's goal can change over time, as can the testing services it offers. The organization is defined by assigning tasks, permissions, and responsibilities to jobs for employees. In addition, processes for an organization are universally defined, set up, and selected so that the processes work as optimally as possible. These definitions are different for each organization; there are no fixed rules for them.

The aim of the permanent test organization is to reduce the lead time and costs in the test process and at the same time to increase the quality of the entire workflow. Specific elements of the test process are to be organized across all projects to gain the following advantages:

- **Optimal use of (scarce) expertise**: There is often a lack of testing experts in an organization. Not only is there a lack of expertise in creating and executing test scripts, but also, for example, in using test tools or setting up a test environment. However, if you combine all the available expertise and consolidate all requests for this expertise in one place, you can optimize a number of challenging points. It is easier to get access to needed expertise if you have insight into all available expertise. In addition, the available expertise can be much better allocated to the individual problem areas. Employees who have specialist knowledge of test environments, for example, can thus be available as service providers for several projects.
- **Predictable product quality**: The services offered by the permanent testing organization are standardized. There are products and processes with associated standards, and the services differ only minimally, so that the service quality is predictable. For example, the service "setting up a test environment" becomes a routine task that can simply be pulled out of the drawer with all the templates, tools, techniques and checklists that are part of the process, and is performed by experienced and qualified employees.
- **Short start-up time**: Due to the standardization of the processes, the start-up time is kept to a minimum. There is no need to attend training courses in advance, nor to try out any parts or select the most favorable procedure. Preparation time, such as setting up a test management tool, can be reduced to a minimum: everything is available

immediately, only the customer's specific wishes and requirements need to be determined and parameterized accordingly.

- **Continuous improvement of processes embedded in the organization**: The test organization is responsible for the processes offered and executes them. It can be determined that an assessment is connected after each executed process. The experience gained from this assessment is then fed back into the organization and integrated into an improved version of the service. Such an assessment and the processing of the results must be embedded in the processes of the testing organization.
- **Consolidation and development of experience**: From the combination of the existing expertise with the above-mentioned evaluation and processing of experiences, a lasting learning effect is obtained. This is further reinforced by synergy effects between individual employees.
- **Easier to plan costs and lead times**: By standardizing tasks and permanently evaluating, processing and improving work, you get a learning effect and strengthen positive synergy effects between individual employees. As a rule, there is also greater flexibility within the organization if employees can be assigned to several projects at short notice. In the best case, this can shorten the test time and avoid idle time.
- **Cost reduction through centralization and scaling**: If testing is performed at different locations in an organizational unit, this often also means that negotiations have to be conducted with external providers at different locations. If all test-relevant activities are centralized, the test organization can conclude framework agreements with all providers, e.g., of tools or test personnel. This is associated with economies of scale, which strengthen the negotiating position and make better conditions possible.

13.2 Conditions for a Permanent Test Organization

A permanent test organization is not possible for every (IT) organization because the organization must meet some conditions:

- The test effort of a permanent test organization must reach a certain order of scale that it is only generally considered for larger companies.
- As part of the corporate culture, it must be formally possible for the permanent testing organization to reach specific agreements with its customers.
- The organization needs to work with recurring processes and projects to enable standardization of services for testing.

- The organization must be able to deal with and allow a central organization, such as a permanent test organization. Central organizations may be perceived as a threat (e.g., due to their size). This is to be avoided.

13.3   Critical Points for Permanent Test Organizations

Once a permanent testing organization has been established and begun, a number of items must be continuously monitored. The following critical points are prerequisites for the continued success of the organization:

- **Testing services**: It must be verified again and again whether the services offered by the permanent testing organization still meet what the client requires. The required quality level is defined by the client.
- **Test professionalism**: The professionalism of the test organization is based on the one hand on the knowledge and expertise of the testers, and on the other hand on the stability of the test personnel in the organization.
- **Reuse**: Cost savings are often cited as one of the most important reasons for a permanent test organization. This can be achieved by reusing testware, test data and test infrastructure, for example. Constant attention must be paid to the actual reuse and its efficient and optimal organization. Experience has shown that the provision of the test infrastructure in particular is a critical factor.
- **Autonomy**: It is important for a permanent test organization to objectively assess the provided software or hardware independently of the rest of the IT organization. At the same time, the test organization remains part of a higher-level entity with overriding interests. This situation brings a considerable challenge and can lead to conflicts of interest.
- **Preventing encapsulation**: Centralizing testing activities creates a separate unit within the IT organization. This could result in an isolation from the common goal of the entire organizational unit, which is counterproductive for the cooperation between developers and testers.

13.4   Test Guidelines

The test guidelines defined in a company determine which elements of the test process are assigned to the permanent test organization and their structure.

Testing policies must apply to all types of systems, infrastructures, and development methods. Since testing is one of the tools for quality assurance, the test policies must also be aligned with the other policies and initiatives related to quality management. Therefore, testing policies must be in alignment with strategic, tactical, and operational company policies. At the strategic level, the importance of the corporate policies in terms of testing must be established for the entire organization. This leads to strategic testing policies that must be implemented and supported from this level. At the tactical level, testing policies must be transferred (depending on the structure of the company in question) to all parts of the company, departments, product groups, programs, or projects. This also includes resources and budgets for clear and unambiguous implementation of the test guidelines.

A consistent implementation of the test guidelines leads to a uniform test approach on the operational level:

- **Strategic:** An IT organization's strategic policies affect all lower-level organizational areas and their activities, including testing. Strategic policies can take many forms. For example, they can set conditions for the internal IT organization, but they can also set quality goals and ways to achieve them. Strategic directives can be shaped by input and requirements from within an organization, but external factors can also play a role. Examples include requirements from external monitoring and regulatory bodies, legal requirements that must be met, or industry agreements and standards.
- **Tactical:** At the tactical level, the strategic guidelines are translated into their operational equivalents. This is achieved by defining rules that set the preconditions and standards by which people, means and methods must be guided to achieve the strategically defined goals. This set of rules describes how a structured testing approach should be set up within an organization, department, product group, program or project (depending on the structure of the organization under consideration).
- **Operational:** At the operational level, a distinction can be made between general support for the test process and its actual execution. Examples of general support for the test process are methodological, technical and functional recommendations for the testers. Examples of test execution are the actual test and test management, both of which can be organized independently. For example, these can be performed in a matrix organization, on a project basis, or partly in line [TMAP2008].

Reference

1. Koomen van der Aalst Broekmann Vroon, TMap Next, dpunkt Verlag Heidelberg 2008

Acceptance Criteria

14

Abstract

Acceptance criteria are measurable performances or properties of the system that are verified during an acceptance test and are relevant for the release of the test object. For the definition of acceptance criteria, as well as for the preparation and execution of acceptance tests, a number of points must be observed.

14.1   Characteristics of Acceptance Criteria

With the acceptance, the client confirms that his requirements are fulfilled, which are described in the project order or specifications or customer specification. Acceptance is a prerequisite for project completion. It also has legal implications, e.g., for invoicing or warranty. The basis for acceptance is the acceptance test, which checks whether all acceptance criteria have been met. It is important that the acceptance criteria are defined at an early stage and are known to all participants.

In IT projects, testing thus links the value-adding project processes (i.e., creation) and the project management processes, e.g., of quality management and acceptance. On the one hand, the testing processes must therefore be integrated into the plan of the respective project, and on the other hand, a testing organization must be established that aligns testing and management processes [PRMG2019].

According to IEEE 610, **acceptance criteria** are those criteria that a system or component must meet to successfully complete acceptance by the user, customer, or authorized entity. For testing, an acceptance criterion is an instruction concerning a requirement that describes the testing and evaluation of the created product or performed process against

© Springer Fachmedien Wiesbaden GmbH, part of Springer Nature 2022
F. Witte, *Strategy, Planning and Organization of Test Processes*,
https://doi.org/10.1007/978-3-658-36981-1_14

that requirement. However, this also means that no additional services or properties may be hidden in acceptance criteria that do not appear in the actual requirements.

Acceptance criteria therefore usually represent contractually defined points by the client, which determine when a product can be handed over by the contractor to the client.

If these points are not fulfilled, the client can reject the product, partially refuse payment and possibly demand improvements free of charge. The contractor thus contractually secures himself against the client. If only less important criteria are not fulfilled and the product is generally accepted as acceptable, a partial release can also take place and the contractor can be granted a period of time for rectification, possibly also during ongoing operation.

It is crucial that acceptance criteria are measurable. When defining the acceptance criteria, the procedure and measurement method must therefore be specified, as they are otherwise open to interpretation.

The acceptance criteria thereby define when a test has been successfully performed.

The acceptance test is the final test phase before the system is released. After acceptance, the system goes into production, whether it is made available directly (for example, via a web application or a mainframe application) or applied to decentralized systems and devices through a rollout.

14.2   Acceptance Criteria Catalog

Enclosed is a possible template for an **acceptance criteria catalog:**

Change history,
Permits and
Distributors.

Table of Contents,
Terms and abbreviations and
other directories.

1.First introduction,
1.1 About the document,
1.2 Product information,
1.3 Project information.

2. Product acceptance criteria:

2.1 Functionality

2.2 Product quality and documentation

2.3 Usability

2.4 Resources

2.4.1 Hardware

2.4.2 Software

2.4.3 Databases

2.4.4 System configurations

2.5 Performance level

2.6 Reliability and availability; and

2.7 Safety.

3.1 Timetable and milestones

3.2 Costs

3.2.1 Development and

3.2.2 Operation.

The following areas may provide guidance on criteria:

- Finance;
- Management: product, changes, processes, structures;
- Responsible;
- Software;
- Platform for operation: hardware, databases, operating system, system configurations;
- Security;
- Monitoring, logging;
- Documentation: user, test, product, technology, service;
- Trainings;
- Warranty and
- Release information [BULL2008].

Defined test cases should be selected as acceptance criteria and made available to the client. For the creation of the test concept, these test cases do not yet have to be defined in detail; it is sufficient to mention the storage location and the document used to define and confirm these test cases. However, it must be planned at which point the acceptance test cases can be described and presented to the client. Acceptance usually takes place in one working day or in a few hours. The scope must therefore be limited and should be restricted to selected, frequently occurring business cases. Usually, it is a reasonable subset of the test cases from the system test. However, this should not mean that only the test cases relevant to acceptance are tested and that other test cases are not tested.

The acceptance criteria are selected individually for each test object. The severity of the acceptance criteria is based on the risk analysis; softer acceptance conditions are set for non-critical test cases than for safety-critical processes. The test effort is therefore concentrated on the essential parts of the test object.

14.3   Organization of the Acceptance Test

It must also be checked in which environment the acceptance test is to be carried out. This is usually the customer's acceptance test environment. The acceptance **test environment** should correspond as closely as possible to the subsequent productive environment. However, testing in the production environment itself should be avoided in order not to negatively influence or endanger the productive operation of running software systems. Because of the different test environments, a test case can fail in the acceptance environment that never caused problems in the system test. The procedures for installing and configuring the system should also be checked as part of the acceptance process [SPIL2007].

In doing so, one must check in advance how hard the acceptance criteria should be: If an acceptance criterion is that the response time must not exceed 1 second, but in the acceptance test 1.1 seconds are measured, but otherwise all functions can be tested successfully, and the system is available as specified, is the acceptance really unsuccessful? Isn't this rather a certain limitation that should be improved in a subsequent release, but not an obstacle to introduce the system?

The acceptance test cases are tested before the acceptance without the client or customer to evaluate the quality of the system. If the result is that significant bugs are still hidden in the system, it is recommended to proactively postpone the acceptance date and not to invite the customer and steal his time with a disastrous acceptance. However, this is sometimes hardly possible with very tight deadlines. It is therefore all the more important to plan for buffer times in advance. If, when defining the test concept, you already realize that the acceptance period is too tight and can probably hardly be kept, you should already register a project risk here.

The definition of the acceptance also includes the organizational clarification of who is allowed to issue the acceptance and who is to be invited to it, or to whom the acceptance test cases must be submitted and what evidence is required for this. Sometimes an employee of the customer travels to the system acceptance, who only makes a recommendation, but does not issue the acceptance himself. It should therefore also be clear from the outset what the **acceptance process** will look like in detail because acceptance usually defines a milestone at which a certain percentage is due for payment. In some cases, planned acceptances are therefore also delayed and postponed by the customer for budget reasons.

14.4   Definition of Suitable Acceptance Criteria

Unfortunately, testers are still often not involved early enough in the project and perfect, error-free requirements are hard to find. Especially under time pressure and with new, inexperienced project teams or vaguely formulated specifications of the client. But it is precisely in these situations that acceptance criteria should not be dispensed with - even if it is often difficult. Often, perfect, error-free requirements are hard to find in the requirements document, especially when there are inexperienced project teams or vaguely formulated specifications from the client. In the agile world, acceptance **criteria** are often the only detailing of user stories, but in traditional projects acceptance criteria also provide another way to design test cases and set priorities. In both cases, they provide orientation and security.

The acceptance criteria also provide indirect support for requirements engineering. When defining the requirements, you have to think about the requirement again and in different words. Many an ambiguity has already come to light through the formulation of the acceptance criteria, and many requirements have been sharpened in this way. Ultimately, agreed acceptance criteria can also protect against legal action [ANEC2016].

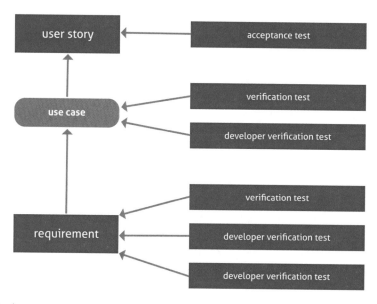

Fig. 14.1 Acceptance tests

The relationship between requirement, use case, and user story is illustrated in the following figure (Fig. 14.1):

In the agile environment, acceptance criteria can be related to requirements artifacts. Acceptance criteria for requirement artifacts define which conditions a requirement artifact or the requirement document must fulfill to be accepted. A requirement artifact is a goal, scenario, or requirement. You can take advantage of this fact when developing acceptance criteria together with the customer. The first step is to develop acceptance criteria for use cases. The description of the acceptance criteria can be based on the corresponding scenarios that make up the use case. The most complete possible coverage of acceptance criteria must be achieved for use cases. You can then go deeper into the description and develop acceptance criteria for individual requirements.

Acceptance criteria do not depend on the implementation of the product or a test environment. Each additional implemented user story expands or changes the scope of the acceptance criteria of the overall product. In addition to the acceptance criteria of the user stories, there are also "unspoken" criteria that are not explicitly mentioned and are usually formulated very openly, such as "there must be no unhandled defects/memory leaks/ crashes" or "readable and clear user interfaces".

To check the quality of the current implementation, explicit test cases are generated for the acceptance criteria. These test cases consider the current test environment (technologies, test data) in which the current implementation is tested. The more openly an acceptance criterion is formulated, the more test cases are needed and the more difficult it becomes to formulate meaningful test cases. To check the quality, the set of these acceptance tests has to be executed. In most cases, manual execution of these tests is no longer possible on a regular basis after only a short project duration and automation of these test cases is therefore essential [CODE2012].

One way to define acceptance criteria for projects in the agile environment is to question keywords. These must first be identified in the requirements text or the **user story, and** then it must be checked whether questions - based on the so-called W-questions (who, when, how often, etc.) – can be provided with a meaningful answer. Questions that do not allow for a meaningful answer in the respective context are ignored. Keywords are full verbs – also known as process verbs, adjectives and nouns. Their questioning must lead to a meaningful answer and supplement or concretize the content of a requirements text or a user story. In the process, a common understanding must be achieved among the stakeholders for the implementation to be aimed for. The answers to the questions make it possible to define specific acceptance criteria that must meet quality criteria. There does not have to be a 1:1 relationship between the answers of the stakeholders and the acceptance criteria, but several answers can be combined into one acceptance criterion or one answer can lead to several acceptance criteria. The formulated acceptance criteria must finally be accepted by the stakeholders. In the final step, test cases are created that correspond to the proven pattern of

- Precondition,
- Test steps to be performed,
- Expected result,
- Postcondition and
- Test data used

The formulated W-questions, for which the keywords must be inserted in the placeholder, represent an excerpt that must be adapted or supplemented for different industries and domains to the respective field of expertise [SIGS2011].

Acceptance criteria derived from user stories are therefore well suited to ensuring a sufficient test basis for acceptance testing. A five-step approach focuses on the definition of acceptance criteria. The goal should be to support team communication and to define specific details for user stories to lay the foundation for a successful acceptance test. In addition, the example of the definition of acceptance criteria can be used to demonstrate how a classic method can be embedded in the Scrum framework by questioning keywords [HOOD2011].

14.5   Properties of Acceptance Tests

According to SCRUM, an **acceptance test** should have the following characteristics:

- **Abstract**: The acceptance test should not include every detail, but should be reduced to the essentials.
- **Trustworthy**: The behavior in the test and acceptance environment must always be identical to the behavior in the customer's actual operating environment regarding the subject to be tested. The test must also be reproducible for the customer.
- **Coherent**: An acceptance test should cover only one (and not several) subject context.
- **Decoupled** (independent): An acceptance test must be independent of all others and must not be influenced in result by the results or availability of other tests.
- **Meaningful and understandable**: the motivation, the content of the test and its expected result should be easily understandable for experts in the test area (domain experts).

- **Non-redundant**: A subject to be tested should only be covered by one test and not more than once.

In this context, an acceptance test is to be understood as a description of how the acceptance criteria are to be checked [OOS2010].

It is recommended to provide the customer or the person responsible for the acceptance with the planned test cases before the acceptance and to plan the scope, i.e., to create an agenda for the acceptance. This ensures a common understanding of the scope and goal of the acceptance right from the start.

Should problems arise during acceptance, it is absolutely necessary to deal with them openly. If the customer gets the impression that certain facts are being concealed, he will feel hoodwinked and will both pay particularly critical attention to the system and develop a general distrust of the development and testing department. A presentation of what was possible and what was not achieved is in any case better than printing around or misinformation. Often it is still possible to achieve an acceptance with certain conditions, which will be improved within an agreed period of time. If an acceptance is not granted, both sides must define and record which points are to be subsequently delivered and by when, so that at least the next attempt at an acceptance does not fail again. The scope should also be defined with the following acceptance, whether only the points complained about are tested after rectification or whether the entire system is checked again.

References

1. https://www.projektmagazin.de/artikel/testmanagement-it-projekten-teil-1_7180, accessed on 9 May 2020
2. http://robert.bullinger.over-blog.com/article-abnahmekriterien-fuer-software-25457484.html, accessed on 9 May 2020
3. Basiswissen Softwaretest, dpunkt Verlag Heidelberg, 3. Edition 2005 – Corrected Reprint 2007
4. http://www.anecon.com/blog/abnahmekriterien-bruecke-oder-kruecke-zwischen-requirements-engineering-und-test/, accessed on 9 May 2020
5. https://blog.codecentric.de/2012/04/akzeptanzkriterien-oder-tests-als-anforderungsdokumentation/, accessed on 9 May 2020
6. https://www.sigs-datacom.de/uploads/tx_dmjournals/becker_OS_testing_11.pdf, accessed on 9 May 2020
7. http://blog.hood-group.com/blog/2011/12/06/akzeptanzkriterien-fur-user-stories-definieren-aber-nur-wie/, accessed on 9 May 2020
8. https://www.oose.de/blogpost/akzeptanzkriterium-vs-akzeptanztest-vs-testfall/, accessed on 9 May 2020

Criteria for Test Discontinuation and Test Continuation

15

Abstract

In certain situations, tests must be aborted or interrupted and continued later. There are certain criteria for this. The resumption after test interruption leads to a rescheduling of the test process.

15.1 Cases of Test Aborts

There are situations where it does not make sense to proceed with the test. This may be the case, for example, if a major component contains defects or is not present at all, or if configuration problems limit the availability of the test environment in such a way that many planned test cases would result in a defect. In this case, a test effort would occur where it is known from the outset that numerous bugs would have to be recorded which, once the triggering problem has been solved, will be solved again anyway. Professional test tools therefore allow test cases to be set to "not applicable" for a test run. In this case, one speaks of a **test abort**.

Another case is when a test object has such a low quality level that acceptance capability is not achieved even after several tests. In this case, it may make sense to remove this object completely so as not to jeopardize the usability of the entire product, but to deliver the product with a smaller range of functions. In this case, too, further test activities must be stopped timely.

Another abort criterion is that the hardware capacities are insufficient. Although this happens much less frequently in recent years than in the past due to the enormous progress in hardware development, it still happens. Porting to other hardware or procuring new

© Springer Fachmedien Wiesbaden GmbH, part of Springer Nature 2022
F. Witte, *Strategy, Planning and Organization of Test Processes*,
https://doi.org/10.1007/978-3-658-36981-1_15

hardware is then associated with additional expenses, and test activities must first be interrupted.

It can also be the case that the central component, which has an impact on numerous test cases, is not faulty, but is developed in a new version, and it is only during the test phase that one decides to use the newer version for the finished product. Sometimes it also happens that the system architecture needs to be changed, that one notices that the application is functionally correct, but the application would have far too long response times, so one needs to make fundamental changes first. Therefore, it may make sense to interrupt a test and then resume it when the development of the new version is complete. This procedure must be defined for each test level, since the component test comes before the integration and system tests in the time sequence. In this case, the entire project planning must be adjusted and the test concept updated.

Another cause can be that another project gets a higher priority before the described project. If several or all testers are pulled from the project to save the other project, the test must be interrupted and continued later. This, of course, has an impact on the schedule situation. Sometimes management has to weigh up whether it is feasible to postpone a deadline for project A to bring forward another project B for strategic reasons or to avert a threatened penalty payment due to a delay in delivery in project B. In such a case, it is important that the testers are not removed from the project. In such a case, it is important that the test manager of project A transparently presents the risks of an interruption.

Sometimes the time allotted for the test has simply run out. Either the product came into the test too late or the test interval was planned too short or there were resource bottlenecks in the test team or a combination of these causes. In this case, the product has to be delivered - if only for contractual reasons – and the initially planned test coverage has to be abandoned. As a consequence, however, this may mean a considerable launch risk. It is therefore particularly important to prioritize test cases so that the most important test cases can still be executed before the product is delivered.

15.2   Restart and Test Continuation After Test Discontinuation

It should be noted that every interruption and every restart is associated with additional costs and risks. Perhaps the test resources are no longer available at a later point, a new training phase has to be considered, and certain documentation and coordination efforts already have to be considered due to the interruption. In addition, an interruption or abort has fatal effects on the project staff in terms of their motivation. In general, a project always becomes considerably more expensive if it takes longer. Sometimes, as a test manager, you get doubts whether management and controlling are really aware of this fact in its entirety.

This procedure must be described in the test concept. This should address whether (project-specific) risks are known that are likely to interrupt the test phase from the outset. The critical core processes and essential components that are crucial for the functionality of the entire application should also be documented.

There are projects where, for legal reasons (e.g., EU-wide entry into force of a regulation) or external circumstances (e.g., relocation of a data center that is terminated at a certain time), the deadline is fixed and an abort or postponement is particularly fatal. If this is the case, this aspect should be specifically mentioned in the test concept.

Test Risks

16

Abstract

Many projects do not run successfully. Project risks must be identified and assessed from the very beginning. There are numerous possible risks to project success that can lead to significant delays and additional costs.

16.1 Project Success

Although the proportion of successfully implemented projects has increased significantly due to improved project management methods, so that the vast majority are rated as successful, there is still great potential for improvement. Many projects are still not successful or only successful in some aspects. The following figures are available from a study surveying project activity in Germany, in which 500 private-sector and public-sector companies were interviewed (Fig. 16.1):

Interestingly, outcome and quality are more accurately assessed than other criteria. This can mean that the quality assurance measures are on a generally high level (this would be the optimistic variant) or that the quality is not considered closely enough (this is more likely in my eyes, if the test was reasonably successful and not too many open defects occurred, one is already satisfied). Problems with the cost and time situation are known, and the values seem plausible, that the stakeholder satisfaction is lower, must not only be rooted in the projects themselves, but in general dissatisfaction with the work, the company, the payment, personnel differences and communication problems.

© Springer Fachmedien Wiesbaden GmbH, part of Springer Nature 2022
F. Witte, *Strategy, Planning and Organization of Test Processes*,
https://doi.org/10.1007/978-3-658-36981-1_16

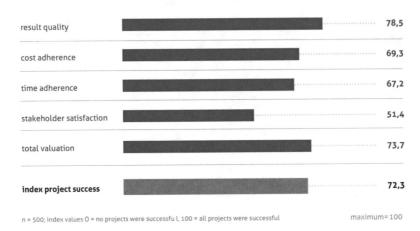

result quality 78,5

cost adherence 69,3

time adherence 67,2

stakeholder satisfaction 51,4

total valuation 73,7

index project success 72,3

n = 500; index values 0 = no projects were successfu l, 100 = all projects were successful   maximum = 100

Fig. 16.1 Characteristics of project success [GPIM2015]

Table 16.1 Calculation of project risks

Risk	Probability of occurrence	Cost of risk	Calculated risk
Risk 1	10%	€50,000	€5000
Risk 2	15%	€100,000	€15,000
Risk 3	5%	€300,000	€15,000
Risk 4	5%	€40,000	€2000

16.2   Assessment of Risks

Many risks are already known at the beginning of the project or in the test planning phase. Therefore, the **test risks** and their possible effects must be described in detail in the test concept.

The individual risks should be weighted and evaluated. What does it mean if the risk occurs, and how high are the costs (Table 16.1)? For this purpose, the costs must be determined and known, which is not trivial in some cases. The probability of occurrence can be estimated based on experience, although this can, of course, be very much off the mark.

The sum of the calculated risks is added. In the above example, the risk is therefore 500 0 + 15,000 + 15,000 + 2000 = €37,000.

You can see from this example that it makes sense above all to avoid risk 2 and risk 3 because these two risks would hit the project much harder than risk 1 and risk 4. So, you can manage your resources better and more purposefully right from the start if you are aware of these risks and assess them.

The regular project reviews should address whether the risk assessment is still up to date, whether any new risks have been identified, or whether any of the risks have materialized.

16.3   Possible Test Risks

It is therefore important to obtain an overview of possible test risks. The enclosed list is intended to highlight possible risks and their impact. The list is by no means complete, but it does show problems that frequently occur in practice and can be used as a thought-provoking aid for the creation of a test concept.

Management
1. The project manager does not have the power to push project goals through and is not sufficiently supported by management.
2. The test is considered to be of secondary importance in the company. The senior management is not interested in the project and neglects communication.
3. There is disagreement about the scope of the project at management level. Some managers do not want the project politically.
4. A change in management leads to a re-prioritization of tasks.

Project Scope
1. The requirements are insufficient, incorrect or contradictory. As a result, the project scope is not sufficiently described.
2. Uncontrolled changes increase the scope of the project.
3. The project team adds product features that are not present in the requirements and also not present in change requests.
4. Estimates are inaccurate or overly optimistic from the start. Testing activities have not been sufficiently evaluated.
5. Dependencies on external circumstances or other projects have an unfavorable effect on the schedule and cost situation of one's own project.
6. Individual activities in the project were not given sufficient consideration in the planning phase.

Cost Management
1. The costs for software, hardware or personnel are not fully collected.
2. There are subsequent changes to the project costs.
3. Delays or idle times due to late realization increase the project costs.
4. Extensive defect analyses and repeated regression tests lead to increasing costs.

Change Management
1. Too many changes or too much dynamic in the requirements will lead to complications, delays and confusion in the project.
2. There is no agreement on changes or their effects. This leads to conflicts in the project.
3. There is no suitable system to track changes.
4. The change management process is missing or opaque. Decision paths are not transparent or are taken by the wrong stakeholders.
5. Changing or inaccurate priorities for changes affect the schedule.
6. The wording of the changes is not precise enough, does not take all aspects into account or conflicts with the existing system, the system architecture or other requirements.

Stakeholder
1. Problems in communication due to lack of stakeholder participation.
2. Stakeholders have expectations of the project that are not defined.
3. Fluctuation and changing stakeholders slow down project activities.
4. Group dynamic processes or conflicts between stakeholders, smoldering conflicts, disagreements, prejudices or personal dislikes. From my point of view, this is one of the most difficult problems. It is estimated that problems in projects are 20% technical or organizational and 80% interpersonal. Consequently, it is estimated that in about 80% of the cases where a project goes wrong, the cause can be traced back to internal power struggles or personal conflicts. Therefore, a well-functioning conflict management is essential for success in the project business [THEQ2020].
5. Negative attitude of stakeholders, stakeholders wish the project to fail.
6. Lack of input from stakeholders: this includes lack of experience and information as well as lack of diligence, low motivation or frequent absences.

Communication
1. Misinterpretation of requirements or inaccurately formulated requirements lead to faulty test cases. Workshops of testers with the clients and the requirements management are unfortunately omitted in many cases or carried out much too late.
2. Lack of communication leads to misunderstandings and dissatisfaction. From my own experience: it is often difficult to find out who needs what information. Either you give information to too many who can't do anything with it, or the individual employee doesn't realize that there is a need for action for him. If affected people are not informed and feel ignored, this can also lead to disruptions and resistance during the project. Too

much communication or information to the wrong stakeholders who are not responsible can also delay the project. Finding the "happy medium" in the scope and goal of communication is an enormous challenge.

3. Mutual recriminations, political acting, alliances and aversions within the project team. It has been shown time and again that personal conflicts within projects are among the greatest risks that prevent project success.

Resources

1. There is a lack of test resources to complete the individual tasks.
2. The training of new employees is more difficult than expected: The learning curves of employees who are new to the job, the company or the project lead to lower productivity. Employees who are already overworked are often entrusted with the induction process. Missing or insufficient training and lack of experience lead to delays during the project.
3. Poor performance, negative attitudes, low motivation or lack of support from line managers can lead to schedule or cost overruns.
4. Fluctuation during the project, especially of experienced employees with inadequate documentation of the work performed. A lot of know-how is only in the heads, but not documented in the right place in a comprehensible way. The handover and familiarization phases are usually too short to have sufficient effect in a project.
5. Key personnel resources have been diverted to another project and are therefore not available.

System Architecture

1. The system architecture does not fit the prescribed principles.
2. The system architecture is not described completely and up-to-date. As a result, it is possible that effects on connected systems and remapping procedures are forgotten and not tested.
3. The architecture is inflexible or deficient.
4. The architecture is difficult to implement, costly, or does not meet the requirements.

Design

1. The design is inflexible or buggy.
2. The product design is not readily convertible or does not fit the requirements.
3. The quality of the product design is not sufficient.
4. Stakeholders or experts reject the design.

Technology and Quality

1. Individual technical components do not sufficiently meet the requirements.
2. Technical components do not scale and do not meet performance requirements.
3. Technological components do not work together and have interface problems.
4. Parts of the system have security vulnerabilities. Information can leak out through these security gaps.
5. Lack of stability or system crashes of individual components lead to problems during testing and delay their productive use.
6. Individual components do not work reliably or fail after a short time.
7. Standards and best practices are not followed.
8. Components are "over-engineered", i.e., bloated with useless functions or design features. This leads to increased complexity and higher risk of bugs during testing.
9. Technical components are not easily expandable with new functions.
10. Failure of critical systems such as test environments or lack of availability of test environments.
11. The collection and administration of test data is much more difficult than initially assumed.
12. Lack of documentation of existing components leads to problems with system integration.
13. Missing updates, lack of hardware support and insufficient maintenance options for components that are no longer supported endanger system stability.
14. Components or products cannot be put into operation because important criteria are not met.
15. The quality of the software is worse than planned, there are delays in the bug fixing phase as a result, and there are more regression tests than planned. Additional deliveries lead to additional work and overtime, especially in the final phase of the project.
16. The tools (e.g., for defect recording or test case definition) are not suitable or different tools are used. Changing tools during the project or using different tools can significantly complicate reporting for the test manager and tie up additional unplanned effort of the stakeholders.

Integration

1. The setup of hardware and software or the provision of the test environment is delayed.
2. The product cannot be easily integrated into operational processes or existing systems.

3. The project result cannot be integrated into the company organization because the project was implemented, but the overall picture was not considered. Example: A sales system has been set up, but there is no sales team.
4. Key components are faulty or are not available on the required date.
5. The interaction of individual components does not work.
6. The project disrupts operational business processes and negatively impacts financial performance.
7. The project disrupts sales processes or compliance processes such as audits and reporting.

Requirements
1. Requirements do not match the corporate strategy or corporate processes.
2. Requirements do not match existing systems.
3. Requirements are ambiguous, contradictory or open to different interpretations.
4. Requirements are incomplete or of insufficient quality.
5. Requirements conflict with existing regulations or legal requirements.
6. Unclear and poor-quality requirements lead to queries and incomplete or incorrect test cases.

Decisions
1. Open decisions delay the progress of the project if no clear deadlines and rules for decision-making are defined.
2. Decisions are ambiguous for fear of taking responsibility.
3. Decisions are made unobjectively or based on incorrect or incomplete information.
4. Incomplete decisions only partially solve problems and lead to further open questions,

Procurement
1. Unacceptable contract elements are included in subcontracted supplies from suppliers that cannot be negotiated.
2. Subcontracted supplies are of insufficient quality and cannot be used in the project.
3. Conflicts between suppliers and clients or conflicts and dependencies among suppliers lead to delays.
4. Suppliers start a task late or deliver it late.

5. Service and advice from the supplier are not of sufficient quality.
6. Suppliers drop out, e.g., due to insolvency, and are therefore no longer able to deliver. Alternative procurement is difficult and delays the overall project.
7. Components or supplies infringe patents.

Power and Authority
1. The project team lacks the authority to implement or impose certain tasks.
2. Authority to enforce project goals is unclear.
3. Conflicting statements and instructions lead to confusion.

Approval Procedures and Bureaucracy
1. Delayed approvals from stakeholders cause problems in the schedule.
2. Failure to provide funds in a timely manner will negatively impact the project.
3. Delays in purchasing processes or the recruitment of employees delays the project.
4. Further education or training does not take place in time. Individual stakeholders are recalled to other projects.

Organization
1. The project does not fit the corporate culture.
2. A restructuring in the company delays the project or influences the goals.
3. A merger or a company acquisition or sale disrupts the course of the project.
4. Other projects get a higher priority, so resources have to be pulled from the project.
5. Responsibilities for certain functions or defect analyses are not clearly defined.

External Risks
1. Legal changes affect the project.
2. Changes in the market (e.g., stock market crashes) or force majeure affect the project. In this case, decisions are postponed or funding is provided late.
3. Technical changes in the industry or business innovations delay the project progress.

Project Management
1. Project management processes are not followed to a sufficient degree.
2. Lack of or inadequate project management leads to lack of adherence to best practices.
3. Defects in project management methods (e.g., faulty scheduling or algorithms) delay the project.

Subordinated Risks

Subordinated risks arise when a risk is shifted externally, e.g., to a supplier.

Customer or User Acceptance
1. The user interface is of low quality, slow or difficult to use.
2. The user interface is not accessible and violates rules.
3. The project is perceived by users as a disruptive factor in their own productivity.
4. Users reject the prototype, requiring rework or entirely new designs.

In general, a distinction is made between project and product risks. **Project risks** threaten the ability of the project to deliver a product. **Product risks**, on the other hand, result from problems with the delivered product.

Risk-based testing considers information about product and project risks and focuses testing activities on high-risk areas [PRLE2019].

References

1. https://projekte-leicht-gemacht.de/blog/pm-in-der-praxis/130-projektrisiken-beispiele/, accessed on 9 May 2020
2. https://www.gpm-ipma.de/fileadmin/user_upload/GPM/Know-How/GPM_Studie_Vermessung_der_Projekttaetigkeit.pdf, accessed on 9 May 2020
3. https://thequaliteers.de/nachrichten-leser/items/10-schritte-start-testprojekt-02.html, accessed on May 2020

Test Data

17

Abstract

Test data management regulates the use and administration of test data. The availability of test data has to be ensured, and special questions have to be answered. Different approaches and tools must be used for this purpose.

17.1 Test Data Management

There are several aspects to consider when **managing test data:**

- People, roles and risks,
- Tools, methods and procedures,
- Defined processes,
- Tasks and necessary skills,
- Technical challenges,
- Security, laws, data protection and regulations as well as
- Efficiency and economy.

Consideration must be given to how test data is made available automatically when needed, how test data is restored to its original state after processing, and how the validity and currency of the test data set can be tracked.

Test data must be provided quickly and efficiently, especially when mass data is involved. Links and dependencies across different systems must be considered.

© Springer Fachmedien Wiesbaden GmbH, part of Springer Nature 2022
F. Witte, *Strategy, Planning and Organization of Test Processes*,
https://doi.org/10.1007/978-3-658-36981-1_17

In test data management, it is necessary to clarify what type of test data should be used: purely **synthetic data** or a **production data dump** that has been processed with **anonymization** (data alienation), or a combination of both methods. This can also vary in a project depending on the test level [TEST2019].

Typical challenges in test data management are the use and management of the data:

- Test cases cannot be executed because data constellations are missing or not available.
    Example: A bank wants to test new personalized offers, but customer data is missing in the depot.
- The test environment is too small for the required test data.
    Example: Several test teams need data for representative regression tests, which are consumed during the tests. Therefore, they need to be provided multiple times.
- The available data may not be used for regulatory reasons.
    Example: Customer data may not be used for testing personalized offers for reasons of data protection.
- The development of a test data set is costly and tedious.
    Example: In a test dataset with several thousand attributes, those that are relevant for compliance reasons must be identified. A decision must be made whether the data is to be generated synthetically or anonymously.
- Comparative data are required for the test evaluation.
    Example: The posting records created in the test must be checked against a reference file.

In many cases, it takes too long for the data to reach the tester. Only very few employees in the development departments have independent access to the data. They have to work with what is provided to them.

To operate agile test data management in software development, the necessary data must be provided as flexibly as possible.

The following steps are required:

- **Data virtualization:** Highly compressed, virtualized data copies are created from any data source to virtualize test data. The copies allow users to quickly access the information they need. This optimizes the resources that a database consumes, increases storage efficiency, and thus reduces costs. Data virtualization is accomplished by connecting to an external solution that virtualizes data in a non-disruptive, minimally invasive, continuous, and efficient manner.
- **Data masking:** In the second step, the data is masked. The information in the original data is thereby all anonymized. This has the advantage that customer and company data

is consistently protected, and data protection is considered without the tester having to completely dispense with sensitive data.

- **Test data provisioning:** The testers and developers can independently access the virtualized and masked data. Care must be taken to avoid time-consuming authorization procedures to ensure agility and efficiency. Testers and developers must be able to concentrate on the data that is relevant to them without losing time unnecessarily in release and waiting loops. It must also be possible to easily reset the test data to any previous state so that the tester can experiment with the test data without any worries.
- **Automated data provisioning**: Automated data provisioning enables testers and developers to work more efficiently and accurately, as well as to save time. They can use this time for productive and non-repetitive activities that require their full expertise and undivided attention [ITDA2019].

17.2   Approaches to Test Data Generation

There are different approaches to create suitable test data. The different types are shown in the following figure (Fig. 17.1):

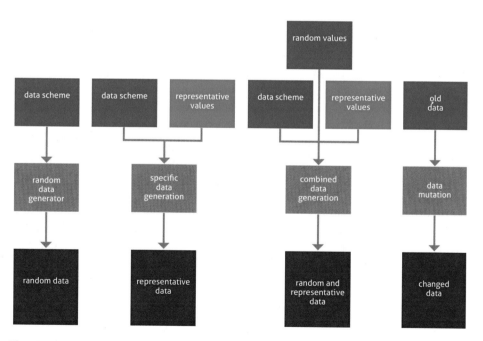

Fig. 17.1 Approaches to test data generation

- **Blind approach:** In the blind approach, random data is generated. The data generator does not consider the specification or the code. Only the data description (type, label and size of the data fields) is known to the data generator. Since the blind test data generator does not know the algorithms in the software, it tries to generate as many value combinations of all proxy values as possible. This approach is very costly, and the chances of testing a particular function and finding bugs in it are very low. Test data generation by a random number generator is very easy to do, but test execution is all the more laborious and test coverage tends to be low. Therefore, this approach is not very suitable for practice.

- **Targeted approach:** In the targeted approach, exactly those data are generated that trigger functions leading to a certain output, i.e., the test data are derived from the function specification. Each test case targets one or more functions with the purpose of passing one of its outputs. The approach is similar to the white-box test method, except that the object of analysis is the specification rather than the code. The advantage of the targeted approach is the higher test coverage with fewer data, the disadvantage is the higher effort to analyze the functions and to specify the test cases.

- **Combined approach:** The combined approach combines the blind and the targeted approach. First, some data is randomly generated for each database attribute as well as for each input variable. Then, based on the function specification, the randomly generated data is manipulated to trigger specific functions in a targeted manner. The advantage of the combined approach is that some critical functions are tested selectively, while others are tested randomly. Thus, one saves some analysis effort compared to the targeted approach and some test execution compared to the blind approach, and increases the test coverage compared to a pure random test.

- **Mutation approach:** In the mutation approach, a specific dataset is manipulated. The test starts with only a few test data, which cause a kind of smoke test. Then the test dataset is gradually expanded, partly by random data and partly by targeted values for testing specific functions. Thus, with this approach, testing can start early and, depending on the time remaining, the test data can be expanded through several iterations. After each iteration, the function coverage as well as the number of defects found should increase. Critical functions are tested first and at a later stage more routine functions are included in the test. The test can be aborted at any time to deliver the product or release. The disadvantage of this is that one tends to be satisfied with a minimum of test data and a correspondingly low-test coverage [SNEE2012].

17.3   Tools for Test Data Generation

Test data generators can support the test designer in generating suitable test **data**. Different approaches can be distinguished, depending on the test basis from which the test data is derived:

- **Database-based test data generators** process database schemas and can generate test data sets from them or to filter out test data from database contents in a suitable form. The same applies to the generation of test data from files of various data formats.
- **Code-based test data generators** create test data by analyzing the source code of the test object. However, no target values can be generated because a test oracle is required for this. Also, (for all white-box methods) only source code that exists is considered. Defect states due to forgotten program statements remain undetected. Therefore, code-based test data generators can only be used in a very limited way.
- **Interface-based test data generators** analyze the test object interface, recognize the definition ranges of the interface parameters and derive test data from them, e.g., through equivalence class and limit value analysis. Tools exist for a wide variety of interface types, from program interfaces (**API - application programming interface**) to the analysis of graphical user interfaces. The tool recognizes which data fields are present in a mask (e.g., numeric field, date field) and generates test data that cover the respective value ranges, e.g., by limit value analysis. Again, the problem is that no target values can be generated. The tools are therefore well suited for the automatic generation of negative tests, since no concrete target values are relevant here, but only whether the test object reacts with a suitable defect message.
- **Specification-based test data generators** derive test data and associated target values from a specification. In this case, the specification must be available in a formal notation. For example, the call sequence of methods can be specified by a UML model, the **sequence diagram**. Such an approach is also called **model-based testing** (MBT). The UML model is created with a CASE tool and then imported by the test generator. The test generator generates test scripts that are passed to a suitable tool for test execution.

A test data generator can apply certain rules (e.g., for limit analysis) to systematically create test cases. However, the test data generator can by no means judge whether the generated test cases are good or bad, important or irrelevant. This still requires the test designer to have a comprehensive understanding of the test object, experience, creativity and intuition. Tools can only support to a very limited extent, but cannot replace a tester. For example, the target response usually has to be added manually. The correct interpretation of the test results also remains an essential task for the test designer [SPIL2007].

17.4   Test Data Types

Test objects can be user interfaces, system interfaces, or database tables or files. Each of these test objects has a different type of test data that is generated in different ways:

- **Databases:** When testing databases, the functionality and structure of the database must be known. There are four levels of data coverage when testing:
  - **Record overlap**: There is one characteristic for each record type or table.
  - **Attribute overlap**: There are at least two different values for each attribute.
  - **Value overlap**: Each representative value occurs at least once in the value range of an attribute (number of records = number of representative values for the attribute with the most values).
  - **State coverage**: All combinations of all representative values are generated.
- **System interfaces:** When testing interfaces, three types of interfaces must be differentiated:
  - Application programming interfaces (API): Interfaces for calling external systems
  - Messages
  - Import/export files

References

1. https://www.testing-board.com/testdatenmanagement/, accessed on 9 May 2020
2. https://www.it-daily.net/it-management/software-development/20587-in-vier-schritten-zu-agilem-testdatenmanagement, accessed on 9 May 2020
3. Andreas Spillner, Tilo Linz, Basiswissen Softwaretest, 2007 dpunkt Verlag Heidelberg
4. Sneed, Bauimgartner, Seidl: Der Systemtest, Carl Hanser Verlag Munich 2012.

Test Documentation

Abstract

The test documentation with standard IEEE 829:2008 distinguishes different integrity levels and different types of documents to be prepared within the test process. The test should be integrated into the organization and the test documentation should follow a structure. For test documentation, suitable metrics are to be defined and collected on a regular basis. The availability of the test system during the project duration should also be documented.

18.1   Test Documentation Objectives and Integrity Levels

The IEEE 829:1998 as an older variant was also introduced to establish a standard for **test documentation.** The goals of the standard are different for the different groups of stakeholders:

- **Project** management: understanding risk, value, cost, requirements and schedule;
- **Development**: Identification of critical areas and documentation of the currently achieved quality level;
- **Test**: Development and execution of the tests within the given time and budget frame.
- **Test manager**: Documentation, control and overview of time and budget frame and quality of the product.

IEEE 829:2008 was developed to bring this standard up to date. Agile projects became increasingly widespread in the mid to late 2000s. This standard is intended to be suitable for both an agile and a conventional systematic approach, and applies to systems as well

© Springer Fachmedien Wiesbaden GmbH, part of Springer Nature 2022
F. Witte, *Strategy, Planning and Organization of Test Processes,*
https://doi.org/10.1007/978-3-658-36981-1_18

as software. The intention was to move away from the previous principle of "documents follow activities" towards a documentation process, conforming to ISO 12207 (international standard for describing the processes of a **software life cycle**) and ISO 15288 (**system life cycle** as a standard for describing the processes within a life cycle of a man-made system). This new type of description should be created task-oriented with input and output. For this purpose, 4 **integrity levels,** depending on the fault tolerance of the system, were defined, and specific documents were proposed for each level:

- **4 - Catastrophic**: Master Test Plan (static), Level Test Plan (dynamic and detailed), Level Test Design, Level Test Case, Level Test Protocol, Level Test Log, Anomaly Report, Level Integration Test Status Report, Level Test Report, Master Test Report
- **3 - Critical**: Master Test Plan, Level Test Plan, Level Test Design, Level Test Case, Level Test Protocol, Level Test Log, Anomaly Report, Level Integration Test Status Report, Level Test Report, Master Test Report
- **2 - Marginal**: Level Test Plan, Level Test Design, Level Test Case, Level Test Protocol, Level Test Log, Anomaly Report, Level Integration Test Status Report, Level Test Report
- **1 - Negligible**: Level Test Plan, Level Test Design, Level Test Case, Level Test Protocol, Level Test Log, Anomaly Report, Level Test Report

In accordance with the V model, several stages are planned for the test; the documents Test Design, Test Case, Test Protocol, Test Log, Interim Test Status Report and Anomaly Report are therefore created for the Component, Component Integration, System and Acceptance Test stages as required. To support the test manager, there is also a template for a Master Test Plan Metrics Report, which includes metrics according to **ISO 91266.** ISO 9126 is a standard for defining the quality characteristics of a software product as clearly and objectively as possible.

As usual, adaptation of the test documentation process to one's own project or company is expressly desired, as long as the requirements for comprehensible test documentation are met. In addition to test documentation, the standard also deals with the integration of testing into the organization. It defines and describes the following forms (ISTQB-compliant):

- Completely integrated into the development team,
- Internal: tester in the development team,
- Integrated: own team parallel to the developers in the same organizational unit,
- Autonomous: own independent organizational unit within the company and
- Independent: completely independent, outside the company, outsourced [BULL2008].

18.2   Structure of the Test Documentation

A test documentation consists of the following:

- A planning document (test plan, test concept),
- The description of the individual test cases and test procedures,
- Documents accompanying test object deliveries (test object delivery notes),
- Automated test scripts,
- The description of the test cases performed,
- Regular test reports,
- Defect reporting,
- Defined statistics and appropriate metrics, and
- A test completion report with a summary of the test results, evaluation and recommendation of a release of the software.

The test concept with its individual chapters is already described elsewhere in this book.

18.3   Test Script

A **test script** defines how the individual test cases are to be executed. It contains information about the prerequisites for starting the test cases and how the test case is to be executed. A test script should be valid for as many test cases as possible with similar prerequisites and a similar procedure. Separate test scripts should be specified for different groups of test cases. Test scripts containing only one test case should be avoided if possible. If multiple test scripts are required, each is given a unique identifier. Include as many sections as there are test scripts.

The individual steps of each test case in this test script should be defined in advance, e.g., to clarify what should happen if the test fails before the test case is executed.

The description of the test procedure should include the following elements:

- Log: Any special methods or formats are to be described to record the results of the test runs, incidents and other important events, e.g., log file in XML format.
- Preparations (optional): This documents what has to be done to prepare the execution of the test script.
- Start: It has to be defined how the test script is to be started.
- Execution (optional): It has to be described what needs to be done during the execution of the test script, e.g., whether further user input is required.

- Observation: This section specifies how measurements and test results are to be obtained (e.g., the response time of a remote terminal is to be tested with a network simulator).
- Abort (optional): What to do to abort the test due to unforeseen events.
- Restart (optional): All starting points and the respective procedure are described at which the test can be restarted.
- Stop (optional): Defines how the test script is properly aborted during the execution of the automated endurance test.
- Cleanup (optional): The cleanup tasks must be defined to restore the original state after the tests. The test system must be in exactly the same state after cleanup as it was before the test was performed, to be able to repeat a test run with the same test conditions, but modified software or configuration, or exactly identical.

18.4   Test Case

A test case is a combination of input data, conditions and expected outputs that serve a specific purpose. It is used to check whether requirements from a specification document are met or whether the program flow actually corresponds to the expected path.

At least the following attributes must be defined:

- Test case ID: unique identification with short designation. It must be ensured that this identification is unique in the project or in the organization and will no longer be changed.
- Description of the test objects and methods executed by this test case.
- Input data required to run the test case.
- Expenditures (target response) that are expected.
- Test environment (configuration).
- Test case specifics.
- Dependencies (does the test case depend on the execution of other test cases), test requirements.

18.5   Test Protocol

The test log contains information about all executed test cases, their results and any deviations from the expected result.

The test protocol contains the following parts:

- Test protocol ID: unique identification with short designation. The test protocol must be archived and retraceable. It must be possible to trace the results of past test runs at any time. Care must be taken to ensure that this identification is unique in the project or in the organization and is not changed.
- Description of the test execution: tested software components, test environment (e.g., operating system, databases, web servers, application servers, configuration details).
- List of the test cases performed: The execution per test case with result (OK, NOK) per test run must be documented. This also includes defect messages, program aborts and messages (which require an action from the tester). Any deviations in the test environment or changes to the test description made specifically for a particular test run must also be described. If unexpected events have occurred, it should be recorded what happened before and after the unexpected events. If test cases could not be executed, the circumstances that led to this problem will be described. Even if no unexpected results occur, this should be noted.

18.6   Summary of the Test Documentation

In a final part of the test documentation, a summary of the test results will be listed. This will list all problems that were addressed and how their solutions were achieved.
The following can be addressed:

- Scope of the test (completeness) compared to scope criteria of the test plan, listing of functionalities that were not tested with reasons why the test was not fully performed.
- If applicable, deviations of the executed tests from the test plan, test script or test cases, the deviations must be justified.
- Summary of test results and evaluation of software quality.
- Summary of all the main activities and the important events of the test [TESD2007].

18.7   Neglection of Test Documentation

In testing and development, you often only just finish your planned work. The developer just manages to finish his component and does not create a sufficient documentation due to time constraints. The situation is similar in testing.

Unfortunately, many employees do not learn from their mistakes either, but only consider their own work when estimating their effort, but not the entire process. Therefore, many effort estimates are set too low.

It is particularly difficult if the effort for the entire project was not estimated exactly in advance, but only approximate empirical values were used, or if one wanted to enforce a completion date politically. In my experience, the task is also repeatedly examined in too little detail and to too small an extent right at the beginning by those who are to implement the project. Raising appropriate open questions at an early stage of the project always pays off later. In practice, however, stakeholders are usually involved too late in the process because they are often still participating in other projects (which are also delayed). One often gets the feeling that one's work is constantly running behind the existing challenges.

But if the program has just been made to run at the last moment, there is no time left to do the documentation. This then falls behind because you are already behind schedule anyway. The effects of incomplete or missing test documentation are usually not noticed immediately, and this is dangerous.

One of the main reasons for delays and poor quality in testing and development, for queries and unanswered questions, is the fact that sufficient documentation was not provided in the past. Thus, the problem continues to propagate: nothing is found and is hardly finished in time because the documentation is missing. Finally, at the end of the cycle, there is no time left to document the lessons learned. In a later release or development stage, there is no time again because you have to search for documentation, which is unfortunately missing or again incompletely created. This quickly creates a vicious circle.

With the agile approach, this problem has unfortunately become even more pronounced. After all, the agile manifesto states, "Functioning software is more important than comprehensive documentation".

In many projects, this is understood to mean that no documentation is required at all and that there is carte blanche for negligence. The addition in the agile manifesto that the values of test documentation are also highly valued, only the functionality is in the foreground, is no longer considered. The problem is not the theoretical specifications themselves, but the fact that people only want to implement what sounds good and involves little effort.

Of course, you have to document in agile projects just like in classic projects. If not, enough time is considered during sprint planning, you will have problems in the short term, but you will pay a lot more in the long term. Unfortunately, this realization has not yet been sufficiently accepted in many companies. One of the problems in this context is the prevailing quarterly thinking and the desire to implement "low-hanging fruits". If too much emphasis is placed on optimizing returns and making shareholder value the top priority, this is exactly what happens. Companies that have been trimmed to this supposed efficiency to a high degree for a while often have to cope with an even deeper crash a few years later. The quality of the test documentation is also an indicator.

18.8   Test Completion Report

The test completion report documents the test results of a specific test stage or the entire test phase. The test completion report is structured as follows:

- Description of the functionality and the test object.
- Notes on maintenance and releases.
- Deviations from the test concept and justification of the deviations.
- Shifting test activities to subsequent test levels because the test level must be completed on time, but not all test activities planned for the test level have been completed.
- Known bugs and their status.
- Defects that are still open at the time of test completion and remediation plan.
- Test coverage and reference to a traceability matrix describing coverage per requirement.
- Assessment of the test progress and release recommendation.
- Risks.
- Test automation for reusable work results.
- Lessons learned for future test phases and projects.
- Assessment legend.

18.9   Metrics

Test documentation also includes the collection of appropriate index values and regular creation of metrics.

Multiple metrics are to be captured across projects:

- Total bugs by effect;
- Number of defects found, classified by defect type/effect (e.g., blocking, high, medium, low);
- Total defect detection rate per week;
- Total defects found vs. completed per week (**defect burndown rate**);
- Efforts for reviews and testing in absolute terms and in relation to development costs;
- Per defect effort for defect correction;
- Efforts for defect correction in total over all defects;
- Average duration of defect recovery per defect;

- Point of origin of the fault (measurement of the distance between origin and detection);
- Per review expenditure for reviews and testing.

These values should be collected separately for production and test.

A metric for defining new test cases is critical when creating a larger scope of new test cases.

The metrics listed above represent only the minimum scope. One can collect numerous other metrics that allow for a more accurate assessment of the overall testing process and can point to hidden problems. These include:

- Requirements-based test metrics,
- Metrics for software quality,
- Effort estimation metrics,
- Metrics for test preparation and test follow-up,
- Test planning metrics,
- Metrics for different levels of testing,
- Metrics for measuring test coverage,
- Test case-based metrics,
- Test object-based metrics,
- Test execution metrics,
- Metrics for performance and load testing,
- Test automation metrics,
- Cost-based test metrics,
- Defect-based test metrics,
- Metrics for test documents,
- Metrics for usability tests,
- Metrics for exit criteria.

Which metrics are collected, how and at what time management is informed, and which persons involved are informed should also be defined during test preparation, unless there is already a cross-project definition.

Especially in larger projects, a project controller is sometimes used to support the project management. **Project controlling** has the following tasks:

- Checking and updating project planning, in particular cost planning.
- Obtaining status reports and review monthly status reports;
- Carrying out special target/actual comparisons and organizing project reviews;
- Preparing project forecasts, in particular on financial resources and
- Deriving recommendations for action for the project management.

The test manager, together with the project controller, should determine the necessary parameters in advance, which are required for the successful control and management of the project regarding quality assurance measures, and be involved in the definition of suitable evaluations and metrics for this purpose from the very beginning.

In the case of massive deterioration of the values from the cross-project definition across the entire company, certain measures must be defined. In plain language, this means that the software development and the quality are endangered in their entirety and that essential company goals can no longer be achieved. Therefore, you should define from the beginning what you mean by "massive degradation". The priority and the effects of the bugs should also be taken into account.

The aim here is not to lose sight of the company-wide perspective when, for example, a project is in particular focus.

When creating a comprehensive test concept, these company-wide metrics should be defined. In addition, a responsible employee must be named who regularly collects, analyzes, and interprets them.

18.10 Availability of the Test System

During test execution, it should also be documented whether the test system was available at all (Table 18.1).

In the above example, it was planned to make a subcomponent available for testing as early as Monday, June 15. However, since the development is not yet complete and the setup of the entire test environment is delayed, the availability of the test system is 0%. On Thursday, 06/18, a partial functionality, which is valued at 60% of the total, is made available, and the test can start. However, since the test environment cannot be released until 10:53 am, only 40% availability is set for Thursday, June 18, and 60% each for Friday, June 19, and Monday, June 22. On Tuesday, June 23, the entire functionality is transferred, but the test environment must be completely set up and reconfigured. It is therefore not available for testing on this day. The availability of the test system is 0%. Finally, from Wednesday, June 24, to Friday, June 26, the test environment and the entire test object are available without restriction. The availability of the test system for these days is 100%. In total, an availability of 44% can be determined for the entire test period.

This allows you to document the availability of the test system in the test completion report as well as for the regular weekly test reporting. Already when creating the test concept, you can set targets for the availability of the test system and also continuously evaluate the deviation from the target. You can also extend this overview in case testers are not available as planned (e.g., due to illness or because other activities have been given higher

Table 18.1 Example availability test system

	Date	Status	Assessed availability per day	Release after handover at	Availability in % period considered
1	Monday, 15 June 2020	Functionality not yet Transferred from development, Test delay	0%		0%
2	Tuesday, 16 June 2020	Functionality not yet Transferred from development, Test delay	0%		0%
3	Wednesday, 17 June 2020	Transfer of a partial functionality, environment is not available for testing	0%		0%
4	Thursday, 18 June 2020	Test release, partial functionality Can be tested	40%	10:53	10%
5	Friday, 19 June 2020	Partial functionality can be tested	60%		21%
6	Monday, 22 June 2020	Partial functionality can be tested	60%		26.7%
7	Tuesday, 23 June.2020	Transfer of the Complete functionality, environment is not available for testing	0%		22.9%
8	Wednesday, 24 June 2020	Test release, partial functionality Can be tested	80%	09:47	30%
9	Thursday, 25 June 2020	Functionality can be tested, test System fully available	100%		37.8%
10	Friday, 26 June 2020	Functionality can be tested, test system fully available	100%		44%
	Total				44%

priority). In all cases, the goal is to achieve better transparency about the possible and achieved test progress.

With the survey of the availability of the test systems one can investigate the causes more closely, why it came in detail to these failures and optimize thereby the test processes purposefully.

Testing usually takes place during development, i.e., it is normal that not all functions are fully available at the beginning of the test period. Nevertheless, it should be checked which minimum requirements the test project must have in order to be able to start testing at all.

References

1. https://www.ibr.cs.tu-bs.de/courses/ss07/sep-cm/templates/testdokumentation.pdf, Softwareentwicklungspraktikum Testdokumentation, accessed on 9 May 2020
2. http://robert.bullinger.over-blog.com/article-testdokumentation-nach-ieee-829-20510038.html, accessed on 9 May 2020

Test Items

Abstract

Responsibilities are to be defined for the individual test tasks. Role descriptions are to be defined for individual areas of activity. Standards (e.g., IEC 62034, IEC 62304) are used to describe regulatory tasks and problem-solving processes. An impact analysis of the change requests is to be performed as part of the regression tests. Suitable test tools are to be used for the optimal completion of the test tasks.

19.1 Types of Test Items

For the **test items,** one needs to think about all the personnel questions: "When, Who, Where, What". This also includes "who" can do "what". In other words, who should take on which "tester role" and which "test tasks"?

Test items include all activities to be performed in connection with the test. Typical test tasks are:

- Creation of the test plan,
- Design of a test concept,
- Specification of the test cases,
- Generation of the test scripts (test automation),
- Provision of test data,
- Setup of the required test environments,
- Execution of the defined test cases (functional tests, load tests, stress tests, surface tests ...) for the verification of the quality characteristics,
- Logging of test results,

- Preparation of bug reports,
- Defect tracking, defect and change management,
- Constitution of the test reports.

In practice, there are several variations of these task types. Tasks should be defined in such detail that one or at most two people can complete them in a few days. The more detailed the tasks are described, the easier it is to control the test progress [SNEE2012].

19.2   Role Descriptions

It is recommended to define **role descriptions** for individual areas of activity for this purpose.

1. **Test manager:**
   - Development of reusable test structures and test standards using professional and technical methods and tools for test execution and test documentation.
   - Overall planning, management and control of all test activities. If required, consolidate work results of the test coordinators, determine and evaluate the work progress of the test activities and report to the project management.
   - Systematic examination (if necessary, in random samples) of the test documentation of the testers regarding formal correctness and content appropriateness of the tests, indication of weak points and tracking of their elimination (if necessary, with delegation to a quality assurance specialist).
   - Monitoring of compliance and conformity with relevant principles, e.g., the specifications of orderly IT-supported accounting systems (GoBS) and the organizational handbook (OHB) of the business unit.
   - Organization of tests for basic changes (service packs, refresh measures).
2. **Test coordinator (in some cases, a test coordinator from the specialist area and a test coordinator from IT with distributed responsibilities are used):**
   - Planning, coordination and control of the internal functional test preparation, test execution, test evaluation and test documentation for the functional and/or the functional chain test.
   - Planning and control of test resources.
   - Definition of test environment requirements and test master data together with the test environment manager.
   - Detailed elaboration of the test concept regarding the functional tests. Identification, definition and prioritization of the functional test objects.

- If necessary, support the testers in the evaluation of test results and prioritization of bugs (defects).
- Carrying out the risk classification for test objects, if this has not already been carried out by the technical coordinator or client.
- Formal quality assurance of the functional test (review of test cases, determination of test coverage and risk assessment).
- Execution of the decentralized defect management (assignment of defects to developers of the project team, tracking of defect removal).
- Determine test coverage and assess test risks.
- Detailed elaboration of the test concept regarding the tests (test objects, risk assessment).
- Decision on retesting and tracking of retesting.
- Issuing release recommendations for the entire tested software package from the tester's point of view.
- Coaching testers in the application of testing methodology standards.
- First point of contact for testers and developers regarding all test-related questions.
- Elaboration of the test concept regarding the tests (test objects, risk assessment).

3. **Test environment manager:**
   - Clarification of the requirements for the test environment and the test master data with the test coordinator. Commissioning and tracking of the set-up of the test environment and the availability of the test master data.
   - Clarification of defects and faults in the test environment.
   - Planning and information about known future downtime of the test environment.
   - Checking of the test environment for refreshes and importing service packs.
   - Maintenance and monitoring of occupancy schedules and reconcile scheduling conflicts as necessary.
   - First point of contact for testers and developers regarding all test-related questions.

4. **Defect manager:**
   - Informing applications about open defects and maintaining the defect status.
   - Global tracking for defects, especially if they are unprocessed or unresolved in the system, and tracking of processing and reminders of accountability.
   - Convene meetings for special defects affecting multiple instances.
   - Delivery of the defect status to the functional test coordinator and decision basis for the release of the transport.

5. **Test analyst (partly different roles for test analyst business and tester IT):**
   - Document review of the business concept and system design.

- Identification and creation of test cases and coordination with the author of the business concept.
- Determination and creation of test data, if necessary, with the support of the IT department.
- Execution of the planned tests and resulting re-tests.
- Documentation of test results.
- Evaluation of the test results, if a deviation is found, determination of the severity of the deviation/defect or deficiency.
- Automation of tests, if necessary, in collaboration with test automator [HETT2019].

The test tasks are to be assigned to the individual persons responsible. The status of the test tasks (open, in progress, on hold, completed) is tracked in the test status report, which must be maintained on an ongoing basis.

Since, for example, the specification of test cases in unit, integration and system tests is usually carried out by different employees, the test tasks must be assigned to the individual test levels as far as possible and reasonable. Meaningful integration steps must be defined and precisely specified in the test concept.

19.3   Standard IEC 62034

The standard describes regulatory requirements for software and system testing. This standard originates from electrical engineering and is also used for testing activities in medical technology in particular, but the pure content of what is described can also be easily transferred to other testing tasks.

This standard requires software system testing for Class B and C software. This requirement extends **Amendment I** (IEC 62304:2006 A1:2016) to all software, i.e., Class A, B and C software. The classes are defined as follows:

- Class A: No injury or damage to health is possible.
- Class B: No serious injury is possible.
- Class C: Death or serious injury is possible.

The Amendment requires software system test records, even for legacy software. Therefore, an auditor may require software system testing for all software systems by reference to the state of the art.

The standard sets out the following requirements for software system testing:

- **Completeness:** Verify that all requirements for the system have been met, typically by testing, and "tracing" that you have succeeded.
- **Pass-fail criteria:** Criteria need to be established for when a test is to be considered successful.
- **Documentation and reproducibility:** The tests (specification, criteria, results) must be documented in such a way that it is possible to reproduce them including the results. This includes documentation and configuration control of the test environment.
- **Problem-solving process:** If defects are found during the test, a defined problem-solving process must be started (see below).
- **Repetition in case of changes:** If the software is changed, the tests must be repeated as appropriate. (It is therefore not written that all tests must always be repeated).
- **Suitable test strategy:** The test methodology/test strategy must be checked for suitability. For example, if you do not test the runtime behavior of applications that are time-critical or where race conditions can occur, you would not meet these requirements.

19.4 Problem-Solving Process

The **IEC 62304 standard** requires that bugs found during software system testing are fed into the problem-solving process. You should think about this in advance. The problem-solving process should apply throughout the company and be defined uniformly for all projects.

The following principles apply:

1. **Avoiding Defects or Finding them before the System Test**

   If one encounters a very large number of defects in the software system tests (whereby it must be defined here exactly what "very large number" means), this means that the preceding quality gates (e.g., review of the requirements, code review, unit tests) were not sufficiently effective. This is definitely the place to start because the defects found in system testing are always just the tip of the iceberg. These defects indicate a real quality problem.

2. **Define the Procedure in the Sprints**

   In some companies, the tests are only rudimentarily carried out during the individual sprints and defects that occur are not managed via a tool or are only communicated internally. An "official" software system test is only performed once after integration of all subsystems, directly before the release. Only during this last test are problems handled via the defined problem-solving process. This approach is allowed, but not recommended because you ultimately undermine the process and establish shadow processes in the company. Here, too, supposed savings are the trigger, which in practice lead to considerable additional costs due to poor quality. It is important to think in processes. For a company, thinking in processes sometimes also means changing the organizational structure. It is no longer the classic **organizational structure** with the typical departmental thinking that is decisive, but the **operational structure** with the defined processes that moves into the central focus. This means that the classic system boundaries are broken down and the individual subtasks in the departments must be integrated into an overall process. This also means that the intersections or seams at the individual transitions between the organizational units must be eliminated. The problem is that egoism and self-interests often avoid exactly these changes, and thus the organization cannot follow the agile approach. I often notice in projects that the operational organization tends to slow down the dynamics necessary for projects instead of promoting them. There are always examples of this in operational practice. I doubt that top management is fully aware of the consequences.

3. **Lean problem-solving process:** The key here is to define a lean problem-solving process. No one should be tempted to bypass the problem-solving process because of the overhead involved. A lean process includes that:
   - The problem reports can be filled out quickly and easily.
   - No unnecessary releases and signatures are required.
   - The process does not require any unnecessary steps.
   - Only those data are collected that are required by regulation or are actually evaluated later [JOHN2019].

19.5   Test Tasks in Regression Testing

Test tasks must also be defined for regular regression testing. This definition usually takes place across projects. These include:

- Ongoing adaptation of the test plan,
- Design of a regression test concept,
- Selection of old test cases for regression and new test cases for extension and change of functions,
- Modification of existing and generation of current test scripts,
- Provision of test data,
- Checking of the existing test environment, if necessary, provisioning as well as
- Execution of the regression tests.

Table 19.1 Example of an impact analysis

Source object

Project	ID	Name	Type	Assigned to	Type	Path
Integrated sample set	AIS-ASTK-2	Shutdown at low Speed	Requirement of the client		Source object	AIS-ASTK-2

Direct relations

Project	ID	Name	Type	Assigned to	Type	Path
Integrated sample set	AIS-ASYS-50	Speed sensors	System requirement		Derived from	AIS-ASTK-2 → AIS-SYS-50
Integrated system sample set	AIS-VAL-12	Shutdown at speed above 6 km/h	Validation		Validated by	AIS-ASTK-2 → AIS-VAL-12

Second degree of derivation

Project	ID	Name	Type	Assigned to	Type	Path
Integrated system sample set	AIS-BUG-4	Development over 6 km/h	Defect		Related to	AIS-ASTK-2 → AIS-VAL-12 → AIS-BUG-4

As part of the regression testing, an **impact analysis of** the change requests must be performed. The aim of this task is to identify the test cases required for the regression test [SNEE2012].

The following table shows a simple impact analysis. In this example, the requirement AIS-ASTK-2 is to be examined. A prerequisite for an impact analysis is a maintained traceability. In this example, two links have been "moved down". First, a system requirement was linked (AIS-ASYS-50). Second, an acceptance test was also created (AIS-VAL-12). However, one of these items also has a link: the test was probably not passed and is therefore linked to a defect (AIS-BUG-4). This can be seen in the "path" column. An impact analysis (Table 19.1) can run over any number of stages [SETR2019].

19.6   Test Tools

The use of suitable tools is crucial for the success of a project. Unfortunately, savings are often made in the wrong place. I have experienced several times that software licenses that would have cost only a few thousand EUR, but would have made testing much easier, were not purchased for "cost reasons". If a tester needs longer time for certain tasks without a suitable tool than with the tool, it may cost many times more than the tool. Nevertheless, unproductive reconciliation of lists and redundant data storage are still practiced, which leads to bugs and reconciliation problems, which can significantly delay projects.

However, these costs do not become directly clear. In some cases, they are no longer even questioned. From experience, the test manager sets 3 months for a certain scope of testing because he already knows that there will be queries, that tests will have to be repeated, that the test environment will not be properly available from the start and that idle times will arise in the project. The test manager also knows that there are other phases where you can hardly finish on time and even need to reinforce resources. Interestingly, the 3 months is usually not questioned further when referencing a similar previous project. But even that example is far from being ideal. The costs for a software license, on the other hand, are transparent and immediately impact the calculation, the costs for delays in the workflow are invisible in the operational calculation and are only reflected in a moderate return in the end.

If the test processes were better, the test manager in the above example would perhaps only need 2 months for the same test scope and at the same time be able to deliver higher quality. This is known, but difficult to change, and because one already knows that one will not get the desired tool through controlling anyway, or that processes, even if they run suboptimal, will not be changed because every change of a process also brings a certain risk with it, one still plans with the higher personnel numbers without exactly questioning the benefit.

19.7   Tasks for the Individual Stakeholders

It is also important that the individual stakeholders are aware of their tasks and know what needs to be done. The delineation between the individual areas is also crucial for the success of the test. Otherwise, the situation can arise where individual functions are tested several times in different test stages and other functions are not tested at all. This is also frequently encountered in operational practice. Technical reviews of the test cases over several test levels are therefore highly recommended. Unfortunately, there is often not enough time for this in everyday life.

References

1. https://www.johner-institut.de/blog/iec-62304-medizinische-software/software-systemtest/, accessed on 9 May 2020
2. https://se-trends.de/was-ist-eine-impaktanalyse/, accessed on 9 May 2020
3. https://www.hettwer-beratung.de/konzepte/testkonzept/testrollen/, accessed on 9 May 2020
4. Sneed, Baumgartner, Seidl: Der Systemtest, Carl Hanser Verlag Munich 2012

Abstract

Suitable test environments must be set up for test execution. Test environment management includes configuration management, availability management, access management, change management, and release management. External test environments and cloud services such as AWS or private clouds can be used for hosting test environments.

20.1 Need for Test Environments

For the execution of software tests, it is necessary to provide one or more separate **test environments.** Testing must never be carried out in the production environment. This is necessary because using the production environment for test execution creates an incalculable risk for production. In any case, this is partly required by regulations. Defects in the test object can affect productive systems or data so that they can no longer be considered trustworthy. Another risk for the use of the productive environment is that a crash of the test system could prevent the use of the productive system in the same environment and thus lead to losses due to lost business or delays in production, i.e., for example, production downtimes and thus consequential damage to property could occur [BOCH2010].

Often, a test environment that is very close to the development environment, in which individual components that are not yet finished are replaced with mocks or stubs, is used for module and integration testing, a test environment without mocks and stubs is used for system testing, and an environment that is close to the production environment is

© Springer Fachmedien Wiesbaden GmbH, part of Springer Nature 2022
F. Witte, *Strategy, Planning and Organization of Test Processes*,
https://doi.org/10.1007/978-3-658-36981-1_20

used for acceptance testing. If non-functional endurance tests (e.g., load tests, performance tests) are scheduled in parallel with the system test, a further test environment must be defined.

If several projects are due to be introduced in parallel for a software release, it may be recommended to carry out the tests on different test environments because otherwise changes from one project can have a negative effect on the tests of another project. This is particularly relevant if the database is changed during the test execution and cannot be easily reset to the defined original state. For each test, it is important that the environmental conditions are precisely defined and known to be able to precisely limit and accurately detect bugs and to avoid recording bugs for any observations that are not bugs at all.

20.2   Adequacy of the Test Environment

In principle, the closer the test level is to productive use, the more production-like the test environment should be. For component tests at developer level, the development computers or emulators of the target systems are often sufficient as a test environment. In contrast, a test environment comparable to the production environment should be available for the acceptance test. An exact replica is necessary if, for example, data migrations in production systems (mergers) are to be tested or load and performance tests are to be performed.

As a rule, it is possible to carry out a test based on a systematic test case determination with a reduced dataset, which comprises only a fraction of the productive dataset. However, if the test environment differs fundamentally (i.e., not only in terms of its performance) from the productive environment, there is a risk that defects will be overlooked in the test or that supposed defects will be found that are not defects at all ("phantom defects").

20.3   Test Environment Management

Since the test environments must be as close as possible to the real production environments and most organizations have a complex system landscape, the test environments are also correspondingly complex. Therefore, adequate test environment management is required for configuration, administration and operation of these environments. The following aspects must be ensured:

- **Configuration management:** knowledge of the contents of the test environment;
- **Availability management:** ensuring availability in accordance with the plan.
- **Access management:** setting up required permissions and accesses, and.
- **Change management** and **release management:** orderly change management and bundling.

It is recommended to use the same tools and configuration management systems in the test environment as in the production environment. This also applies to the hardware and infrastructure used. Apart from the performance, the test and production environments should only differ in the version of the test object.

The timely provision of the test environment (availability management) and regular stocking with updated data and software must also be considered. Delays due to the late or incomplete provision of test environments lead to delays in the test process and thus for the entire course of the project and unproductive idle times. For this purpose, the test processes should be outlined in advance to be able to carry out necessary actions on schedule. Experience shows that the availability of the test environment must be made transparent to all testers so that tests are not carried out for which the test environment is not sufficiently prepared. To provide the necessary access rights to the test environment, particular care must be taken to ensure that testers do not gain access to sensitive data that is outside their authority and that their regular testing activities do not prevent other tests from being performed. This is especially true if automated scripts manipulate the data and are therefore no longer available for other test cases to the extent required.

An important point for the management of the test environment is that there must be no uncontrolled changes within the test environment. Changes are not always avoidable because, for example, the production environment changes and this change must be considered in the test environments. If uncontrolled changes are made to the test environment, the test result may not provide reliable information about the test objectives and is therefore worthless. Therefore, any change must be planned, communicated, controlled and monitored by change management to ensure that changes do not affect completed, running or planned tests. If test impacts occur due to necessary adjustments, they must be coordinated with all parties involved and documented in an adjusted test plan. Controlled changes to the test environment can also result in a complete repetition of all previously executed test cases, and this fact must be considered in the scheduling of the project.

20.4   External Test Environments

When working with external IT service providers, external test environments may be used. In addition, there is the necessary system integration for external test environments if data is also exchanged with the company's own systems. In such a case, the test manager must coordinate the following points with the software operator:

- Type of test environment(s) required,
- Scope and time frame of testing,
- Required test data and their management as well as.
- Changes due to the new release.

It is important to ensure that consistent data is available on all systems involved in the test environment. For this purpose, processes that ensure this consistency should be defined together with the external service provider. Experience shows that the coordination and introduction of these processes requires a certain amount of preparation time and should therefore take place in an early project phase.

The test environment is provided in different ways. These can be divided into two groups; whereby mixed forms also exist:

- **Internal provision**: The IT service provider sets up its own test environment on the user's premises.
- **External provisioning**: The IT service provider sets up a test environment in its own company. The user accesses this test environment via a remote connection.

Regarding the use of **access rights**, the following variants (and their combinations) can be distinguished:

- **Exclusive access rights**: The test environment is exclusively available to a tester or subproject. Access by other testers or subprojects is excluded.
- **Semi-exclusive access rights**: The test environment is only partially available exclusively to a tester or a subproject. In this case, it must be clarified exactly which parts are provided exclusively and which parts are provided non-exclusively. The test cases must be adapted to this. Test cases where collisions can occur due to non-exclusive use must be marked accordingly and coordinated with the other users to prevent impairment of the test execution. It must also be checked to what extent it is possible to encapsulate the test environment or to set up different clients on the test environment.

- **Institute-exclusive access rights**: This feature applies primarily to tests in the banking sector. All testers or test sub-projects of an institution must share the test environment and coordinate the test activities within the institution.
- **Non-exclusive access rights**: The test environment is made available to many customers simultaneously by the IT service provider. The coordination of test times or test windows across many organizations must be ensured by the IT service provider in the form of a test calendar and exact schedules. In this form of provision, particular care must be taken to ensure that no confidential or personal data can be viewed by each other.

20.5   Test Environment in the Cloud

There are a few options for hosting test environments - the most exciting is probably the cloud. A few years ago, only a few people knew about the cloud, but today it is hard to imagine the private sector without it, for example from smartphones (Dropbox, Evernote) or TV (Netflix, Amazon Prime). In the business sector, large providers are pushing into new market areas with end-user solutions, such as Microsoft with Office 365. Beyond these obvious applications, the cloud also offers solutions for everyday problems in the areas of software testing and development - and therefore also for the hosting of test environments.

"Cloud" in this context refers to services for renting hardware from large providers such as Amazon or Microsoft. Especially with Microsoft's Azure Cloud, emphasis is placed on integrating common Microsoft tools (e.g., Visual Studio, SharePoint or Team Foundation Server). The following advantages result for IT organizations:

- Versioned source code repository,
- Automated build and deployment processes,
- Seamless integration of the fault management system,
- Monitoring of the hardware used and
- Transparent presentation of the costs incurred.

Amazon Web Services (AWS), on the other hand, offers a large marketplace where templates for machine configurations can be obtained for small amounts of cents. Here, virtual servers with a number of pre-installed tools (such as Apache servers) can be set up with just a few mouse clicks. The negative side effect is that Amazon and Google will once again obtain information about user behavior and with the additional revenue potential gain additional power and advertising potential, as is already the case for numerous areas of private life, be it health data or movement profiles.

Compared to cloud-only solutions, an **"on-premise approach"** is often used in practice, in which the hardware for testing and development is hosted by and in the company itself. The big advantage of this is that the organization is controlling the entire administration. However, this is also the biggest disadvantage: there is a lot of effort for maintenance and operation. While this solution may be a viable path for small or medium-sized organizations or projects, it quickly reaches its limits for larger undertakings.

Another option is external data centers, or **"private cloud"**, where a third-party provider takes over the management of the infrastructure. The difference to "real" cloud solutions is that in this case not only the operation, but also the control and the setup, are usually taken over by the third-party provider. An application must therefore be submitted to the third-party provider for each new server or cluster, the processing of which can take some time depending on availability.

When using cloud solutions, however, this is exactly where the difference lies: via the easy-to-use and clear web interfaces of Amazon and Microsoft, the control and setup is decoupled from the maintenance and care of the hardware.

The advantages are obvious - the provider more or less guarantees 24/7 availability and maintenance, while the user is in control of how the hardware is used and combined. Of course, hybrid approaches are also possible, in which in-house hosted test environments are extended by additional instances from the cloud. The possibilities here are very diverse and require special attention in the planning phase to ensure that the right approach is chosen for implementation in the cloud and that the test environment ultimately corresponds to everyday life.

A sample process for creating test environments using AWS and Docker or Puppet might look something like this (Fig. 20.1):

In addition to the web interface, commands on the command line can also be used to operate the AWS services. Thus, the AWS setup can also be automated via script. The setup is done in several steps:

- Configuration: the desired hardware and system parameters are defined (e.g., CPU, RAM, operating system, IP address) with which a particular instance (i.e., server) is to be equipped.
- Initial instantiation: the new server is created from the configuration using the "Run-instances command". You connect to this server via remote desktop connection to perform the setup.
- Setup: In a further step, Docker and Puppet can now be installed so that this server can subsequently be used as a target machine for these two tools. However, an AWS machine can also be used for other purposes, such as:
  - License server,
  - Repository,
  - Server for a third-party system that is required in the test environment or.
  - Monitoring instance.

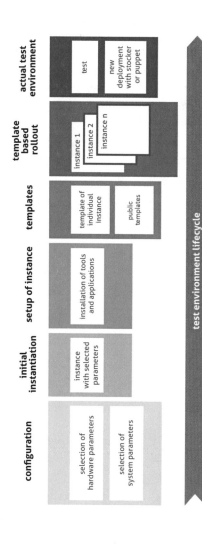

Fig. 20.1 Sample process for setting up a test environment in AWS

A template can be created from an AWS machine. However, pre-built templates from the community are already available in the Marketplace. These templates can subsequently be started again as a new instance with different hardware configurations. In this way, for example, the system behavior can be tested during load and performance tests on differently dimensioned hardware. The instances – based on the templates – are started with the rollout.

At the end of this process, you get one or more current test environments. If individual systems running on these environments change, nothing stands in the way of a flexible redeployment using Puppet or Docker. Alternatively, the underlying AWS template must be changed and the rollout restarted. However, the disadvantage of this option is that the rollout of many instances can take longer than changing individual systems with Puppet or Docker. In addition, the management of IP addresses quickly becomes confusing when constantly creating new instances.

Reference

1. Bochynek, Diaz: Testen in der Finanzwelt, Diaz & Hilterscheid 2010

Responsibilities, Accountability and Communication

21

Abstract

Well-functioning cooperation between the individual team members is crucial for successful tests. Communication in projects becomes increasingly complex as the size of the team increases and represents a particular challenge for test management. The precise definition of responsibilities and the use of a communication matrix help to plan the flow of information within a project in a structured manner. The RACI method serves to improve communication within the company.

21.1 Determination of Areas of Responsibility

For the distribution of **responsibilities** among the individual stakeholders and the distribution of **responsibilities,** the test process must be precisely defined. The basis for this is that one describes the individual test stages, specifies the content of the individual work packages, and precisely describes the transitions between the individual activities.

In the context of test activities, e.g., provision of the test environment, definition of the test cases, automation of scripts and execution of the test cases are individual activities. It is recommended to define these steps as finely granular as possible. In principle, each individual activity must be described in such a way that it can also be performed by someone other than the intended employee. Experience shows that this is problematic for very specialized activities and employees with many years of experience, but there is no way around it.

Companies often are often concerned about outsourcing know-how or would like to build up know-how themselves. This may be the subliminal reason for not specifying work steps precisely. However, specialist know-how is only ever available to individual

© Springer Fachmedien Wiesbaden GmbH, part of Springer Nature 2022   163
F. Witte, *Strategy, Planning and Organization of Test Processes,*
https://doi.org/10.1007/978-3-658-36981-1_21

employees, never to an organization as such. This is particularly noticeable when long-serving, highly specialized employees resign or retire.

If the interaction works well, the team is successful together. But far too often the responsibilities are completely unclear. You run from pillar to post looking for the person responsible. The chaos is perfect when someone is ill, on holiday or unavailable for other reasons. The result is lack of clarity, unfinished tasks, defects as well as postponed decisions, which make progress tedious. Therefore, it is important to clarify the responsibilities in the company in the initial phase of the project to work more efficiently. This also means defining the basics again in the "generic test concept" so that a project can access it with its test concept. Often, however, the project's test manager searches in vain for precisely these definitions and has no choice but to define them on a project-specific basis. In many cases, it is not even transparent from the beginning what has to be done at all.

21.2 Communication in the Project

In addition, the **complexity of communication** as a central problem in larger projects is usually underestimated. The following formula clearly shows how much complexity increases:

$$K = n\,(n-1)/2$$

where n is the number of participants.

This means that with 5 employees, there are 10, with 10 stakeholders, there are already 45, and with 20 participants, there are 190 communication relationships. A larger project, however, may well have 50 to 100 involved stakeholders, i.e., with 50 stakeholders there are 1225 (!) communication relationships, and even if not, everyone is connected to everyone else, the formula still shows how many disruptive influences are possible.

Typical causes of communication breakdowns are different self-interests, insufficient information, different levels of knowledge and experience, internal alliances, prejudices or historical aversion that may have nothing to do with the specific project and the specific problem. Especially in hectic phases, this can lead to disputes or mutual recriminations, which in the end help the project and the common goal even less.

In general, "soft influencing factors" for project success are often underestimated. For the success of project, are key influencing factors.

- Methodology,
- Instruments,
- Expertise,

- Experience and
- Psychology

21.3 Definition of Responsibilities

Responsibilities are especially important when it comes to general activities. A classic is the flipchart in the meeting room. Who puts it away and makes sure that internal information doesn't get stuck? Let's say there's a calculation on it with the note "20 percent profit markup" or a note "massive quality deficiencies in the application." If the responsibility for preparing the meeting room for the next customer meeting is unclear and the customer is already standing in the doorway for the acceptance meeting and sees the flipchart, then he unintentionally has an opportunity for a topic that he urgently wants to discuss.

Therefore, a list of the individual persons, with names, contact details and preferably also with a picture, the responsibilities in the project and for each of these persons one or more representatives, should be included in the test concept.

It is also possible to store only the names in the test concept and to maintain and link the list of responsibilities company-wide. The advantage is, in the case of reorganizations, that the department name is maintained centrally in one place, or changes to telephone numbers or the office in the case of relocations do not have to be maintained by the test manager. In this case, however, the description of the activities must also be stored there in such a finely granular way that it can be seen at first glance. Experience has shown that it is always difficult and a source of defect to have different sources of information with different data available.

For the specific procedures, process descriptions and corresponding checklists for the case of substitution are to be created.

This can ensure that the appropriate tasks are completed and that there are no waiting times. It is not only useful to list and describe the activities and responsibilities. It can also be useful to arrange them chronologically.

Furthermore, it should be checked whether there are activities that have to be completed at certain intervals, e.g.

- Weekly,
- Monthly,
- Quarterly,
- Semi-annually,
- Annually,
- Sporadically,
- Per release or
- Per test level.

The substitute should be asked whether he/she has understood the individual description of the tasks and whether he/she finds it comprehensible. It is ideal to complete the tasks step by step together with the substitute based on the description.

The clarification of responsibility is also important for the familiarization of new employees. New employees should be able to become productive as quickly as possible. Using the table of responsibilities, a plan can be drawn up for new employees for the first few days, clarifying who the new employee needs to speak to and what the topics are that they should learn there. The appropriate responsible employees know best what their responsibilities are and can best explain them and answer questions themselves. This way, the new employee gets to know his colleagues and at the same time how the company works. During the familiarization phase, the new employee should be asked specifically in the next few weeks when the responsibilities are not yet clear to him. This will help to further optimize the table. Because at least as important as the documentation of the responsibilities is the monitoring of the actuality [BUKA2019].

Especially in the case of transitions between individual areas, responsibility must be defined. If several manual steps are to be carried out by employees 1, 2 and 3 within the scope of a test processing, then employee 2, for example, must be informed by employee 1 when he can continue with his work. If it is not known who then informs whom and when, a process can quickly get bogged down. The test manager as the superior instance should therefore always be informed about the status of the individual steps to be able to intervene in an emergency. Especially in larger projects, this requires communication beyond the boundaries of one's own department or division, which is often lacking.

The causes for expensive software bugs, extreme project delays or large additional costs are usually not technical challenges, but missing, misdirected or unclear communication.

It is therefore recommended to draw up a communication matrix at the beginning of the project:

21.4 Communication Matrix

Every process and every work package within a project should have a fixed place in the exchange of information. The smoother, more targeted and trouble-free the communication, the more successful processes and work to be done will be. This applies not only to internal team work, but also to communication across various interfaces, such as interdepartmental work.

When sending and receiving information, each individual sets different priorities. Communication senders and recipients must process the same information differently and send it via different channels. Furthermore, to avoid a flood of information, it is important to communicate only the really relevant information. A communication matrix is useful for the representation of these processes.

Within the communication matrix, not only is it defined who should communicate when via which channel, but also which conscious content is communicated. Levels of detail and focus can be tailored to the respective sender and recipient.

The resulting advantages of the regulated exchange of information and the optimization of the flow of information and communication create transparency and clarity in the project.

"Communication" is generally defined as the exchange or transfer of findings, experience, knowledge and information. A communication matrix (Fig. 21.1) offers the possibility to determine which participant is informed in which project situation with which measure. It is therefore a good tool for planning communication in the project and not forgetting any of the participants, even in tightly scheduled project situations [KOMM2019].

Clear communication channels with as few interfaces as possible are to be preferred.

It must also be clear who can give which instructions to whom and who is responsible for which area.

Within project management, there are primarily three **communication channels,** two-way non-targeted communication (shop talk, gossip, small talk), two-way targeted communication (discussions, answering a question or solving a problem) and one-way targeted communication (usually **delegation**).

WHEN ? / WHO ?	at start of project	by dates of milestones	in case of delays	in case of individual problems	at end of project
applicant	start workshop		personal discussion note		final project presentation
project manager	kick-off				
assistant project manager	kick-off				
Team	kick-off				
stakeholder 1	info per mail				
stakeholder 2					

Fig. 21.1 Communication matrix

Communication can take place on three different levels:

1. **Matter Level**

   On the subject level, mainly pure information is communicated. Information is transmitted via direct language means such as written documents, graphics or words via certain channels such as e-mails or telephone calls. An example of pure factual information is: "Mr. Meyer was 20 minutes late today".

2. **Emotional Level**

   Within the emotional level, a feeling is added to the actual factual information. This happens subconsciously through body language, facial expressions, gestures or tone of voice. Furthermore, affection or aversion as well as empathy or place of communication resonate on this level and emotionally charge what is said. The same example could read as follows on the emotional level: "Mr. Meyer came much too late again today; someone should finally intervene"!

3. **Structural Level**

   On the third level, time, place, hierarchy, formal aspects or values change the mentioned information. For example, the exact same information is communicated differently with a partner or a friend than with a superior in the company.

The term **communication planning** refers to the structured planning of the information flow within a project, communication at interfaces and communication to and from the project. Furthermore, communication planning includes the determination of the communication and information needs of all stakeholders. The **communication matrix** is the output of communication planning. Within this matrix or table are all the communication senders and receivers of communication that are of interest to the project. An alternative form of a communication matrix is shown in Fig. 21.2.

21.5   Selection of Recipients Information

Before talking about reports, content and channels, it is important to be aware of who should receive which information in the first place. For example, it would be unreasonable to inform several employees of a department individually if the respective department head is also sitting in the project and could distribute the information to his team.

The basis for the decision should be a completed or at least very advanced **stakeholder analysis** showing who holds or represents which role and attitude in the project.

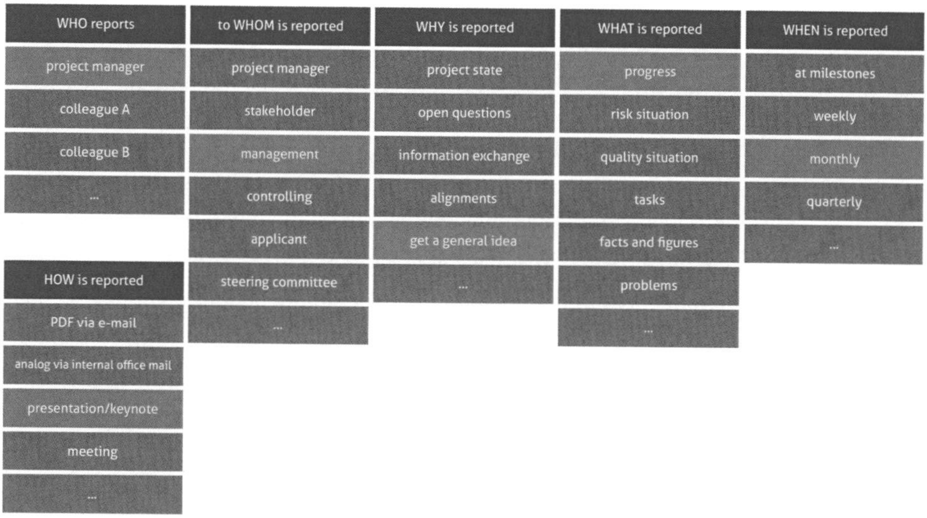

WHO reports	to WHOM is reported	WHY is reported	WHAT is reported	WHEN is reported
project manager	project manager	project state	progress	at milestones
colleague A	stakeholder	open questions	risk situation	weekly
colleague B	management	information exchange	quality situation	monthly
...	controlling	alignments	tasks	quarterly
	applicant	get a general idea	facts and figures	...
HOW is reported	steering committee	...	problems	
PDF via e-mail	...		...	
analog via internal office mail				
presentation/keynote				
meeting				
...				

Fig. 21.2 Communication matrix [PRMA2019]

It is necessary to decide who should receive information. The specific deficient information strictly to be kept internally can also be an instrument of project management.

For example, the stakeholder analysis can define:

- Responsible,
- Business partner,
- Leaders,
- Steering committee,
- Department head,
- Suppliers,
- Third-party vendor,
- Subcontractor,
- Customers,
- Opinion leader,
- Steering groups/staffs,
- Management/board of directors or
- Controlling.

The following thoughts should be made in advance:

- Which person/group relies on what information to perform/plan/coordinate work?
- Are there persons/groups that should/should not explicitly receive information (on certain topics)?

21.6   Definition of Communication Objectives

After that, the **communication goals** must be defined: To this end, all stakeholders who are to be informed must first be documented. The second step is to define the objective of the communication. In doing so, it must be considered why this person or group needs information. Without these communication goals (what is the purpose of providing information), communication will occur, but nothing will be accomplished. Sometimes you get emails where you think to yourself, "Now what am I supposed to do with this"? Then there was either no communication goal or a wrongly defined one.

For example, the communication objective for a department manager in a functional department might be, "Communicate the planned resource assignments for the next two weeks."

21.7   Determination of Information Content

The third step in creating the communication matrix is to add to the table the specific, actual factual information that the recipient expects. This includes at least:

- Current project status,
- Milestone trend analysis,
- Current TARGET/ACTUAL situation of expenses and costs,
- Current TARGET/ACTUAL situation of the defects,
- Problems in the current project phase and
- Need for decision.

This step should be described as precisely as possible. This will help later not only in the execution, but also in the automation of sending information.

After that, the communication channel must be defined. In a test project, this is usually e-mails with corresponding reports, but it can also be meetings, presentations or newsletters.

The test manager is responsible for the functioning communication, i.e., as a sender, he must deliver the defined information to the defined recipients in a timely manner. However, the test manager is also a recipient and depends on deliveries, feedback and status updates.

21.8   Advantages of the Communication Matrix

A communication matrix has the following advantages:

- **Time saving:**
  Especially in larger projects or projects with many stakeholders, as a test manager, you get emails almost daily asking for a status. Even if you only need 10 minutes to answer each mail (including searching for the desired information), this quickly adds up. Therefore, you should refer to existing and upcoming reports or send the standard report of the last week and, depending on the situation, remain consistent – this can save you a lot of time.
- **Communication does not break down:**
  Through the regulated and regulated exchange of information, the flow of information, no matter from and in which direction, does not stop. By actively requesting and forwarding information, the project remains in a state of flux.
- **All on the same stand:**
  It is annoying, error-prone and time-consuming to have many people with different knowledge sitting together in a meeting. If everyone has to be informed first, the air is out right at the beginning. With a proper information base, however, all employees are on the same level and the topic can be started immediately.
- **Also works in case of substitution:**
  Everyone is sometimes indisposed, because of illness, training, vacation or an appointment away from home. The recipient of the message does not even have to notice this circumstance, with a well-thought-out plan, the assistant or the substitute can also send all the required information without having to make additional phone calls or provide extra excuses.
- **Relationships with stakeholders will improve:**
  Through the constant flow of information, all participants feel taken seriously and well-informed. This feeling will upgrade the test manager to the project manager, and he will be respected in case of problems. Furthermore, the constant contacts also strengthen the interpersonal relationship with the respective stakeholders.

21.9   Project Communication Requirements

The following principles have proven effective for communication in the project:

- **Clear and unambiguous:**
  Only factual information should be used, and it should be clear and precise.
- **Efficient:**
  Planning must be designed in such a way that all information needs can be provided with as little effort as possible. Unfortunately, this becomes difficult when different tools are used in a larger project or tools are newly introduced. Every tool break is a massive project risk and should also be marked as such.
- **Written:**
  The statements are to be documented in writing. Every meeting must be minuted and - if not already clarified from the beginning - the keeper of the minutes must be appointed at the beginning of the meeting. It is also very important to send the minutes to all participants (in draft form, if necessary) immediately after the meeting and not to wait for days. If the minutes are not sent immediately, the meeting will already have been forgotten and some of what was said will already be out of date, so the minutes will already look out of date. It is recommended to share the minutes directly with all participants during the meeting on a beamer or online while they are being taken. Taking minutes of statements and meetings has a high priority and is unfortunately often neglected.

21.10 RACI Method

The RACI method is used to improve communication within the company.

The term RACI is composed of the first letters of the terms **responsible, accountable, consulted** and **informed.**

These terms play a key role in the application of the RACI method. The RACI method is particularly suitable for clearly defining and assigning the responsibilities and activities of specific stakeholders within an organization. The primary goal of the RACI method is to achieve a structured way of working and to optimize communication in the project by clearly presenting the responsibilities.

The RACI method is divided into four basic responsibilities:

- "Responsible" assigns the performance of a specific activity to a selected person. This person is understood as responsible in the disciplinary sense.
- "Accountable" describes the person who bears responsibility in the legal or commercial sense. For example, the legal, political or even economic responsibility of the activity is assigned to him.

RACI	[1] preparation				[2] back office												
	1.1	1.2	1.3	1.4	2.1	2.2	2.2.1	2.2.2	2.2.3	2.2.4	2.2.5	2.2.6	2.2.7	2.2.8	2.2.9	2.3	2.4
project manager																	
name of pm	A	A	A	A	A		A	A	I	A		A	I	A	I	A	A
stakeholder																	
stakeholder 1					I		I	I	A	I			A				
stakeholder 2																	
stakeholder 3																	
colleague																	
colleague 1	R	R	R	I	C		C				R		R			C	C
colleague 2	C	C	C	I	R		R	R	R		A	R	R	C	A	R	R

R responsible
A accountable
C consulted
I informed

Fig. 21.3 The RACI method

- "Consulted" means for a person who is not directly involved in the implementation of the activity, but has relevant information for all parties involved, that he or she can be consulted as an expert for the further course of work.
- "Informed" finally describes a person's competence in recording and communicating progress and results in the workflow.

The clear delimitation of these activities primarily ensures that all parties involved concentrate on the task assigned to them.

In addition to the classic RACI method (Fig. 21.3), three further variations are distinguished. These are variants that can be individually adapted to the activity to be performed.

RASCI describes the additional step Supportive, which provides a supplementary worker for support. RASCI is used, for example, for more extensive tasks.

VARISC requires two additional persons to be involved. By checking based on predefined criteria, one person ensures that the work performed to date is correct. Afterwards, another person is appointed to confirm and finally release the work result.

RACIO, which includes the word "omitted", describes the exclusion of a certain person from the project. Here it can be helpful to determine in advance which people should deliberately not be involved in an activity.

21.11 Common Sources of Defects

The following sources of defects are particularly common:

- **Use abbreviations and do not explain them:**
  If abbreviations are not clear, they must be defined and explained. The creator himself knows that in his communication planning the abbreviations "MTA, CA" stand for "milestone trend analysis and cost overview", but his substitute in case of illness or the like does not. Abbreviations used should be known throughout the company or at least explained in the footnote on each page.
- **Select the wrong medium:**
  Favorite media and file types must be discussed with the other party. Thus, the recipient does not wait in vain for an e-mail if the information has already been sent in writing by post.
- **Trying to please everybody:**
  For example, there are 10 stakeholders in the project, each of whom has different preferences regarding the desired way of receiving the information and the information density. The project manager or, in the case of a test project, the test manager decides on the type and scope of the information, determines the basic tenor and must also adhere to it.
- **Set time periods too tight:**
  Your project has a duration of more than 12 months, but the time span of deliveries is set to two weeks – it is then guaranteed to happen more often that work packages take longer and progress is hardly visible on the timeline. Therefore, reports should be produced from the outset to show progress, so that does not look like nothing has happened at all. Another disadvantage can be that there is no time to create the reports at all, if there is no automatic export function of an overarching project management software.
- **Ignore the danger of overplanning:**
  The scale of the plan and the scale of the team are important. Especially in small companies or agencies, a lot runs informally - and it runs well. In corporations, entirely different guidelines often apply, whether internal or acting legislation. One's own plan and test concept must be scaled compared to the planning. One should not describe more than is necessary.

References

1. https://www.buero-kaizen.de/mit-zustaendigkeiten-zu-mehr-effizienz/ accessed on 9 May 2020.
2. http://projektmanagement-manufaktur.de/kommunikationsmatrix, accessed on 9 May 2020.
3. https://projekte-leicht-gemacht.de/shop/produkt/vorlagekommunikationsmatrix/, accessed on 09 May 2020.

Personnel, Familiarization, Training

22

Abstract

The individual stakeholders in the test project must be defined. In this context, the necessary familiarization and training for new employees must also be considered. Good conflict management and relationship management have a significant influence on the success of the project.

22.1 Test Personnel

As part of the test concept, it must be described which stakeholders are planned for the individual activities in the project (e.g., creation of test specifications, manual execution of test cases, test environment management, test automation) and to what extent.

The planning of activities must be broken down at least to the calendar week, or better still to the day. Planning for longer periods of time is too imprecise to be able to intervene in time in case of delays.

The existing **test personnel** is usually already available (at least as far as possible). If there are bottlenecks or special skills are additionally required in the project, the task must be precisely described in a job advertisement.

It should also be noted that every new tester needs a certain phase for familiarization, during which they cannot yet be 100% productive. This is due to the onboarding process, which sometimes drags on for weeks, especially in larger companies, and is sometimes very tough and slow. The workstation must be set up, permissions must be in place, and the new employee must understand the requirements of the project. In addition, the new employee needs to get to know the organization, the other stakeholders, and the specific challenges of their new work environment. Experience has shown that this takes a few

© Springer Fachmedien Wiesbaden GmbH, part of Springer Nature 2022
F. Witte, *Strategy, Planning and Organization of Test Processes*,
https://doi.org/10.1007/978-3-658-36981-1_22

weeks, and when projects are scheduled for very short periods of time, there must be deliberate reductions. In addition, existing employees who have been with the organization for years assume many things are known and cannot empathize with the newcomer's problems. Essential information or contexts are missing, and many details can only be read between the lines in corporate communications. The existing documentation usually does not provide sufficient orientation for this. It is a good idea, for example, to bring in new employees in addition to taking minutes at a meeting. The first minutes probably have many defects and gaps, the new employee lacks the "red thread" and essential background information, but with a subsequent discussion of the minutes before publication and a review in the round, the employee quickly becomes productive and make the best experiences about the gaps.

There are naturally differences in motivation, education, personality structure and experience of the individual employees.

There are numerous treatises in the literature about the individual **personality traits**, from the Enneagram types (1–9) to individual animals (whale, shark, dolphin, owl) or color types (red, yellow, green, blue). Projects are most likely to be successful when individual strengths and weaknesses are known and employees are supported accordingly. The topic of personnel development and conflict management must be dealt with outside of test management, but it has a direct impact on project success. Unfortunately, it can be observed time and again that employees are in positions that do not correspond to their strengths, but on the contrary, make their personal weaknesses particularly visible.

22.2 Conflict Management

Conflicts in the project can require considerable effort. If disturbances in team development are perceived, the causes of the described disturbances in the team must be analyzed. Possible disruptive factors are:

- **Competence problems:** Team members have very different levels of knowledge, e.g., in terms of professional competence, so that there is no synergy in teamwork.
- **Decision-making problems:** The work in the team does not really progress because one cannot bring oneself to make the necessary clear decisions.
- **Information problems:** Problems in cooperation are sometimes due to difficulties in the exchange of information between the parties involved.
- **Organizational problems**: There is no agreed work plan, in particular a time and activity plan. This has to be reworked accordingly.

- **Role conflicts:** Roles and functions are often not clearly defined. In this case, the role concept must be discussed again and a clear definition of the responsibilities and competences of management and team must be made.
- **Relationship problems:** For example, "dominance games" take place among team members. Old conflicts, perhaps even historical dislikes from earlier projects and past times, break out. If relationship problems between team members are ignored, this can lead to real crises, where even factual appropriate information and arguments are no longer heard and considered.

Suitable measures for coping with the aforementioned disturbances consist primarily in optimal **relationship management** vis-à-vis all cooperation partners, as well as in a carefully coordinated **exchange of information**. In this respect, it is obvious that – depending on the cooperation partner – an adapted and differentiated cooperation behavior is also necessary:

- The IT management should try to exemplify the characteristics of top teams and motivate the environment in the team at regular intervals. Customer orientation should be the essential guiding principle of action in the team.
- Another success factor is the attitude of the individual team members. It is positive if each team member tries to reach a common wavelength with the cooperation partner. Since the individual cooperation partners can naturally be highly diverse, this is not always easy. In any case, team members need a large repertoire of behavioral alternatives.
- To jointly achieve the goals, it is also necessary to repeatedly check whether the content of the work steps and partial solutions correspond to the team goal. Then it must be considered whether the type of cooperation (distribution of roles and tasks, team climate, distribution of power) and the type of procedure (methodology) are goal-oriented.
- In addition, each team member should take note of the effect he or she creates on the respective counterpart and view it as a reflection of his or her own behavior. This sometimes requires the courage to leave well-worn tracks and the willingness to learn new ways of behaving. However, such efforts are sure to be rewarded because each time a new opportunity for personal development presents itself in the process.

An important task for project management and test management is therefore to control team development regarding the goals to be achieved. Because teamwork is limited in time, a functioning working basis must be created quickly. IT management is responsible for moderating the team, agreeing on team rules, and regulating responsibilities.

Projects ultimately fail not because of technical challenges or complex software, but because of communication, personal differences, different ideas, personal ambitions, mutual blockades, envy. Sometimes they also fail due to the fading out of reality and unrealistic goals.

Abstract

The COCOMO model is suitable for estimating the test duration. Precise data is required for detailed cost estimation and scheduling. For scheduling, the individual test phases and mutual dependencies must be considered. The determined costs and schedules together with the personnel utilization plans must be permanently reviewed during the project duration. Delays on the "critical path" can lead to a delay of the entire project. The COCOMO model can also be used to determine test productivity.

23.1 Determination of the Test Duration

As part of the test planning, a precise plan is to be drawn up as to when which work is to be carried out and by whom.

The **COCOMO model is** suitable for estimating the test duration.

According to this model, there is an algorithmic relationship between the effort expended on a project and the project duration. The equation for the duration of a software development is given in COCOMO-I:

$$TDEV = 2.5 \times (\text{expense})^{\text{exponent}}$$

where the exponent is chosen as follows:

- 0.38 for standalone systems,
- 0.35 for distributed system and
- 0.32 for embedded real-time systems.

According to the original COCOMO I formula, the duration of a distributed systems test project would be an estimated 275 person-days or 14 person-months:

$$TDEV = 2.5 \times (14)^{0.35} = 6.3 \text{ months}$$

This would be the minimum duration of the project with two testers. However, COCOMO-I assumes that development is a task that can only be divided to a limited extent. However, test projects, like migration projects, are more divisible. Except for the initial phases of analysis and planning, testers can better work side by side. This allows the duration of the test project to be compressed, not entirely, but significantly. Therefore, the COCOMO-II time formula is more suitable for testing. In the new COCOMO-II model, the equation is:

$$TDEV = (C \times (PM)^{F)} \times (1 - (SCED\% / 100))$$

where F = (D + 0.2 × (E-B))
In this equation, the parameters are defined as follows:

- B = Lower limit of the scaling component = 0.91,
- C = Multiplier = 3.67 for new development,
- D = Time base coefficient = 0.28 for new development,
- E = Scaling component of development = between 0.91 and 1.23,
- F = Scaling exponent for the project duration,
- PM = Estimated effort in project months,
- SCED % = Percentage compression of the project,
- TDEV = Time for development.

After that, the duration of the test project is calculated as follows:

$$F = 0.28 + 0.2 \times (0.96 - 0.91)) = 0.29$$
$$TDEV = 3.67 \times (14)^{0.29} = 3.67 \times 2.15 = 7.89 \text{ months} (\text{rounded } 7.9 \text{ months})$$

This is the calculated result for the test duration when using two testers, as in the earlier project (see above). But now the **schedule compression factor** is added, which is relatively high when testing. In this assumption, the time to test can be reduced by at least 60% by distributing the work among several testers.

$$TDEV = 7.9 \times \left(1 - \left(60/100\right)\right) = 3.16\,months\left(rounded\,3.2\,months\right)$$

Accordingly, 5 testers could be used, for example. Requirements analysis and test planning are performed by two testers. After completion of the planning phase, three additional testers are added who, together with the first two, create the test case specifications, generate test data, provide the test environment, perform the test and evaluate the test results. As a result, the entire test project could already be completed after about 3 months [SNEE2012].

To what extent this is feasible in practice, however, depends on the distribution of roles and the project organization. The availability of the testers for the project, the general availability (vacation, illness) and possible delays from the environment (development, environment management ...) can also have a negative effect. In addition, the productivity and deployment options of the individual testers vary.

The above formula also presupposes that the corresponding data is consistently collected in the company in the first place. Many projects are not only about software development, but also to a considerable extent about configuration and parameterization of the systems. All of these influences must be adequately considered in the calculation of effort.

23.2 Detailed Work Planning

It is recommended to plan the effort per task and per employee and day in a **work plan** (Table 23.1).

Table 23.1 Work plan

Activity	Tester	Monday 15 June	Tuesday 16 June	...
Test case creation	A	1	1	
	B	0	0	
Test execution	A	0	0	
	B	0	0	
Test management	C	1	1	
Activity	**Tester**	**Week 20**	**Week 21**	**...**
Test case creation	A	5	...	
	B	4	...	
Test execution	A	0	...	
	B			
Test management	C	5	5	5

23.3   Cost Estimate

The test manager should have an overview of the planned and incurred costs at all times. However, it must also be ensured that he can get an overview of additional expenses in a timely manner. If it can take days or weeks until the test efforts incurred become transparent for the test manager (for example because they are only recorded in a central tool), there is a cost risk right from the start that should be named in the test concept. It should also be clarified from the beginning whether the test manager should be assigned an overview of or responsibility for costs.

Regression tests are required especially for new releases (e.g., a function extension of an existing software). Depending on the scope and frequency of these regression tests, a recalculation of the test costs may become necessary. The cost development must therefore be checked continuously during the project.

23.4   Planning of the Individual Test Phases

The individual test phases are summarized in a timeline in the test concept to present the project progress transparently. In addition, a timeline for the individual test phases (Fig. 23.1) should be documented:

The "**critical path**" must always be considered: What happens if a phase starts later or is not completed on time?

The critical path method uses the activity arrow form of representation. In **networks (CPM plans)**, the activities are represented as arrows, the events as nodes and the

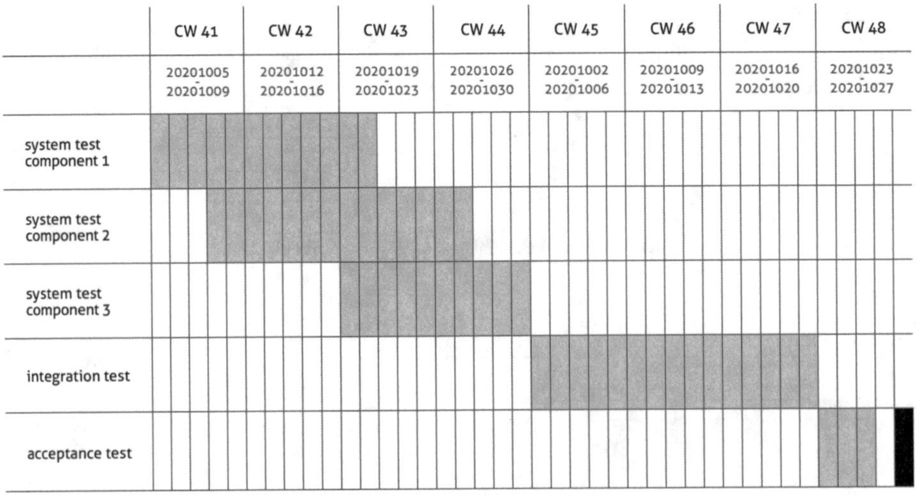

Fig. 23.1 Timeline of the test phases

relationships as arrows. A prerequisite for being able to work meaningfully with a network is that all the activities of the project are correctly related to each other with their respective individual durations.

The following rules must be observed:

1. An operation can only start when all preceding operations (predecessors) have been completed. In this case, the start event coincides with the finish event of the preceding operation (exception: first operation).
2. If several operations must be completed before a subsequent operation (successor) can start, they end in the initial event of the successor.
3. If more than one successor can start after a predecessor has ended, they start in the final event of the predecessor.
4. If two or more operations have common start and end events, their clear identification must be ensured by inserting mock operations. For clarity, mock operations should be represented by a dashed arrow.
5. If in an event several operations start and end, which are not all dependent on each other, the uniqueness must also be achieved by dummy operations.
6. Any number of mock operations can be inserted in a sequence of operations. They serve as a logical link and can increase the overview. Mock operations should be considered a necessary evil and should therefore generally be used sparingly.
7. If an activity can start before the predecessor is complete, the predecessor must be subdivided. This rule does not necessarily increase the clarity of the network.
8. Each process may only run once, no loops may occur.

Gantt chart: For the detailed planning of projects, the Gantt chart and the staff workload plan are recommended. Gantt charts can be created with Microsoft Project or Excel, for example. Figure 23.2 shows a graphical representation and Fig. 23.3 shows a representation with Excel.

It is recommended to plan the individual activities and availabilities on a daily basis. Planning on a weekly basis is usually too roughly granular and does not adequately represent too many idle times. Planning on an hourly basis is usually not feasible in day-to-day operations.

Alternative representation:

After the logical structure of the project has been made based on a network plan, the actual scheduling can be carried out. This results in activities in which the test is involved.

Scheduling is normally done with a Gantt chart, as shown in Figs. 23.2 and 23.3. In this, starting from the critical path, the intervals with durations of all the activities are plotted on a suitable consistent scale, maintaining the relationships established by the network.

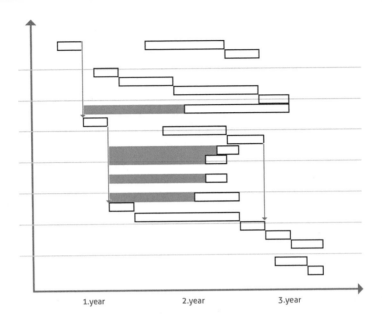

Fig. 23.2 Bar chart

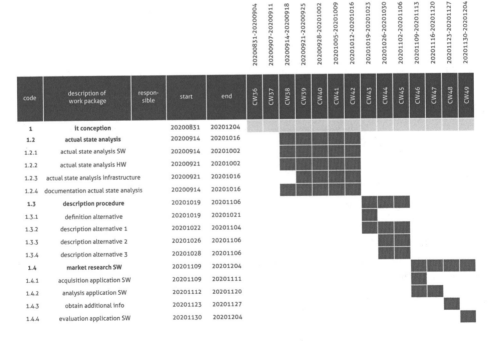

code	description of work package	respon-sible	start	end	CW36	CW37	CW38	CW39	CW40	CW41	CW42	CW43	CW44	CW45	CW46	CW47	CW48	CW49
1	**it conception**		20200831	20201204														
1.2	**actual state analysis**		20200914	20201016			▓	▓	▓	▓	▓							
1.2.1	actual state analysis SW		20200914	20201002			▓	▓	▓									
1.2.2	actual state analysis HW		20200921	20201002				▓	▓									
1.2.3	actual state analysis infrastructure		20200921	20201016				▓	▓	▓	▓							
1.2.4	documentation actual state analysis		20200914	20201016			▓	▓	▓	▓	▓							
1.3	**description procedure**		20201019	20201106								▓	▓	▓				
1.3.1	definition alternative		20201019	20201021								▓						
1.3.2	description alternative 1		20201022	20201104								▓	▓					
1.3.3	description alternative 2		20201026	20201106								▓	▓	▓				
1.3.4	description alternative 3		20201028	20201106								▓	▓	▓				
1.4	**market research SW**		20201109	20201204											▓	▓	▓	▓
1.4.1	acquisition application SW		20201109	20201111											▓			
1.4.2	analysis application SW		20201112	20201120											▓	▓		
1.4.3	obtain additional info		20201123	20201127													▓	
1.4.4	evaluation application SW		20201130	20201204														▓

Fig. 23.3 Gantt chart with Excel [PROJ2019]

The project deadlines that apply to the individual activities and events can be read from this representation. The Gantt chart can also be used immediately for personnel planning. This is done by assigning the target staffing levels for the individual work packages in the network to the bars that now represent the work packages and adding the corresponding values in the vertical axis. This results in the "first approximation" of the personnel utilization plan in the project.

In practice, there are often postponements that affect the entire project. Therefore, the scheduling must also be checked regularly and adjusted if necessary. If you consider sufficient buffer times when planning the individual test phases, you will have fewer postponements during the project and thus save a lot of effort and stress in the end.

23.5   Staff Utilization Plan

The first version of the manpower utilization plan (Fig. 23.4) usually leads immediately to a rescheduling of the project. Unless, by extraordinarily fortunate circumstances, a reasonably balanced "manpower mountain" has been created right at the first time, no personnel manager will accept his staff being delegated in and out of a project in a short time. Apart from the purely technical frictional losses that occur in the process due to the learning

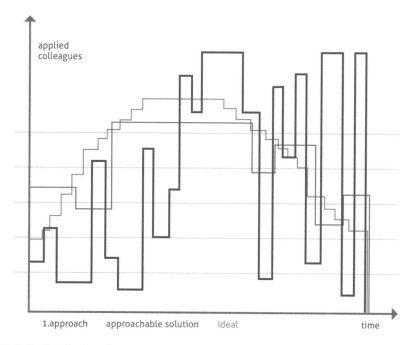

Fig. 23.4 Staff utilization plan

phases that occur at short intervals among employees, no qualified employee would participate in such a project for a long time.

Consequently, the Gantt chart must be discussed again, which leads to a review of the assumptions in the network, and so on. So, the whole thing is an iterative process.

In many cases, however, several projects run in parallel in the company, all of which access the same resources. For the line manager, who allocates the testers to individual projects, it is necessary to collect the requirements from the individual projects and then allocate the testers accordingly. When a tester is deployed to multiple projects, dependencies and idle time can always occur because the deployment is then either on the critical path or shifts prevent a test object from being available. This is especially important to consider during the test execution phase.

23.6   Detailed Test effort Planning

For a detailed test effort planning, it is recommended to plan the test efforts per day in a table (see Table 23.2).

If individual test phases are postponed, this document must be adapted.

For each day, it is determined to what extent an employee is available for the project. Holidays, distributed locations and dependencies between testers must be considered. The critical path is to be observed.

Values above 0.8 should never be set for the workload per working day to have sufficient buffer for unforeseen events and sufficient cycles for necessary night tests. Unproductive times, such as for the ongoing update of the test environment, should also be considered.

Table 23.2 Work plan per employee

		Week 29					...	Total
Activity	Employees	Monday 13 July	Tuesday 14 July	Wednesday 15 July	Thursday 16 July	Friday 17 July	...	
Test case creation	Meier	0.8	0.8	0.8	0	0	...	
Test case creation	Müller	0	0	0	0.5	0.5	...	
Test performance, analysis of results and retesting	Meier	0	0	0	0.8	0.8	...	
Test performance, analysis of results and retesting	Müller	0	0	0	0	0	...	
Load and performance test	Schmidt	0	0	0	0.2	0.2	...	
Test coordination	Huber	0.8	0.8	0.8	0.8	0.8	...	

If there are several testers in different teams, it is recommended to keep another column for the team to which the individual employees are assigned. This allows you to show when which employee is involved in the project. In the example in Table 23.2, tester Müller is only called in later and does not yet start testing in week 30. At the end of the period, a sum per line and a total sum is formed over the individual values.

If different components are delivered at different times during the test, this can also be visualized by the table.

If the project extends over several releases and the effort can be allocated to the individual releases, this can also be mapped in the table and totals can be formed for certain time intervals, from which the test effort can be broken down to the individual release. The share of effort for regression will increase in later releases, especially if test automation is not yet sufficiently advanced. Test automation efforts should also be recorded in this table.

The following example shows how difficult test planning can sometimes be:
There are 3 testers and 3 bricks up for testing.

- Tester 1 tests component A in week 1;
- Tester 2 tests component B in week 2;
- Tester 3 tests component C in week 3.

C depends on module A and B being fully tested.

Each module should take 1 week to test. The testers have specified the tests and know the project.

Attached are a few possible glitches:

1. Tester 1 is sick in week 1, tester 3 is still tied up in another project. Tester 2 can take over module A.
2. Tester 1 is sick in week 1, tester 2 and 3 are still tied up in another project. Tester 4 is available, but he does not know the project, does not know the test cases and must first familiarize himself. This causes a delay, which can still be absorbed: Tester 4 continues testing module A for a few days in week 2, and tester 3 can start module C in week 3 on time.
3. Component B is not finished in time in development. Tester 2 is available in week 2, but cannot start the test execution on time on Monday, but only on Wednesday. This puts the project on the "critical path" because the test is at risk in total. The test of module C can also start in week 3 with a time delay. Therefore, tester 1 and tester 2 should be called in for module C to finish on time. At this point, however, tester 1 is already involved in another project that has an even higher priority than the project under consideration, and is therefore not available for strengthening the test activities.

4. Module B is of such poor quality that partial integration becomes impossible, and it does not have sufficient prerequisites for testing module C. The rework in development continues throughout week 3. The test of module C is only possible in week 4, whereby the critical path has been left, and the project is already delayed.

The examples described here still seem relatively trivial. Especially in the case of several parallel projects, these problems add up. In the case of mutual dependencies, project planning is often confronted with complex challenges. Therefore, it is recommended to take certain idle and buffer times into account as early as the personnel resource planning stage. Each employee should therefore generally only be utilized to 60% or 70% in the planning.

23.7   Estimation of Test productivity Using the COCOMO II Method

The relationship between effort and time is not linear, i.e., you cannot reduce a project from 12 man-months to 6 man-months by doubling the number of project participants. The increasing number of participants significantly increases the effort for communication, administration and organization. Productivity per employee decreases, sometimes significantly. A key in the mutual influence of time and effort is the determination of productivity. The following diagram (Fig. 23.5) shows how test productivity is determined.

To create a productivity indicator, the so-called "**test points**" are first introduced here. They allow each test object to be evaluated according to its complexity, and thus make it possible to differentiate between the difficulties of individual test activities. A test point is valued at 1.5–3 working hours.

On the one hand, a distinction is made between the dynamic test points, i.e., the number of logical test cases executed according to the requirements. For example, if 1000 test cases (1000 dynamic test points) are executed in 150 working days, this results in a test productivity of 6.6 test points per day.

This dynamic productivity can be recorded and determined in the long term, as in Fig. 23.5. On the other hand, there are the static test points. These result from the number of test objects. In system testing, for example, these are the interfaces, user interfaces, or databases to be tested. The formula for calculating the test points is as follows

$$\text{Test points} = N_{\text{Test cases}} + \left(N_{\text{Panels}} \times 4\right) + \left(N_{\text{Reports}} \times 2\right) + N_{\text{Services}}$$

Since productivity depends to a large extent on the experience of the testers and the degree of test automation, the statistics of previous projects (Fig. 23.5) must be used. In

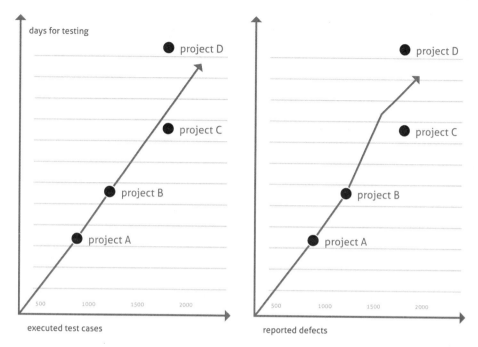

Fig. 23.5 Determining test productivity

addition, special influencing factors and test circumstances must be considered, so that the **test productivity** results as follows:

$$\text{Test productivity} = (\text{Test points} \, / \, \text{Tester days}) \times \text{Days of operation}$$

The idea of this formula, which is still not very detailed, is further taken up in the so-called COCOMO-II equation for estimating testing effort with quantities besides test productivity.

The three other factors considered here are:

- Project conditions,
- Product quality and
- System type.

The **project conditions** can in turn be divided into the following five conditions:

- Degree of test repeatability,
- Stability of the test environment,
- Knowledge of the application,
- Togetherness of the test team and
- Maturity of the testing process.

The final scaling exponent is the arithmetic mean of the scores for the five project conditions. Each of these conditions is rated using the following scale:

- very low (1.23),
- low (1.10),
- medium good (1.00),
- high (0.96) and
- very high (0.91) [IWTB2017].

References

1. Sneed, Baumgartner, Seidl: Der Systemtest, Carl Hanser Verlag München 2012
2. https://dieprojektmanager.com/terminplanung-balkenplan-gantt-diagramm-chart/, accessed on 9 May 2020
3. https://iwt-bodensee.de/wpcontent/uploads/2017/07/140505_literaturuebersicht_stand_der_technik.pdf, accessed on 10 May 2020

Planning Risks and Unforeseeable Events 24

Abstract

In the case of postponements, the target amounts of the alternative courses of action must be made clear and possible alternative decision paths must be evaluated. Methods such as investment appraisal and argument balance are suitable for this. SWOT analyses, consequence tables and decision trees, utility and risk analyses are further helpful methods for evaluating and controlling unforeseen events during projects.

24.1 Unforeseeable Risks

Chapter 16 has already dealt with the need to assess risks that are identified in advance for the test.

There may be delays in schedule, cost and quality due to identified risks or problems that arise during the project.

Postponements during the project duration are sometimes only acceptable if the functional scope of the test object is reduced afterwards.

However, it happens again and again that one has not even recognized problems that arise during planning, or has recognized them but considered both the risk of problems arising and the resulting delay to be low. If the general conditions in the company change, if priorities shift, or if new demands are placed on the organization or the project from outside, the entire planning must be questioned and restarted.

In these cases, it is necessary in any case to report the circumstance to the management and to submit proposals showing different alternative courses of action and to

© Springer Fachmedien Wiesbaden GmbH, part of Springer Nature 2022
F. Witte, *Strategy, Planning and Organization of Test Processes*,
https://doi.org/10.1007/978-3-658-36981-1_24

evaluate these alternative courses of action. It is important to react quickly and flexibly in such cases.

The following procedure is recommended:

24.2   Making the Target Contributions of the Alternative Courses of Action Visible

With the description of the decision situation, goals and framework conditions are defined that are important for a good decision. With the solutions and alternative courses of action, the possibilities are shown among which the decision-maker can choose and decide for or against. Now, in the next step, possible consequences, implications or results must be shown which an individual alternative course of action has when it comes to achieving the objectives and results and observing the framework conditions.

The possible consequences and results that the choice for an alternative action can lead to should be worked out as comprehensibly, understandably, plausibly, justified and substantiated as possible. For this purpose, information must be compiled that decision-makers can evaluate. This presentation should help the test manager or other decision-makers to make the right decision in the sense of: this choice contributes best to the achievement of the objective.

24.3   Methods and Tools as Decision-Making Techniques

There is a wealth of methods and tools that help to compile, evaluate and present the information in such a way that the decision-makers are able to evaluate the consequences and implications. These decision-making techniques all have the purpose of bringing transparency to the decision-making situation and making visible which alternative would be best in light of the objectives and evaluation criteria. They help to reduce the uncertainty of the decision maker.

Which decision-making techniques, methods and tools are most suitable is primarily determined by the following questions:

- What is to be decided?
- Which goals play the most important role?
- Which evaluation criteria should therefore be considered and assessed?
- What are the important framework conditions?
- Who are the decision-makers?
- What interests do other stakeholders have?
- How complex is the decision?

- How far-reaching are the decision and the associated consequences? (Time horizon, risk or opportunity potential)
- What kind of solutions are there?
- What information is available?

Against this background, the following decision techniques, methods and tools are mostly used in business practice – individually or in combination to make different aspects of the decision consequences more visible.

24.4   Methods of Investment Appraisal

These methods focus on business calculations. These include profit, profitability, economic efficiency, profitability or productivity. The alternative courses of action should help to improve these. These methods reveal the extent to which this succeeds in individual cases, and which decision therefore makes business sense:

- Cost comparison accounting,
- Profit comparison statement,
- Profitability calculation,
- Amortization calculation and
- Cash flow calculations (with different variants such as: net present value, discounted cash flow or economic value Added).

This includes calculation methods that assume that costs (or expenses and disbursements) on the one hand and sales and revenues (or income and receipts) on the other are known, calculable or at least can be reliably estimated.

24.5   Balance of Arguments

If no reliable figures on economic efficiency, profitability, profit, revenue or costs are available, qualitative methods must be used to evaluate options for action and their consequences. Here it is a matter of finding arguments that speak for or against a solution. These arguments must be comprehensible and conclusive. This can be achieved if suitable evidence, i.e., examples, indicators, key figures or expert experience, is mentioned and defined.

A simple method for an appropriate qualitative evaluation is the **argument balance**. It forces the user to name his essential evaluation criteria and to make them transparent – especially for other persons. Implicit evaluation criteria are presented explicitly. In this way, subjective opinions become visible and are put up for discussion.

As in a business balance sheet with assets and liabilities, two sides are compared for each option for action that is up for decision: Pro and Con. In both columns, the main arguments for or against an alternative are briefly and concisely stated. The arguments should explicitly refer to the goals and desired results as they were worked out with the decision situation. The user of the argument balance must then decide for himself which arguments he wants to use for the overall evaluation of the solution and which convince him. In doing so, pros and cons are weighed up. Each of the alternatives can be given a score, and the alternative with the higher score wins.

In an argument balance, all arguments for both sides should be compiled as objectively and neutrally as possible, and not a preconceived opinion should flow into the selection and formulation of the arguments. This is often a difficult undertaking. If the balance of arguments is drawn up in a team, the danger of a one-sided view prevailing and one person getting their way with their opinion is reduced. For this, however, the alternatives must be noted down by all participants (as in a brainstorming session), so that not only the spokespersons prevail.

24.6   SWOT Analysis

The **SWOT analysis** (abbreviation for Strengths, Weaknesses, Opportunities and Threats) is a strategic planning tool. It is used to determine the position and develop the strategy.

Arguments for or against an alternative course of action can have different weights. This is mainly due to how reliable they are and how certain or uncertain the corresponding consequences and outcomes are. This differentiation can be presented thanks to a SWOT analysis. With the analysis of the strengths, weaknesses, possibilities and opportunities as well as dangers and risks, the quality of the alternatives in relation to the present (largely certain consequences and events) and the future (rather uncertain consequences and events) are illuminated. Thus, with this SWOT analysis, arguments in favor or against an alternative are elaborated and presented in a more differentiated way. The strengths and weaknesses become very significant, especially when they coincide with opportunities or threats in the environment. The following figure (Fig. 24.1) shows the questions of a SWOT analysis:

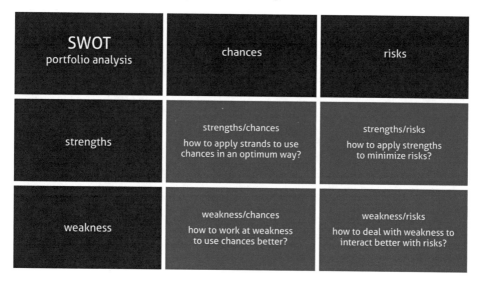

Fig. 24.1 SWOT analysis

24.7 Consequence Table

The basis for the evaluation and decision is that you make all consequences associated with a possible action as visible as possible. The consequence table helps you to do this. It compiles all consequences as clearly, concisely and comprehensively as possible and thus makes the alternatives comparable at "a glance". The table shows: What would be the consequences if the decision-maker opted for the alternative under consideration?

The information in the table can be additionally explained and justified. Examples or key figures are often necessary as supporting documents. These must be extrapolated or estimated for the future. Sometimes it is possible to use a **consequence table** to directly identify the options for action that are in any case worse than other alternatives. The following table (Table 24.1) is an example of a consequence table.

In the following example, an integration test of a software is imminent. Component B is to be newly developed with new functions, but development is not yet complete. However, there is an existing component B with a smaller range of functions that could be integrated immediately, but which is not innovative and has the same software status as the previous product. The new function from component B could be discontinued, but this would be detrimental to the company's image.

Table 24.1 Consequence Table IT

Objectives or evaluation criterion	Alternative			
	1	2	3	4
	Use more developers to complete component B, start integration test a little later	Postpone the start of the integration test because component B is not yet ready.	Use existing component B, new one in a future product (reduce project scope)	Start integration test with existing component B, replace and re-integrate new component B later, but ship out
Costs	Higher costs compared to calculation	Nearly cost-neutral	Lower costs compared to calculation	Higher costs compared to calculation
Dates	Can still be held	Can become critical at the end of the project	Deadline targets can be reliably met	Can become critical at the end of the project
Quality/technical risk	Possibly slight loss of quality due to later test start	Depends on how many testers can be used for integration testing	Quality targets are not critical	Depends on how many testers can be used for integration testing
Image with the customer	Neutral	Neutral but risky path	Negative	Neutral but risky path
…				

24.8 Decision Tree

The decision tree also provides an overview of possible actions (alternatives) and their probable or less probable consequences, impacts and effects – especially in relation to the goals and expectations. With the decision tree, a picture is developed in which, starting from the actual situation and the decision question, the alternative actions and possible decisions are presented as branches and then linked to possible consequences, impacts and effects.

The respective possible consequences can be evaluated with the likelihood of their occurrence. In addition, expected values can be used to determine the probability of a goal being achieved if a decision is made in favor of an alternative. In this way, the individual alternatives can be evaluated based on probabilities of occurrence and expected values, and the favored alternative can thus be determined. The following figure (Fig. 24.2) illustrates this using an example decision tree.

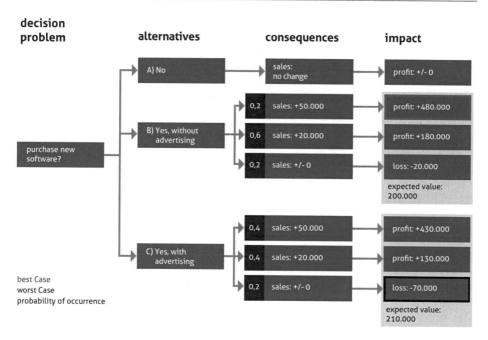

Fig. 24.2 Decision tree for software procurement

In this example, it can be seen that the choice of alternative C would be the best because it is associated with the highest expected value for the goal "maximize profit". However, it is also associated with the worst case, the maximum possible loss. Now the decision maker must weigh which factor is more important to him. If, for example, the maximum possible loss is to be avoided in any case, the second-best alternative can also be deliberately chosen as a result.

The decision tree can be used to show when there are consequences that are not permissible under any circumstances. Then all possible actions from this branch are eliminated. However, a preferred effect can arise within the framework of the evaluation. In this case, an attempt should be made to implement this preferred effect in the corresponding actions.

24.9 Utility Analysis

If several objectives and criteria play a role in the evaluation of options for action, but these have a completely different character, they can be made comparable with the help of the utility analysis. In this method, the contribution made by each alternative to a single objective or evaluation criterion is examined. This target contribution is first specified in the form of an indicator that adequately represents the target contribution. This indicator is then converted into a utility value (points or score value) in a second step; the more points, the better the alternative is in relation to the objective under consideration. In the

Table 24.2 Utility analysis

Evaluation criterion	Weighting	Alternatives												
		1 Use more developers to complete component B, start integration test a little later			2 Postpone the start of the integration test because component B is not yet ready.			3 Use existing component B, new one in a future product (reduce project scope)			4 Start integration test with existing component B, replace and re-integrate new component B later, but ship out		
		Form of indicator	Utility	Weighted utility	Form of indicator	Utility	Weighted utility	Form of indicator	Utility	Weighted utility	Form of indicator	Utility	Weighted utility
Costs	20	Higher	3	60	Related	7	140	Neutral	10	200	Higher	3	60
Dates	40	Neutral	10	400	Risky	5	200	Neutral	10	400	Risky	7	280
Quality/technical risk	30	Slight loss	8	240	Risky	5	150	Neutral	10	300	Risky	7	210
Image with the customer	20	OK	10	200	A little risky	8	160	Negative	0	0	A little risky	9	180
Total	100		29	720			670			900			730

end, all points are added up across all objectives and evaluation criteria. The sum corresponds to the quality of the alternative; the one with the highest score is the best.

It can also be considered that not all objectives and evaluation criteria are equally important for the decision-makers. They thus receive a target weighting that is included in the calculation of the point value. Table 24.2 shows the structure of a utility analysis. Again, the above example with the 4 alternatives for component B was used.

In the example from Table 24.2, the weighted utility value of alternative 3 is the highest. The conclusion is therefore to first integrate the existing component and thus test it further, and to use the new component B in a future product. The project scope is reduced to be able to guarantee the achievement of the objective.

24.10   Risk Analysis

If no reliable or comprehensible indicators are available to show how well an alternative course of action contributes to the achievement of the objective, an evaluation is very difficult. The alternatives cannot be evaluated directly. At best, qualitative possibilities or opportunities on the one hand and dangers or risks on the other hand can be defined. This is done with the SWOT analysis. Some decision-makers pay particular attention to the opportunities, others to the risks.

In the case of far-reaching effects and consequences that are difficult to assess, it can be helpful to take a closer look at the possible risks and analyze them – to make visible what can happen in the "worst case". This makes aspects visible such as:

- the risk must be avoided in any case, or
- even in the worst case, the consequences are so manageable that the possible opportunities should be exploited.

24.11   Selecting and Using Decision-Making Methods and Tools

At the beginning, the decision situation and the decision question should first be written down: What is to be decided?

Afterwards, possible alternatives and solutions should be compiled from that the decision-maker should use to make a decision. The effects, impacts and consequences that can be associated with these alternatives in terms of objectives, evaluation criteria and framework conditions are analyzed. For this purpose, information has to be researched and indicators have to be named that make these interrelationships visible. In the process, key figures are measured or effects are estimated.

Subsequently, one or more decision-making techniques as well as methods and tools are selected. The information, indicators or key figures determined are incorporated into these, processed and provide a picture of the quality of the alternative. Finally, it is examined which decision technique is helpful for the underlying problem. For example:

- Business ratios (costs, profit, profitability, economy, cash flow, amortization, etc.),
- Argument balance,
- SWOT analysis,
- Consequence table,
- Decision tree,
- Utility analysis or also
- Risk analysis.

These decision-making techniques can also be combined to provide a more comprehensive picture of the alternatives and possible consequences. However, decision-makers must always be able to process all this information and evaluate it for their decision.

Suitable templates for the individual techniques can be found on the Internet.

24.12 Showing Decision Problems, Alternative Actions and Possible Consequences

For the decision problem or the underlying issue, the individual alternative actions and choices can be evaluated with regard to selected key figures. This can be presented clearly in the form of a decision tree. In the following templates, this is to be noted:

- Scenarios as possible alternative courses of action;
- possible consequences of these scenarios in the form of quantitatively measurable indicators or ratios;
- Expected values in percent for these consequences;
- possible effects for an individual consequence – also in the form of an adequate key figure (impact factor).

Then an expected value of the respective scenario is calculated from this in relation to the **impact factor.** In this way, the "value of the scenario" can be determined quantitatively.

With the presented decision techniques and their methods and tools, the consequences and effects are made visible to the decision maker and shown which relationships exist to his goals, expectations and wishes. This facilitates the decision and also makes it more comprehensible for others, for those affected. With these procedures, above all, the arguments are worked out that speak for or against a possible course of action or alternative. This is precisely what is important in this decision-making process.

However, despite all the systematics and even the methodical approach, wrong decisions can always be made. Because every decision is based on a subjective evaluation. It is important to be aware of this and to know the possible pitfalls that can occur.

The longer test projects take and the more extensive they are, the higher the risks for unforeseen events.

Approval and Release

25

Abstract

A release recommendation is made in the test completion report, followed by approval of the release. The release process with the recommendation of the use of the tested software is to be defined in advance.

25.1 Recommendation for Release

The department responsible for the test generally only gives a **release recommendation**, not a final **release** after test completion for a specific test object or project. Based on the test activities, a certain quality level is determined, from which it is derived whether the use of the software is recommended or not. A test completion report is required.

As a rule, a test completion report is created at the end of each of the test stages: integration test, system test and acceptance test.

The **test completion report** is structured as follows:

- Designation of the project, the test object and the test phase;
- Information on whether maintenance tasks are affected;
- Releases and environment level;
- Deviations from the test concept;
- Known bugs: all bugs that occurred during the project (with ID, name and status) and bugs that were still open at the end of the test phase, i.e., not yet successfully retested;
- Selected metrics, e.g., test development, defects by status and impact, defect trend;

© Springer Fachmedien Wiesbaden GmbH, part of Springer Nature 2022   203
F. Witte, *Strategy, Planning and Organization of Test Processes,*
https://doi.org/10.1007/978-3-658-36981-1_25

- Test coverage and coverage levels with reference to traceability matrix;
- Release recommendation and rationale for recommending unrestricted, conditional, or no release;
- Remaining risks for the productive introduction or the next test stage;
- Reproducibility of work results, status of test automation;
- Lessons learned, summary of positive and negative experiences gained during the test phase for special consideration in future testing activities.

The **release process** must be defined in general, who decides on the use of the tested software. A specific person issuing the release must be defined in the organizational plan at the beginning of the project. Depending on the hierarchical importance of the processes, this can be a work package manager, a subproject manager, the project manager himself or the steering committee [PRMA2020].

If software was used whose use was not recommended, the test management has ensured with the documentation in the test completion report that the risks are described, and possible problems are transparent in the event that a release is granted.

The test concept must also be released. It is recommended to create a version 0.1, which is subjected to a review. During the review, a list of findings is created that shows which passages should be changed and in what form. After the test concept has been revised, a version 1.0 is created with which the test activities start. Ongoing revisions can be made with further versions 1.x, a released version would then be 2.0 or higher.

Stakeholders from testing, development, project management and other core functions should be involved in the review. A separate review meeting is highly recommended. Afterwards, the test concept must be released by the project management.

It has to be determined in advance who is allowed to release the software and who has to bear the consequences of this decision.

In the event of non-approval, criteria must be defined as to which functions must be improved by when and which work must be carried out in detail, so that approval can be granted. It should also be specified that these criteria must be adhered to, i.e., that the next release must not include further points that were not criticized the first time, as otherwise the release will be further delayed and this can lead to infinite release loops.

In the case that the customer gives an acceptance, to which payment obligations are bound, it can happen that the customer has no interest at all in giving the acceptance quickly, but rather drags out the project, as it can then also be stretched financially. Some reason for refusing acceptance can certainly be found with a sufficiently profound analysis. Therefore, contractual agreements with the customer and clearly defined acceptance criteria are important in advance.

Reference

1. https://www.projektmagazin.de/glossarterm/freigabe, accessed on 29 May 2020.

Project Organization

Abstract

In practice, different forms of project organization are encountered, which have an effect on the organization of the test project. The matrix organization is the most common organizational form encountered in practice. Different indices can be used to evaluate the progress of the project.

As a rule, the form of **project organization** is already predetermined. The following typical forms of organization can be found in practice:

26.1 Staff Line Project Organization

The staff line project organization (Fig. 26.1) is also called an influence organization. The project manager has neither technical nor disciplinary authority and often has no fixed project team.

The project manager can exert his influence in this regard. Often, projects of this kind are carried out with the direct support of the management or at least of a high-ranking department. The project manager can use this influence to make progress in the project.

Example: A new process for quality and test management is to be introduced in the company. This process is to be implemented across departments and employees are to be trained. This project is given high priority by the management. The project manager now acts as a consultant or coordinator in the affected departments. In doing so, he can flexibly

© Springer Fachmedien Wiesbaden GmbH, part of Springer Nature 2022
F. Witte, *Strategy, Planning and Organization of Test Processes*,
https://doi.org/10.1007/978-3-658-36981-1_26

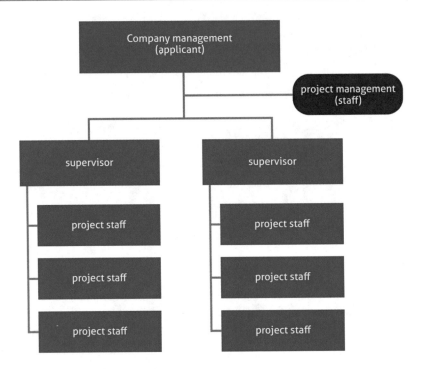

Fig. 26.1 Bar line project organization

Table 26.1 Advantages and disadvantages of the staff line project organization

Advantages	Disadvantages
The organizational structure will not be changed The project organization can be set up and dissolved again quickly Project staff remain in their departments and can draw their expertise from there	The project manager has no direct right to issue instructions Coordination is very time-consuming Measures are often difficult to enforce

access resources and demand additional work with the backing of the management. The staff line project organization has the following advantages and disadvantages (Table 26.1).

Areas of application of the staff line project organization:

- Small and non-critical projects, and
- Strategic and cross-departmental projects.

26.2 Pure Project Organization

The pure project organization (see Fig. 26.2) is also called **autonomous project organization.** For this form of organization, employees are completely detached from their department for the duration of the project and work exclusively for the project. For this period, the project manager assumes not only the technical but also the disciplinary right to issue instructions. This form of project organization is the most distinct from the regular organization.

Example: A company sets up its own development and test department for a product line abroad for expansion purposes. The infrastructure connection is part of the project.

The project team is composed of various experts who leave their positions in the respective departments for the duration of the project and work exclusively for the project. The pure project organization is characterized by the following advantages and disadvantages (Table 26.2).

Areas of application of the pure project organization are above all:

- Particularly large projects,
- International projects or
- Time-critical projects.

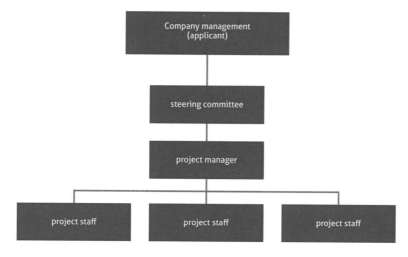

Fig. 26.2 Autonomous project organization

Table 26.2 Advantages and disadvantages of the pure project organization

Advantages	Disadvantages
High identification of the project staff with the project	High effort for reintegration of project
Clear structures and both technical and disciplinary	staff into the line organization
right of instruction by the project manager	Knowledge exchange with specialist
Direct communication	departments difficult

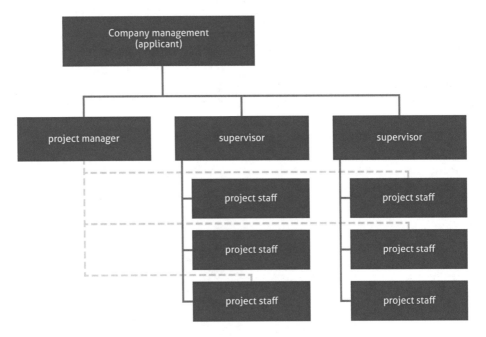

Fig. 26.3 Matrix organization

26.3   Matrix Organization

The matrix organization (see Fig. 26.3) is most frequently used in practice and represents a kind of hybrid form between staff and pure project organization.

The project employees remain in their specialist departments and are available to the project to a certain percentage. The department head continues to exercise the disciplinary right to issue instructions and the technical right to issue instructions for requirements of the line organization. The project manager has the right to issue technical instructions regarding the project content.

Example: In a software company, a new product is to be developed. Several employees from different research, development, and quality assurance departments are available to the project in different proportions of their working time. During the project, they report to both their project manager and their department manager regarding their day-to-day tasks. This can lead to conflicts and resource overlap or issues of prioritization of tasks, so communication is of great importance in this organization. The matrix organization has the following advantages and disadvantages (Table 26.3).

Areas of application of the matrix organization:

- Medium to large projects and
- Deadline-critical projects.

In summary, depending on the organizational form, the project manager has different powers of instruction and must coordinate with the superiors of the individual departments [ERFP2019].

26.4   Balanced Matrix Organization

To mitigate the possible disadvantages of a matrix project organization - such as conflicts between the head of department and the project manager - it can be useful to place a steering committee before the project manager. This committee is then responsible for resource allocation, among other things (▶ above) [PROR2019].

If the relevant department heads are then also represented in this steering committee, this usually reduces resource conflicts between project tasks and day-to-day business, since the department heads are involved in these decisions (see Fig. 26.4).

26.5   Powers and Responsibility for Objectives of the Project Manager

Table 26.4 shows an overview of the project manager's authority and responsibility for objectives for all 3 forms of organization.

Table 26.3 Advantages and disadvantages of the matrix organization

Advantages	Disadvantages
Employees remain in their departments, so that reintegration after the end of the project is not necessary.	Conflicts between project and department management possible (employees have two superiors)
Employees can benefit from the knowledge and exchange in their specialist department	Problems with prioritization between line and project work
Flexible access to resources	

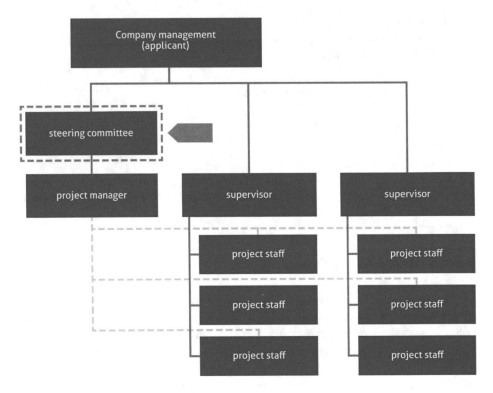

Fig. 26.4 Balanced matrix organization

Table 26.4 Powers and responsibility for objectives of the project manager

Project Manager	Project organisation		
	Autonomous	Matrix	Rod line
Technical authority to issue instructions	Yes	Yes	
Disciplinary authority to issue instructions	Yes		
Goal responsibility	Full	Full	

26.6   Formulas for Assessing the Progress of the Project

In project management, project success can be evaluated using various formulas. Some of them are particularly interesting for test projects, as they can express the status in figures (see Table 26.5).

Table 26.5 Formulas for assessing the progress of the project

Cost development index Cost performance index (CPI)	Completion value (EV)/actual cost (AC)	A value >1 means that the costs were lower than originally planned. <1 consequently means the opposite
Term development index Schedule performance index (SPI)	Completion value (EV)/planned costs	A value >1 means that the project progress is faster than the plan. A value <1 means accordingly the opposite
Expected residual costs Estimate to complete (ETC)	BAV - EV (continues as before, CPI is 1) or (BAC-EV)/CPO, planning is corrected for CPI	In variant 2, the CPI is included in the residual cost estimate. If the CPI has been 1.2 up to now, for example, it is assumed that this value will also be reached in the future and the residual costs are corrected accordingly
Time deviation Schedule variance (SV)	Completion value (EC) - Planned costs (PV) Earned value - Planned value	The calculation determines how far the current percentage of completion deviates from the planned percentage of completion. In doing so, the deviation in time is determined in a monetary value Example: At time x, work packages worth €120,000 are to be created, but services worth €160,000 were actually created in the planned time. In the planned time, services to the value of €40,000 more were performed than planned
Cost variance Cost variance (CV)	Activity value (EV) - Actual cost (AC) Earned value (EV) - Actual costs (AC)	This determines the extent to which the actual costs deviate from the earned value. A negative cost variance indicates that less work was performed with the costs incurred than originally planned. As a rule, one has a monetary value here (euro, dollar ....

References

1. [PROR2019] : https://projekte-leicht-gemacht.de/blog/pm-methoden-erklaert/projektorganisa-tionsformen/, accessed on 9 May 2020
2. [ERFP2019] : https://erfolgreich-projekte-leiten.de/projektorganisation/, accessed on 9 May 2020

Test Methods

27

Abstract

Several models, such as TMMI, TPI or TMap, support the methodical approach during the test process. This allows test processes to be optimized in a targeted manner and with the right priorities. Different maturity levels define the progress of the corresponding test organization.

27.1   Use of Test Methods

In software projects, testing swallows up a significant portion of the available time. To shorten this time, IT managers often fall into actionism. Instead, it would be much more effective to improve the maturity of the test organization.

An essential characteristic of mature test organizations is a methodical approach, as has long been standard in the quality assurance of aircraft and automobile manufacturers, for example. For software developers, this approach still comes up short. The reason is "time-to-market". In addition, the maturity level of IT is generally not yet as far advanced as in traditional industries. More often than in other industries, the approach is still rather creative and artistic. However, the use of suitable **test methods** is necessary for the sustainable success of the test measures, precisely because of the increasing industrialization of the development process and software testing.

The development cycles until the next release have shortened rapidly in recent years. At the same time, IT projects have become more complex and IT plays a business-critical role everywhere in the company today. If systems fail due to software defects, this usually has a damaging effect for the business.

To ensure software quality, testing takes up more project time today. In large projects, it swallows up at least 30% of the total project time; often the share adds up to 40–50

© Springer Fachmedien Wiesbaden GmbH, part of Springer Nature 2022   215
F. Witte, *Strategy, Planning and Organization of Test Processes*,
https://doi.org/10.1007/978-3-658-36981-1_27

percent. As a result, to meet the customer's deadline and stay within budget, software developers play it safe and often let their test management slide. Especially when time for development is already tight, time in the test phases is shortened and effort is saved rather than omitting planned features or strengthening the development team. The way out of this dilemma of time pressure and increasing quality demands is to make testing more efficient, for example, to accelerate the processes.

When it comes to improving processes, however, IT managers often fall into actionism instead of first analyzing exactly how their own test management is doing. Popular ad hoc measures include automating software tests to save testing costs and outsourcing certain tests to specialists. These measures are correct in principle. However, for both, test management should already have a certain level of strategic and methodical approach. One must also be aware that test automation must also be permanently maintained and is by no means a foregone conclusion.

For effective test automation, for example, the test cases should be reproducible and standardized. And to use outsourcing effectively, comprehensive documentation of all processes related to testing supports collaboration with service providers.

27.2   Appropriate Test methods and Test Strategy

Terminology should also be clearly defined and laid down in a **test strategy**. The client and the test service provider thus speak the same language, which helps companies avoid unnecessary costs due to communication breakdowns.

If this strategic approach is missing, the risk increases that the costs for additional coordination rounds, superfluous training and unnecessary tool licenses will rise. In the worst case, the investments even exceed the targeted savings. Because automating chaos tends to lead to further chaos instead of eliminating it.

A major reason for this actionism in many companies is that they are often not even aware of the stage their test processes are at. However, there are now various assessment methods that take companies by the hand and provide a framework for determining the status quo of test management and improving it step by step.

The methods, for example TMMi, TPI or TMap, can be seen as a guide. Test managers can use defined criteria to assess the maturity of their processes and recognize whether planned investments in certain improvement measures are currently at all sensible or whether other steps are not initially much more important [CIOD2019].

27.3 Testing Maturity Model (TMMi)

The Testing maturity model integration (TMMi) is a method often used for this purpose. The assessment procedure is the further development of the TMM, a maturity model for test processes that was developed by Ilene Burnstein and her team at the Illinois Institute of Technology based on SW-CMM.

TMMi comprises five levels, each of which describes a maturity level of test management (Table 27.1).

Companies that test software according to the "trial and error" principle or "debugging", for example, are classified at the lowest level, level 1. Software tests are primarily used to find and eliminate programming and functional defects. At the top level, level 5, companies have integrated the process improvements derived from the levels below into the testing procedures. The test then not only helps to find bugs, but also to actively avoid them [CIOD2019].

Since TMMi is closely aligned with CMMi, all generic objectives and generic practices apply (except for GG1, since TMMi exists only as a Staged Representation) as they do in CMMi. Thus, the topic of reviews is addressed in GP 2.9 OBJECTIVELY ASSESS PROCESS COMPLIANCE and GP 2.10 REVIEW IMPLEMENTATION WITH HIGHER MANAGEMENT. Reviews are meant here in a general sense, i.e., as a review in any form

Table 27.1 The five levels of the maturity model

Level	Level	Features	Necessary improvements
5	"Optimizing"	Retroactive effect of the improvements on the process	Organization of production on an optimal level Continuous process improvement established
4	"Managed"	Quantitatively recorded and understood process	Change in technology Problem analysis Problem avoidance Process improvement proposals based on key figures
3	"Defined"	Process qualitatively defined and institutionalized	Analysis and "measurement" of the process Quantitative quarterly plans Uniform processes established
2	"Repeatable"	Intuitive, person-dependent mastery of the process	Training Technical practices (reviews, tests) Focus on standards and teams
1	"Initial"	Process flow "chaotic" and management "ad hoc"	Project management Project planning Configuration management Software quality assurance

by one or more persons. These reviews can be equated more with audits or other reviews of process conformity and as management reviews rather than document reviews.

Two TMMi process areas are dedicated exclusively to **peer reviews**. These include a process area that describes the performance of informal reviews as well as walkthroughs, technical reviews, and inspections in accordance with IEEE Std 1028–2008, and a process area on advanced peer reviews at maturity level 4, which represents the anchoring of these peer reviews as a strategic part of the overall testing process (i.e., test strategy, test planning, and test approaches) with corresponding metrics. The description of the peer reviews largely corresponds to the criteria of IEEE Std 1028–2008 for formal reviews. The specific objectives and specific practices required are independent of the review type and focus on the specifics of reviews in testing. This is most evident in the specific practice SP 2.2 "Testers review test basis documents" with the typical work products of "testability defects" and "testability review report".

The institutionalization of peer reviews, i.e., the application of the generic objectives and generic practices, are a good source for the activities that organizations need to consider when introducing and optimizing reviews. The organizational policy regarding reviews, which precisely also defines the generic objectives and planning of the reviews and requires the trainings, is a basis for the successful introduction of reviews in organizations. In addition, TMMi provides the most important content for the training of reviewers and for the training of review moderators. Of particular note is the clear requirement that the review checklists provided must themselves be subject to review by the "peers" and potential users of the checklists. It is more problematic to determine and also evaluate the key figures that are important for the company. To achieve this, one must first check from the set of key figures whether they exist at all without further ado and how they can be generated. In addition, one must be clear about which index values result in which interpretations, and what follows from this in detail for operational practice.

During the test process, work products are repeatedly created, and consequently TMMi also requires the review of these work products in suitable specific practices. In TMMi, reviews have a high significance, which is already evident in the requirements for achieving maturity level 3. The contents of the specific practices for peer reviews are compliant with IEEE Std 1028–2008 and clearly formal. The review process is presented and formally described regardless of the review type and regardless of the supporting documents to be reviewed. In individual specific practices, the specifics are presented when testers act as reviewers [QUAL2010].

27.4   TMap (Test Management Approach)

TMap is a model in the area of testing and quality assurance of software in which all arising aspects, the environment and the procedure are structured.

This makes TMap (developed in 1995, registered trademark of Sogeti Nederland B.V.) and standard in many organizations worldwide. It can be contrasted with **TPI** (**Test process improvement**) from the same group of companies. While TMap structures the tests themselves, TPI aims to optimize the entire test process. Thus, TPI is at management level, while TMap is to be used in a specific project. TMap is based on practical experience and is therefore not a theoretical but a pragmatic method. The method can be used universally and across all industries, and can be adapted to the specific needs in the respective test project or test situation.

The test process is divided into 4 areas, the so-called core modules:

1. Business-based test management,
2. Fully structured test process,
3. Complete tool kit and
4. Adaptive, flexible test process.

Business-driven test management approach (**BDTM**) means that the **business case** is the justification for a project and answers the questions of why the project is being executed, what investment is required and what the customer wants to achieve with the results.

During the project, the business case is verified at defined points in time to ensure that the resulting deliverables are still valid for the customer. TMap supports the justification of IT and transfers it to the test activities. TMap assumes that a project approach based on a business case has the following characteristics:

- The approach aims to achieve a predetermined outcome.
- The overall project to achieve this result will be implemented within the available duration.
- The cost of the project to achieve this result is reasonable compared to the profit the organization is seeking to make.
- The risks during commissioning are known and as low as possible. All this is within the framework conditions defined by the above characteristics.

The four factors of **IT governance** described above (outcome, risk, time and cost) are found in these characteristics. For the successful execution of a project, it is important that the testing process is in line with the business case. The relationship between the business case and the testing process is established through the BDTM approach. The BDTM approach has the following steps:

- Formulation of the assignment and compilation of the test objectives: Test objectives must always have relevance for both the customer and the client or their representatives. Test objectives are often formulated in relation to IT-supported business processes, implemented user requirements or defined risks.
- Determination of the risk class for each combination of feature and sub-object: A generic document ("**master test plan**") is used to determine the planned test stages. A risk class is defined for each test objective.
- Determination of how thoroughly the combination of a feature with a sub-object must be tested. From the previously determined risk class, the result for each test stage is documented in a strategy table.
- The overall estimate for all tests is performed, and the test planning is created. After presentation to the customer and other stakeholders, the risk class and strategy table are adjusted accordingly, if necessary.
- Finally, the right test technique is selected from the combination of feature and subobject. When the customer and the other stakeholders agree on the estimation and planning, the test designer finalizes the test design table. In the process, the decisions about more or less thorough testing are translated into concrete statements about the desired test coverage.
- During the test process, the test manager reports on the progress of the test process, the quality and risks of the test object, and the quality of the test process.

TMap supports a structured test process. The master test plan specifies which functions must be tested and with what intensity. Both for the master test plan and for the individual test stages (module, integration, system, acceptance test), a well-functioning process must be set up for the activities of planning, preparation, execution and control. In addition to these processes, certain aspects need to be managed centrally rather than individually for each project. This includes supporting processes for:

- Test guidelines: Determine how people, resources, and methods will be used in conjunction with testing processes and define core support.
- Permanent test organization.
- Test environments.
- Testing tools.
- Testing experts.

TMap supports the correct execution of the structured test process with a complete set of tools. This focuses on the topics

- Techniques for test effort estimation, defect management, metrics creation, product risk analysis, test design, and product testing. These topics describe how to test.
- Techniques for the infrastructure that define where and with what testing takes place. These include test environments, test tools and workstations. Test tools are divided into test planning and test control tools, test design tools, test execution tools, and tools for troubleshooting and code analysis.
- Techniques for the organization describe who executes the test. For this purpose, test guidelines, permanent test organization, test organization in projects, test experts and test roles must be defined.

TMap is an approach that can be used in all test situations and with all system development methods. The tester chooses which elements of TMap to use depending on the situation. This makes TMap an **adaptive method.** Adaptive means that an element can be split into sub-elements which in a different situation result in a new, valuable element for the specific situation.

The adaptability of TMap can be expressed by four properties:

- Respond to changes: If the test strategy and the estimate and plan derived from it are not acceptable to the client, the plan is adjusted. This gives the client control over the testing process and allows them to manage it based on a trade-off between outcome and risk on the one hand and time on the other. The test manager may decide to adjust various aspects of the test plan in consultation with the client.
- (Re)use products and processes: Thanks to a large set of tools available in the form of test design techniques, checklists and templates, products and processes can be quickly deployed. TMap offers various forms of permanent test organization to anchor the reuse of products and processes in the organization.
- Learning from experience: Evaluation of the test process is built into TMap as an activity. Another important tool is the use of metrics. For the test process, metrics about the quality of the test object and about the progress and quality of the test processes are important to control the test process, to justify test recommendations and to compare systems or test processes with each other.
- Try first, use later: Adopting the test base (using a testability report), test infrastructure, and test object allow them to be tested before use [TMAP2008].

27.5   Advantages of TMap

- The method is based on experience from numerous projects.
- TMap takes current trends into account.
- The focus is on the test process.
- TMap optimizes risk coverage and depth of testing.
- Stakeholder engagement is maximized.

References

1. https://www.cio.de/a/test-methoden-tmmi-und-tpi-im-vergleich,2301883,3,   accessed   on   9 May 2020
2. https://thequaliteers.de/nachrichten-leser/items/reviews-in-test-maturity-model-integration-tmmi.html, accessed on 9 May 2020
3. Koomen van der Aalst Broekmann Vroon, TMap Next, dpunkt Verlag Heidelberg 2008

Abstract

TPI Next evaluates the maturity level of test processes and provides suitable best practices to sustainably improve a test organization. For this purpose, the test process is divided into different core areas. Certain criteria must be met for each of the maturity levels.

The internationally recognized TPI model has established itself as the standard for determining and improving the maturity of test organizations. Therefore, it will be highlighted as a test method in the following.

28.1 Determining the Maturity of the Test Process

The goal of **TPI Next** is to sustainably improve test processes and to provide suitable best practices for this purpose. The **TPI model** is used to determine the maturity level of the test process.

In general, the test process should have the following characteristics:

- Transparency: The current status of the tests should be available at all times. All employees have a picture of the overall process and know what needs to be worked on next and when the current tasks need to be completed.
- Manageability: The test activities are divided into individual work packages.
- Traceability: Decisions and results should also be traceable by third parties in retrospect.

© Springer Fachmedien Wiesbaden GmbH, part of Springer Nature 2022

223

F. Witte, *Strategy, Planning and Organization of Test Processes*,
https://doi.org/10.1007/978-3-658-36981-1_28

- Predictability: Process milestones are included, and empirical values are used to estimate the effort required for the work packages at the test object level.
- Efficiency: Redundancies are avoided and an optimal use of resources is designed [HETT2019].

TPI thus serves to evaluate the overarching view across all projects of the operational organizational unit and not just for a single project measure. However, the **maturity levels** determined have a direct impact on the individual project. Many weaknesses and problems in test processes identified in projects can be substantiated and explained using the TPI Next criteria. The use of the TPI Next method is intended to enable a step-by-step improvement of the test processes.

For this purpose, the TPI model divides the test process into 20 different core areas, so-called key areas, to each of which levels are assigned. The levels can be used to determine the maturity of a core area – similar to TMMi. Each higher level is better than the previous one in terms of time, money or quality. To help users determine whether a core area meets the requirements of a level, the TPI model defines a set of checkpoints for each level. They serve as a checklist that enables an objective and transparent assessment of a core area.

A structured test process has the following advantages:

- The approach can be used in any situation and is independent of the business area, the organizational structure or the chosen approach to system development.
- The approach provides information about the quality risks of the tested system.
- Important defects are found at an early stage of the development process so that the defects can be corrected early and costs can be significantly reduced as a result.
- Bugs in future development products are avoided by testability reviews.
- Costs caused by material or immaterial damage are prevented.
- Test cases and test products are reusable.
- Testing is on the critical path of the entire development cycle for as short a time as possible, which can shorten the overall project duration.
- The test process is understandable and controllable.

For this purpose, first the TPI model and later the TPI-Next model were developed. In the TPI-Next model, compared to the TPI model, the maturity categories are emphasized more strongly, the checkpoints are represented in a **test maturity matrix,** and the core areas have been revised. Dependencies and priorities between core areas were replaced by groups, and the model was extended to include test support in iterative and agile development processes.

In addition, improvements have been made that constitute the business-based nature of the new model:

- Grouping of **checkpoint**: A group consists of a number of related checkpoints from different core areas. Even if TPI Next is used as part of a general software process improvement initiative, the use of this basic grouping is recommended. All situations where the classic TPI model was sufficient are covered by the base grouping of the TPI Next model. However, if the test process improvement is to be directed towards a specific outcome - e.g., reduction of test costs or improved time-to-market - the groups can be restructured, which means that the most effective optimization measures are at the top of the list. This makes TPI Next very versatile.

- **Enablers:** Testing is an integral part of software development that is interrelated with numerous adjacent processes. This mutual influence of testing, development and operation is illustrated by the introduction of enablers: processes that are closely interrelated with testing and that have a positive influence on test maturity if adequately considered, and vice versa. However, when inadequately considered, the influences are negative. As a result, enablers play an important role in identifying potential "quick wins" as well as ensuring close alignment with general software process improvement models such as CMMI or SPICE.

28.2 Test Organization in the Maturing process According to TPI Next

TPI Next evaluates the **test process based on** different maturity levels. Among other things, test process management, reporting, communication, metrics and methodical procedures are evaluated. One of the criteria in this evaluation is the test organization, which is discussed in more detail below.

The term test organization as used in TPI Next includes all test functions, facilities, operations, activities, responsibilities and authorities, and their respective relationships to each other. A test organization uses ways and means to provide test products and/or test services. It pursues common goals, controls its own performance, and bears responsibility for its own results.

To be able to adapt quickly to changing circumstances, the test organization must be flexibly structured and adapted to the test process. This is particularly necessary when additional projects are pending or an internal reorganization is carried out. A test organization offers various products and services and has different levels of maturity.

28.3   Classification of Maturity

Each test process can be classified in a certain maturity level.

Starting with the maturity level "initial", a test process can develop through the maturity levels "controlled" and "efficient" to "optimizing", the highest maturity level. Once a higher level is reached, the maturity of the test process increases and the business value increases.

- **Initial:** The test process consists of inadequately documented ad hoc activities. The focus is on whether a software works at all and not on whether the requirements and specifications have been met. Such a test process provides insufficient or unsystematic information about existing risks and the quality of the test process itself.
- **Controlled:** All important activities of the test process are planned and executed. The process is controlled and managed. The test process thus allows earlier and better insight into the quality and allows timely corrective actions. This reduces the risk of delays due to poor product quality.
- **Efficient:** The activities of the test process are coordinated in such a way that a more favorable cost-benefit ratio is achieved. The way of test execution is improved, and the critical defects are identified at minimum cost and time.
- **Optimizing:** The achieved state of the test process is maintained, analyzed and constantly adapted to changing requirements. The level of testing activities is maintained in the future. Control points of the "optimizing" maturity level contain the measures that are necessary to keep the process quality stable even in changing situations and framework conditions.

28.4   Maturity Process for the Test Organization

Individual criteria are evaluated to assess the maturity process:

- Experience of the testers, equipment with test competence and specific expertise, e.g., in the application area or in test-specific knowledge:
  - Support for product risk analysis,
  - Development of a test procedure for the entire project (master test plan),
  - Experience with test effort estimates,
  - Coordination of test projects and
  - Test automation.

- Description of the test process, templates and training materials for structured testing.
- Test tools, tool licenses and scripts.
- Communication and reporting structures.
- Basic procedures for defect management.
- Test process improvement.

Many of the test products and test services listed are also relevant to other core areas to a certain extent. The test organization thus provides the link between the individual core areas.

28.5   Maturity Level "Initial"

The people involved in testing are distributed across mostly technically organized departments. Their roles mostly concern specific subtasks. Common views on testing and quality assurance hardly exist. The sharing of information is poor, the results of testing activities are hardly compared, and the people are rather randomly assembled and devote only a not exactly defined part of their working time to testing systems.

28.6   Maturity Level "Controlled"

Within the software lifecycle, different testing activities and associated responsibilities can be identified. Design, development and maintenance are organized to a certain extent and recognized as specific functions. Testing is organized to some extent, but is highly dependent on the maturity of the other processes and their organization.

Checkpoints

- All parties involved know who or which department is responsible for the testing services.
- A structure of control and accountability is in place within the test organization.
- Test tasks and responsibilities are defined and documented and assigned to a person or organizational unit.
- The products and services of the test organization are known to its customers.

Enabler

- Knowledge management is established in the company, which the test organization can use for knowledge consolidation.

Suggestions for Improvement

- In a small company, a person responsible for testing should be designated to act as the point of contact for all testing-related issues.
- In a larger organizational unit, based on the nature of the established test organization, the best possible (local) placement of the test team can be decided.
- The exchange of knowledge, experience and best practices between testers and other people who perform testing tasks is organized through regular workshops and meetings.
- Stakeholders learn the need to distinguish between different roles and responsibilities for commissioning testing, product acceptance and test execution.
- Products and services of the test organization are documented (e.g., "Creation of the test planning", "Execution of a test level")
- A marketing and communications plan for public relations (What do we sell? Who does our product appeal to?) is in place.

28.7   Maturity Level "Efficient"

Different departments and teams may be involved in the test process, some of which may not even know what testing activities are being performed elsewhere in the company. They may have an entirely different way of working and use different tools. To reach the maturity level "Efficient", one should coordinate the separate activities holistically.

In an efficient test organization, testing resources are made available to projects in the form of services covering the following activities:

- Execution,
- Support (coaching and training courses),
- Control (audit and review),
- Maintenance and
- Research and development.

Test services can also be provided by external service providers. In the case of outsourcing, the test responsibility can be taken over externally in whole or in part. If the resource requirements of the individual projects change, a redistribution of resources to the individual projects takes place.

At this maturity level, the test organization is more focused on the actual requirements of a customer than at the "controlled" maturity level. As a result, the focus is less on the activities and more on the results. The test activities are identified, organized and monitored to this end.

To better plan the scope and quality of test results, certain procedures are defined and communicated through training. The need for tools and other aids is analyzed and covered accordingly.

The test strategy of the organizational unit is defined by the company management and the test organization and documented in a test guideline. Corporate management ensures compliance with and implementation of this test policy.

Control Points

- Different people or departments providing testing services coordinate the organization of their work among themselves.
- The test organization provides the agreed test resources and test services to the projects.
- The decision of where and how to position the test execution is well-thought-out.
- The test guideline is followed.

Enabler

Organizational units that provide services in the areas of personnel, development environments, tools, and processes may also provide services and resources in testing.

Suggestions for Optimization

A study of the needs of the various test projects will be conducted. The needs are categorized by types of resources and types of services per resource. A bill of quantities with different types of resources and services is compiled. Based on a business case, it is decided which services should be provided by the test organization. A permanent improvement of the test organization is shown by concrete measures and goals.

28.8   Maturity Level "Optimizing"

Improvement and innovation and relationships with groups and individuals outside the test organization play an important role. The test organization functions at all levels and for the most important processes.

At the "optimizing" maturity level, the focus on internal and external quality leads to better results. This includes the maintenance of the service specification, insofar as it reflects the need to adapt supply to demand. The test organization focuses on providing the appropriate personnel with relevant experience and expertise when needed.

The test organization continuously improves itself by evaluating and adjusting internal processes. Comparisons are made with external service providers and used to support when they can offer better services.

Checkpoints

- The products and services of the test organization are evaluated regularly. New services are added when they are economical.
- The test organization bears responsibility for the success and failure of test assignments.
- The performance of the test organization is regularly compared with the performance of external service providers or similar test organizations.

Enabler
A test organization can improve its performance if the interrelated parts of the organization have the same level of maturity and work together proactively.

Optimization Suggestions

- The demand for the services offered is monitored and regularly adjusted to changes in demand.
- At regular intervals, a check is made to see whether there is demand for new test services and a decision is made whether these services should be included in the service specifications.
- The cost of services is reviewed and compared to external service providers and/or test organizations of similar maturity.
- The internal processes of the test organization are reviewed and optimized where possible [TPIN2011].

28.9   Differences TMMi and TPI

When comparing both method construction kits, it is noticeable: TMMi has advantages if a company already relies on CMMi to improve software development overall. This gives test managers a 360-degree view of the IT organization that covers software development and testing in equal measure.

Synergies and a broader view of all processes can thus be achieved when improving the processes. For example, if a test organization reaches level 3 according to TMMi, this is comparable to level 2 in the area of "Verification and Validation" at CMMi.

Although TMMi goes into great detail, it does not cover areas that TPI does. These include the **office environment**, **reporting**, and **testware management**. However, all three areas are important parts of the test process. This provides TPI with some advantage over the TMMi approach. Another difference between the two approaches is the gradation between maturity levels. Each core area in TMMi requires a certain maturity level. This means: to reach level 3, all requirements of the Key Area "Test Training" have to be fulfilled, among others [CIOD2019].

References

1. Sogeti: TPI Next – Geschäftsbasierte Verbesserung des Testprozesses, dpunkt Verlag Heidelberg 2011
2. https://www.cio.de/a/test-methoden-tmmi-und-tpi-im-vergleich,2301883,3, accessed on 9 May 2020
3. https://www.hettwer-beratung.de/konzepte/testkonzept/testrollen/, accessed on 9 May 2020

Special Features of the Test Organization in Agile Projects

29

Abstract

Test management in agile projects must consider the stronger dynamics of the test processes. Organizational forms, roles, and methods necessary for agilization also affect software testing. Special principles must therefore be observed for agile testing.

29.1 Agile Projects

If the task for test planning and test organization is an **agile project**, the challenges for test management increase significantly. Processes running in parallel and changes in functionality within a time window lead to considerably stronger dynamics.

More efficient communication between all project participants, optimized time-to-market, mastering the increasing complexity and, above all, ensuring the required quality are essential reasons for agilizing processes that affect test planning and test organization.

Instead of presenting a final result at the end of the project, agile teams involve their customers in the process and regularly deliver new software versions for them to evaluate. However, it is not enough to identify customer requirements at an early stage – efficient implementation is at least as important. The software is therefore subject to frequent and often far-reaching changes. The advantages are obvious: short development cycles with rapid implementation successes.

But to keep up with the fast pace, testing must adapt to agile working methods, as it has now become an indispensable part of agile software development. For a long time now, the

© Springer Fachmedien Wiesbaden GmbH, part of Springer Nature 2022
F. Witte, *Strategy, Planning and Organization of Test Processes*,
https://doi.org/10.1007/978-3-658-36981-1_29

discussion has not been about whether agile methods should be used, but rather how they can be used correctly and scaled if necessary.

29.2   Agile Methods

Testing is therefore inextricably interwoven with development. One of the best-known agile methods is **Scrum,** which implements the principles of the agile manifesto. However, neither the agile manifesto nor the Scrum description deal with test activities or the test organization in any depth. While **test-driven development** or **continuous integration** approaches are recommended, a systematic testing approach is not described. There may be testers, i.e., specialists with a focus on quality assurance and acceptance testing, but a separate testing track does not appear in most of the process models. **Kanban**, the software development method underlying the agile approach, deliberately leaves this open. However, testing activities and test organization play a critical role in the success of agile methods. Testing in agile development projects differs from traditional methods primarily in that it is a preventive measure and that tests must be executed much more frequently in so-called **sprints** than in the classical test model (such as in the V model). As a rule, the duration of a sprint is one to two weeks, at the end of which the tested software is to be delivered to the customer. Successes and problems are recorded and evaluated in regular retrospectives, which further increases the quality and the test coverage achieved.

For agile teams, however, a model has now become established that represents the different test perspectives in a somewhat simplified, but all the more effective way. The so-called four test quadrants by Crispin & Gregory (Fig. 29.1) divide the test task into a more IT-technical and a more functional perspective for the tests. In addition, tests are differentiated according to what has already been worked out in advance ("**supporting the** team") and which problems are only encountered during completion ("**critique the product**").

This also allows different types of tests (e.g., unit test, usability test) to be subdivided, for which there may be different groups of employees who are responsible in each case. Especially for load/performance tests, security tests and reliability tests, assistance from partners outside the project team is often necessary.

The regression test is not considered here because it is not a separate test. The regression test is always part of a test and should be considered in every test, even if it is possibly outsourced organizationally (e.g., use of offshore employees) or technically (through automated tests).

Once you have clarified the perspectives of the test and thus, if necessary, the division of labor in the test, you should consider what the object of the test is in the first place.

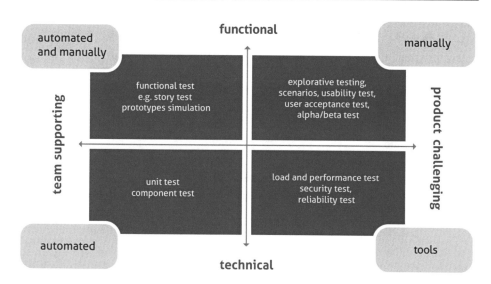

Fig. 29.1 Test quadrants as a model for testing activities in agile projects

On the one hand, the functions/features (or as they are called in the project) should be mentioned in this context. Here you have to distinguish exactly which functions are to be tested and which functions are not. Sometimes a function is better delimited by excluding what is not part of the functional scope. In the case of a web shop, for example, you could promise the cancel function for shopping, but it makes things clearer for the client if you restrict that the customer is not (yet) able to go back to the checkout with the same shopping cart.

On the other hand, the non-functional quality characteristics should be considered in addition to the individual features. Reliability, security and usability are central criteria in IT projects. Here, it is recommended to take a look at the quality model of **ISO 25010**, which should be gone through in sequence as a checklist [PERF2017].

For the success of a project, it is essential that all test procedures relevant to a project (unit, functional and load performance tests) are scheduled early and implemented at all levels. This helps the tester to identify and resolve problems in time. Automating tests makes it possible to run them several times a day or in regular test runs at night and on weekends. Regression testing ensures that new features do not affect existing features. Since the automated tests must be adapted to the revised digital product after each iteration, the efficiency of the method must be continuously weighed.

In addition to running test cases, automated or not, it is important to combine them with exploratory testing, where the software is tested without a predetermined test plan. Human acumen and creativity are needed to find both shallow and deep bugs that cannot be planned in the lab. The quality of the testing activities ultimately determines the quality of the final product.

29.3   Organization and Goals of Agile Projects

At the center of the team organization is the **product owner**, who keeps an eye on the big picture, defines goals and is the technical representative of the customer. In addition to the product owner, there are the individual test teams. The cross-functional organization and collaboration gives agile development teams the chance to work more freely and to think outside the box. Developers and product owners talk to each other regularly and exchange ideas directly with those responsible for testing. This allows for quick adjustments and reactions when needed.

Defining the goals gives the teams a clear idea of what they are working on. Only when these are clearly defined can the teams test efficiently and complete each sprint successfully. Although testing is quality assurance, the testers can never find all bugs. Therefore, the real goal of testing efforts should be to continuously improve the software. Moreover, the goals can be too ambitious if developers want to implement too many features. As a result, the goals are not thought from the user's point of view and the teams test past the core of the problems. What good is an offer that no one takes advantage of? It is therefore elementary to know your own users and, for example, to test on devices that the target group also uses. How high is the CPU load, how much data volume does the app consume, and what loading times are acceptable? These and other factors should definitely be checked during the test.

This is where methods like **crowdsourced testing** or **crowd testing** come into play. This type of quality assurance of a website, mobile app or connected device relies on a community of testers outside the company to perform the tests. With crowd testing, products are tested not in a sterile lab environment, but by real people, on real devices, and in common everyday situations around the world. The results reflect the actual or potential user experience much better than would be possible through in-house or lab solutions. Another advantage of this method is that it is compatible with the speed of agile processes, as many testers can test at the same time, generating hundreds of hours of testing in a single day. However, defect capture is problematic, since defects are usually not described as precisely and comprehensively as with experienced, trained testers, and defects are often captured multiple times by different testers. This means more comprehensive defect management, with more queries and elimination of duplicate defect entries. The organization and work preparation can also become complicated and costly. In addition, this approach is generally only suitable when dealing with an Internet application or an app that addresses a broad customer base (such as an online shopping platform), but the method tends to be unsuitable for very specialized applications that require a special infrastructure.

29.4   Agile Projects and Traditional Organization

Test data management is often underestimated, but it is essential. Testers promote the exchange of valuable information and insights. How many test cases were executed, what is the defect rate, etc.? These are all questions that provide material for extensive and detailed reports, and are certainly of high relevance for the project manager and the product manager. But the question is: Who else could be interested in this data? Because at its core, agile methods are all about optimizing workflows and spending only as much time as absolutely necessary on reporting. It is therefore recommended collecting data that is also useful for other departments. Preparing the data in the form of best practices or cases can help to increase the performance of the teams and improve the development of the software.

Such comprehensive changes naturally present companies - especially management - with challenges that must be mastered: The teams repeatedly encounter resistance at the interfaces to the traditional organization. A segmented planning approach, the increased coordination effort or the reduced documentation often cause uncertainty. To counteract this, full backing from management, clear definition of decision-making competencies, timeframes and budgets, and clarification of the interfaces with functional units outside the agile process are required [ENTW2019].

29.5   Necessary Requirements for Test organization in Agile Projects

When organizing testing, you need to consider the following points in agile projects:

- You have to define an overview of the test object, the test objectives and the delimitation to the interfaces (scope).
- The functions of the test object must be mapped in a suitable structure.
- For each component, the respective test coverage must be recognizable at any time.
- Each individual work package is compared to the remaining time and the appropriate adjustments are made for time, money and performance.

In practice, it is recommended that a document containing the compilation of test-relevant information, which is divided into functional components, is used for implementation. The following components should be included in the document:

- Graphic of the desired representation,
- Acceptance criteria,
- Comments from meetings,
- Test-relevant conversions with reference to associated test cases,
- Authorizations of the roles and
- Other relevant information.

The aim of the working document is to obtain an overview of the current status of the test activities in the agile team at any time. This enables a targeted response to changes in the agile project with short reaction times and the identification of necessary adjustments at short notice. The component should be quickly locatable, adapted and the affected test cases visible. These test cases can then be changed, extended or removed accordingly. Test cases that should be additionally created can be easily identified [BLDS2019].

29.6 Principles for Agile Testing

The following principles should be followed in agile testing:

- Scheduling of test activities, quality assurance as a core task: Development work is often delayed in agile teams, which leads to the fact that the test is not given the necessary attention. Test experts are not always available in agile teams. However, only regular, early testing brings the benefits of short feedback loops in Scrum to bear.
- Methodical test case creation: Unit tests should be represented the most, complex end-to-end or system tests the least. Especially with complex applications and issues, there are often too many variations to be able to examine all cases in a timely manner. Therefore, special attention should be paid to the reasonable selection and sufficient test coverage.
- Coordination of testing activities: Especially in the context of Scrum and interdisciplinary teams, it is advantageous to mix teams with qualified test experts. Depending on the subject and the number of teams, a test manager should be appointed to take over the internal and cross-team coordination. In any case, care should be taken to manifest test know-how in all teams in the long term. Certification in the ISTQB area is also recommended in this context. In agile teams, quality assurance becomes problematic above

all when development assumes a more powerful position than software testing and the topic of testing is regarded only as an appendage.

- Agile test charter: The **test charter** is similar to a test concept, but it is revised iteratively during the project. It is also possible to include aspects of testing in the **definition of done**, e.g., there is an automated test case for each **product backlog item** (often: user story). The following points should be present in the test charter: distribution of test cases to test levels, application of methodology and metrics, use of test environments, derivation and handling of test data.
- Use of test automation: The creation of automated test scripts should be focused on from the beginning, starting with the unit test. Only by successively creating and maintaining suitable automated test cases (e.g., also by transferring manual tests), it is possible to continuously deliver the product in the sprint rhythm (continuous delivery & integration). Test automation is a necessary prerequisite for successfully agilizing projects [SCRU2019].

At some test levels, such as unit testing or integration testing, the advantages of agile methods are more apparent than in system testing. Agile methods are superior to classic methods, especially when the requirements are only worked out during development.

Therefore, there are also mixed forms in which testing is still performed according to the V-Modell at the higher test levels and according to agile methods at the test stages close to development. This results in a better systematic test execution. However, these mixed forms mean a particularly high demand for communication among the stakeholders and the organization of test processes.

References

1. https://blog.doubleslash.de/testmanagement-im-agilen-projekt-ein-erfahrungsbericht/, accessed on 9 May 2020
2. https://www.scrum.de/5-tipps-fur-agiles-testen/, accessed on 9 May 2020
3. https://entwickler.de/online/agile/agiles-testing-579801504.html, accessed on 9 May 2020
4. https://www.informatik-aktuell.de/entwicklung/methoden/das-perfekte-testkonzept-in-6-schritten.html, accessed on 9 May 2020

Artificial Intelligence and Cognitive Testing

30

Abstract

New trends, such as artificial intelligence and the use of cognitive technologies, will increasingly influence software testing and lead to new test procedures and changed processes.

30.1 Artificial Intelligence

Artificial intelligence (AI) is a trendy topic that will bring about a significant upheaval in everyday life and daily work in the coming years. Artificial intelligence already has many cognitive properties. Cognition, however, has been attributed by humans primarily to themselves, so artificial intelligence is first seen as a competitor to human work. The new trends in the use of cognitive technologies will also have an impact on software testing.

Through the use of artificial intelligence, it will be possible to verify software systems that are becoming more complex in less time. In addition, real-time monitoring of productive software and forecasts of future changes and deviations will be possible before defects occur. Furthermore, analyses of large amounts of data are possible, for example to identify defect taxonomies or to increase test coverage.

Many tools already offer automated visual matching of the user interface and can thus be used for acceptance testing. A few tools are already capable of autonomously designing, executing, and maintaining test cases after training. Furthermore, most AI-powered testing tools monitor changes in software performance (e.g., runtimes, memory usage) and regularly check information security. Based on historical data and targeted training, these

© Springer Fachmedien Wiesbaden GmbH, part of Springer Nature 2022
F. Witte, *Strategy, Planning and Organization of Test Processes*,
https://doi.org/10.1007/978-3-658-36981-1_30

tools can provide early warnings before quality limitations occur. As a result, trouble-shooting can be initiated even earlier or, by recognizing specific patterns, can be detected in advance before bugs have an operational impact.

After risk-based and agile testing, AI again means a rethink for software testers. In the future, collaboration with AI-supported tools will become even more important. But to do so, these systems must be trained with meaningful data, such as a sufficient number of images for a given term. A basic understanding of mathematical and algorithmic principles is therefore an essential prerequisite. Software testing thus becomes a bit more technology-oriented again. Artificial intelligence takes over essential tasks of software testing, for example the test execution or the design of test cases. However, it will not be able to completely replace humans as software testers in the foreseeable future. As always in history, certain, more reproductive activities will fall away, other, creative and intellectually demanding tasks, will shape software testing and will rather increase the need for organized and well-designed testing activities and thoughtful testing processes [SQMA2018]. AI will not make testers redundant. Job descriptions change over time, but just as certain activities will no longer be necessary or can be automated in the future, new professional challenges will arise that cannot even be accurately predicted today.

When AI is mentioned, there are sometimes wild associations such as omnipotent supercomputers hell-bent on destroying humanity, voice-controlled assistants like Alexa or Siri, computers as chess opponents or self-driving cars. The buzzwords are mostly used in a political context, without defining them precisely, and in part to present science fiction scenarios that have very little to do with reality.

30.2   Fields of Application of Artificial Intelligence

It is also important to realize that the scope of what is meant by AI changes over time. For example, there was a time when Optical Character Recognition (OCR) was considered the state of the art in AI. Similarly, Siri and Alexa's questions and answers were once considered state of the art, but are now largely taken for granted and not considered AI in every case. The same will happen with software testing tools: Today's automation innovations will be taken for granted as new capabilities become available.

The use of artificial intelligence in software development is still in its infancy; the **degree of autonomy** here is still far lower than in more developed areas such as self-driving systems or voice control. Nevertheless, the development is clearly aiming in the direction of autonomous testing. AI use in software testing tools is focused on making the software development lifecycle simpler. By applying reasoning, problem solving and in some cases machine learning, AI can be used to help automate and reduce the amount of tedious routine work involved in developing and testing software. At this point, it would be appropriate to ask if test automation tools are not already doing that. The answer is a resounding yes, albeit with a few caveats. Consider, for example, that most (or even all) test automation tools are used to run tests for developers and deliver results. Because most tools don't know which tests to run, they just run all of them or a predetermined selection. So, what if an AI-enabled bot could evaluate the current test status, recent code changes, code coverage, and other metrics to decide which tests are still needed based on that, and then run those tests? Incorporating decision making based on changing data is an example of using AI. This effectively enables the software to replace the developer or tester in this decision-making process.

AI can always show its full strength in software development when it comes to removing these limitations, or when the tools used to automate software testing should provide even greater benefits to developers and testers. The benefit of AI comes from reducing the direct involvement of developers or testers in the particularly mundane tasks. (Human intelligence, on the other hand, is still exceedingly sought after in the application of business logic, among other things) [EMBD2020].

References

1. SQ Magazin, ASQF, Ausgabe 48/2018, Intelligence of Things, Markus Höber "Kognitives Testen"
2. https://www.embedded-software-engineering.de/was-bedeutet-kuenstliche-intelligenz-beim-software-testen-a-817057/, accessed on 9 May 2020

Epilogue

Numerous challenges and problems that will be encountered by the test manager in the project can already be assessed in the concept development phase.

Therefore, it is important to start creating a test concept early, several weeks before the first tester is involved in the project. This way, many experiences and risks are already known before the project even starts.

Of course, one might ask why more resources, more time, fewer functions are not planned for a project right from the start. If one has evaluated those basic prerequisites are difficult – be it the availability of the test environment, the quality of the requirements management or the structure of the projects – one could optimize these things proactively and specifically. Every other project would benefit from this optimization.

After the successful introduction of a project, it is often difficult to directly summarize the deficits that have arisen during the project phase and to motivate oneself to analyze them. After the biggest problems have been solved by the subsequent correction delivery and the introduction or rollout has been accomplished, a certain project fatigue usually occurs among those involved. Now there is plenty of reason to celebrate the successes.

You should actually have a longer phase available in which no project is carried out at all and the operational process and the test processes are optimized in a targeted manner before you start the next project. However, only projects bring in the necessary money to justify the existence of the IT department in the first place. This is especially true for external support, which could be used to adapt and renew processes. So longer phases, in which "first of all calm needs to be restored in the company", in which the necessary adjustments are carried out, remain wishful thinking. This can be seen very clearly time and again in economic crises – such as at the turn of the millennium, in the financial crisis around 2010, and in the Corona crisis in 2020. Actually, there would now be sufficient time to finally improve the processes, to catch up on the documentation, and to clean up.

© Springer Fachmedien Wiesbaden GmbH, part of Springer Nature 2022
F. Witte, *Strategy, Planning and Organization of Test Processes*,
https://doi.org/10.1007/978-3-658-36981-1

However, if there is more time to tackle elementary problems due to a declining order situation or a more difficult economic situation, this quickly leads to financial problems, staff cuts, savings with the red pen and even greater restriction to the essential. The optimization of the processes is then rather downstream, if one does not know at all whether the organization can continue to exist in this form or it will face the thread of an insolvency.

Companies usually make the crucial mistakes when they are doing (too) well: They have enough revenue anyway and expect a respectable return, so they can afford less productive processes. Whether all defects are discovered or not, is not a decisive factor. If necessary, an improved software version is rolled out, as there are enough financial resources available anyway. The bottleneck is more likely to be the available personnel that is not able to finish on time due to work overload. Certainly, you might not be working efficiently, but that is not considered that important in this case. Experience shows that efficiency is a secondary criterion anyway; if it were actually about that, process improvements would be tackled much more aggressively. However, if the company is currently experiencing a decline in sales and a slump in profits, people think more about how they can leverage optimization potential and are therefore more anxious not to make mistakes and not to generate additional effort.

One speaks of the balance between "brain" and "capital": In times of crisis, when less capital is available, it is particularly important to achieve improvements through mind, knowledge and innovation and to return to one's strengths, rather than in times when deficits can rather be compensated by money. This can be observed in projects, but also in daily life. A country that has a lot of raw materials does not have to worry as much about innovation as a country lacking in raw materials. Those who have inherited richly need to make less effort to increase money, but only to be careful not to lose it through thoughtless functions. If you compare countries rich in raw materials like Russia or Saudi Arabia with a country lacking raw materials like Germany, this becomes particularly clear.

Since there is little that can be done about the general conditions, it is even more important to point this out and also not to expose oneself to too much pressure to succeed. I have already experienced that projects that were started with great enthusiasm were stopped or stretched. The purpose is not clear to the observer, and in purely economic terms, it is also a bad decision, at least in the medium term. However, since quarterly thinking and shareholder value have come to the scene in companies, it usually happens that some useful improvements that can only take effect over a longer period of time are not made at all, but instead mainly "low-hanging fruits" are harvested. Therefore, it is not unusual if the risks from project A in year 1 can be taken over almost as they are for project B in year 2. The advantage with project B is simply that you already know from the past how to deal with it and, in the best case, the calculation for project B already takes these restrictions into account. In many cases, however, you inherit a project as a test manager and were not even involved in the effort estimations. You are often working within a narrow, predefined framework.

If you look at testing activities generically and can introduce new processes as a staff department or quality department, you are more likely to be able to set new standards in this regard. However, a blunt analysis of the operational reality is an absolute prerequisite for this. To this end, the individual test departments should also be strongly involved. The quality department is often seen as a theoretical and abstract group. Norms and standards, however, must be translated for everyday operational use. Quality assurance will only find acceptance if it shows concretely, using examples and real functions, how internal processes can be optimized without generating only additional effort for the departments involved (development, test, system design ...) to create new documents.

From concept to implementation, the individual actions to be completed during the test are recorded in a plan and the completion is tracked. However, it is often not known who depends on whom, which actions are interrelated or build on each other. The documentation usually does not provide this information, and workflow documents are rare. That's why you often have to ask around. Especially in corporate groups and large projects with numerous internal and external participants, this overview can become very complex. However, as a test manager, it is highly recommended being aware of the dependencies and to understand the technical requirements to a certain extent, otherwise you will not be sufficiently accepted by the testers.

It is becoming increasingly important to think in terms of processes. Process structure versus functional structure – this contrast inhibits the development of process excellence in companies. Promising process management projects often cannot fully develop their effect due to the existing functional structure because a coherent process responsibility does not exist. The long-term structural element in companies are few but essential business processes which are necessary for a successful business model in every company. With a real process structure, a company becomes less dependent on individuals and decision makers who frequently change jobs and companies. Sustainable successful process excellence in companies requires a reorientation of the leadership and corporate culture, an integrated thinking and acting in processes. Process responsibility must be established as the sole management principle [ZANG2009].

Thanks to a real process structure, it is easier to develop a suitable test strategy. This also helps during the project with the test activities from the creation of the specification to test execution and test automation to the reporting of the results.

Every project, every industry, every requirement is ultimately individual. Again and again, entirely new challenges arise in a new project. There are also always things that are so special in the organizational unit being analyzed those standard suggestions can no longer be applied to them, and one has to live with the deficit. It is always important to name this as a risk in advance and to address it in a appropriate place.

From the concept phase, there is a smooth transition to the implementation phase. But a test concept must develop, it must not be set in stone but rather be adapted to the operational needs. The more you refer to the test concept again and again, the more likely it is to become a central document in the development and testing process and not just managed as an alibi document.

Test management is evolving. The agile transformation has reached many companies. Often, however, the implementation of the specifications has only been carried out to some extent. Due to changes in the environment of agile processes, test management is faced with new challenges that go hand in hand with a higher degree of test automation and new structures and therefore also require a conceptual realignment. New technological trends, from artificial intelligence to blockchains to quantum computers, will continue to lead to a high level of dynamism in software development and make well-thought-out test management even more important in the future. The biggest growth will be in companies where software is not a tool that supports workflows, production or communication and that you buy later as an add-on, but is increasingly becoming a mindset that is part of the core product and thus one of the most profitable benefits. With the introduction of a pure IT implementation and the introduction of a few agile methods and tools in the daily work routine it is no longer done, software must be a central self-image in all areas of the company. As a result, the pressure for technological change will continue to increase. Software development and therefore also test management will reach a stage of higher product maturity, in which classic industries such as mechanical engineering or vehicle construction have already been for a long time. The processes of industrialization and standardization of test processes, which have already been observed for several years, will increase as a result. As software testing is changing and will continue to grow in importance, the need for strategic planning and organization of test projects thanks to clearly structured and complete test concepts will increase.In my book, I have pointed out in several parts how important communication is in projects and how often projects fail primarily because of poor communication and not because of technical or mathematical challenges. This includes agreeing on the terms used in the organizational unit. Everyone must understand the same thing by the name of a test environment, a software, a document or an abbreviation, otherwise a Babylonian confusion of language is pre-programmed. I have explained the terms in the text and added an index at the end of the book. This procedure should also be a matter of course in companies. A separate glossary or a list of abbreviations and clear explanations of the procedures used are important in order not to talk past each other. Due to different organizational locations, different training and professional experience, different cultures but also different characters, the challenges of communication are complicated enough as it is. These are all problems that a test organization or even a good test concept can only influence within a narrow framework. In most cases, you have to deal with the existing framework conditions and still try to save the project.

Reference

[ZANG2009]: http://dodo.fb06.fh-muenchen.de/zangl/downloads/Prozessphilosophie.pdf Thinking and acting in processes. Prof. Dr. Hans Zangl, Munich University of Applied Sciences, 2009, accessed on 9 May 2020

Index

A

A/B test, 86
Acceptance
  criteria, 22, 107–114, 204
  tests, 4, 7, 8, 10, 14, 22, 46, 64, 65, 75, 80,
    81, 91, 94, 107–115, 136, 156, 203,
    220, 228, 234, 241, 247
Acceptance criteria
  catalog of criteria, 108–110
  processes, 107, 110, 112
  test, 22, 107, 109–113
  test environment, 112
Access
  management, 207
  rights, 157–159
Action alternative, 191–194, 196, 200
Adaptive method, 221
Agile
  procedure model, 43
  projects, 2, 10, 33, 42, 43, 60, 77–81, 111,
    112, 135, 140, 152, 233–238, 248
  testing, 10, 42, 43, 80, 94, 233–239, 242, 248
Amazon Web Service (AWS), 159–162
Amendment I, 150
Anonymization, 130
Application programming interface (API),
    133, 134
Area of impact
  factor, 200
Argument balance, 194, 200
Artificial intelligence, 241–243, 248
Automated data provision, 131
Autonomous project organization, 209
Availability management, 157

B

Balanced matrix organization, 211, 212
Balanced scorecard, 16–19
Black-box
  procedure, 72
  test, 74, 80
Blind approach, 132
Business-driven test management approach
    (BDTM), 219, 220

C

Change
  management, 2, 56, 84, 121, 122, 148, 157,
    247, 248
Chat, 51
Checkpoints, 224, 225, 227, 230
Client, 22, 31, 42, 46, 55, 62, 75, 89, 97, 101,
    102, 104, 107–111, 122, 125, 149,
    153, 158, 216, 220, 221, 235
CMMI, 12, 225
COCOMO
  II method, 180, 188–190
  model, 179
Code inspection, 90, 97
Combined approach, 132
Communication
  matrix, 166–171
  planning, 168, 174
  target, 167
  way, 5, 172
Complexity
  of communication, 164
  size according to Rechenberg, 81

© Springer Fachmedien Wiesbaden GmbH, part of Springer Nature 2022
F. Witte, *Strategy, Planning and Organization of Test Processes*,
https://doi.org/10.1007/978-3-658-36981-1

Component test, 22, 46, 73–75, 97, 116, 156
Computing times, 52, 53
Configuration management, 14, 84, 157, 217
Conflict management, 122, 176–177
Consequence table, 195–196, 200
Continuous integration, 86, 234
Contractual penalty, 46
Controlled, 15, 56, 157, 226–229
Cost
    development index, 213
    deviation, 213
    estimates, 182, 213
    performance index (CPI), 213
    variance (CV), 213
Cost and financial plan, 30
CPM plans, 182
Critical path, 52, 182, 183,
    186–188, 224
Critique the product, 234
Crowd
    sourced testing, 236
    testing, 236
Customer perspective, 17
Cyclomatic complexity, 81

D
Dead-lock situation, 85
Data
    masking, 130
    provision, 54, 104, 157, 159
    virtualization, 130
Date
    plan, 30, 33, 52
Decision
    problems, 25, 200–201, 242
    technology, 193, 200, 201
    tree, 196–197, 200
Defect
    classes, 133
    detection curve, 40, 41
    source, 133, 165
Defect burndown rate, 141
Defect classes, 46–47
Defect guessing, 76
Defect manager, 149
Definition of done, 239

Degree of autonomy, 242
Delegation, 148, 167
Documents, 1–8, 10, 14, 21, 22, 27, 32, 33, 38,
    39, 42–47, 61, 65–66, 75, 84, 90, 97,
    108, 109, 111, 112, 136–138,
    140–143, 149, 168, 186, 195, 218,
    220, 238, 247, 248

E
Efficient, 77, 80, 84, 96, 104, 130, 172, 216,
    226, 228–229, 233
Enablers, 40, 225, 228–230
EN 50128, 12
Estimate to complete (ETC), 213
Evaluation of the progress of the project,
    212, 213
Expected residual costs, 213
Exploratory testing, 13, 76–77, 235
External test environments, 158–159
Extreme programming, 80

F
FCC CUTS VIDS touring heuristics, 76
Feature list, 65
Features, 3, 4, 10, 29, 40, 63–65, 76, 83, 89–91,
    121, 124, 159, 216, 217,
    220, 233–239
Financial perspective, 17
Functional tests, 74, 83, 85, 147–149
Function points, 23, 33, 34

G
Gantt charts, 183–186

H
Hardware, 11, 12, 14, 33, 52–54, 66, 75, 85, 91,
    96, 104, 109, 115, 116, 121, 124,
    157, 159, 160, 162
HICCUPPS, 76

I
IEC 61508, 12
IEC 62034 standard, 150, 151

IEEE 829 Standard for Software Test
    Documentation, 1, 2
Impact analysis, 153
Impact domain, 67
Incremental integration, 74
Influencing factors test effort, 70
Information
    contents, 33, 68, 168, 170
    exchange, 167, 176, 237
    problems, 5, 23, 51, 176
Initial, 3, 11, 62, 80, 81, 95, 160, 164, 180, 183,
    217, 226, 227
Integration
    strategies, 10–13, 74, 78, 79, 81
    tests, 7, 10–13, 22, 27, 74, 75, 77, 79–81,
        86, 94, 116, 136, 150, 151, 188, 195,
        196, 198, 217, 239
Integrity levels, 6–8, 135–136
ISO 12207, 6, 136
ISO 15288, 6, 136
ISO 25010, 235
ISO 26262, 12
ISO 9126, 7, 136
ISO 91266, 136
ISO/IEC/IEEE 29119, 2
IT Governance, 220

K
Kanban, 234
Kick-off meeting, 61, 62

L
Launch events, 61
Load tests, 21, 27, 85, 97, 147, 156

M
Managed service model, 49
Master test plan, 7, 136, 220, 226
Master test plan metrics report, 7, 136
Matrix organization, 105, 210–211
Maturity
    process for the test organization, 226–227
Meeting, 50, 51, 56, 60–63, 75, 90, 149, 165,
        170–172, 176, 204, 228, 238

Method of investment calculation, 193
Metrics, 2, 5, 7, 15, 16, 22, 23, 64, 87, 136,
        137, 141–143, 203, 218, 221, 225,
        239, 243
Mock objects, 96
Model-based testing (MBT), 133
Multivariate tests, 86
Mutation approach, 132

N
Network, 75, 96, 138, 182, 183,
        185, 186
Non-incremental integration, 74

O
Object model, 67
Object points, 33
Office environment, 231
On premise, 160
Operational structure, 152
Optimizing, 140, 217, 218, 226,
        229–230, 237
Oracle, 76, 77, 133
Organization
    plans, 9, 22, 52, 103, 107
    problems, 151, 191, 234, 246, 248
    structure, 11, 54, 104, 105,
        152, 248

P
Peer reviews, 218
Permanent test organizations, 101–105,
        220, 221
Personality traits, 176
Planning and control, 56, 59–61, 148
Potential perspective, 17
PRINCE 2, 56
Prioritization, 84, 93–99, 148, 149, 211
Private clouds, 160
Problem solving process, 151–152
Procedure-oriented strategy, 74
Process excellence, 247
Process perspective, 17
Product risks, 127, 221, 226

Project
   communication, 51, 53, 71, 121,
      164, 166, 167, 171–172, 188,
      211, 233
   conditions, 29, 41, 156, 189–191, 246
   controlling, 55, 117, 142
   director, 169
   documentation, 91
   employees, 52, 56, 123, 168, 176, 186, 188,
      207, 209–211, 234
   lights, 25, 26
   management culture, 56
   organization, 12, 13, 22, 29, 31, 41, 53–56,
      66, 105, 107, 125, 136, 138, 139,
      172, 181, 188, 191, 207–213,
      219, 233
   planning, 29, 31–34, 40, 43, 52, 55, 62, 66,
      116, 120, 121, 142, 148, 167, 172,
      180, 181, 183, 185, 188, 191,
      217, 233
   product documentation, 5
   risks, 6, 10, 12, 30, 42, 62, 66, 84, 110, 120,
      121, 123, 127, 172, 187, 191
   schedule, 13, 30, 116, 157, 180
   situations, 17–19, 111, 116, 167, 219
   steering committee, 55–56, 204, 211
Project and sprint test strategy, 78
Pure project organization, 209, 210

Q
Quality
   targets, 12, 197, 236

R
RACI method, 172–173
RACIO, 173
RASCI, 173
Refactoring, 79, 80
Relationship
   management, 9, 177
   problems, 171, 177
Release
   management, 157, 204
   notes, 6, 65
Reporting, 2, 5, 24–26, 31, 64, 125, 137, 227
Report plan, 31
Requirements, 1, 7, 9, 10, 12, 14, 17, 21–24,
      32–33, 38, 40, 42, 43, 46–47, 49, 55,

      60, 63, 65–68, 70–72, 75–77, 83–85,
      87, 90, 96–98, 103, 105, 107, 108,
      111, 112, 121–125, 135, 136, 138,
      141, 144, 148–151, 153, 171–172,
      175, 181, 186, 188, 210, 218, 220,
      224, 226, 229, 231, 233,
      237–239, 247
Requirements management, 84, 122, 245
Resource plans, 30
Responsibilities, 2, 26, 32, 49, 54, 62, 76, 89,
      102, 125, 126, 148, 163–174, 177,
      182, 211–212, 225, 227, 228,
      230, 247
Review, 6, 30, 39, 50, 61, 90, 91, 121, 141, 142,
      149, 151, 154, 176, 186, 204, 217,
      218, 224, 228
Risk
   analysis, 63, 66, 110, 199, 221, 226
   -based testing, 98, 99, 127
   plan, 2, 98, 110, 154, 221
Roller
   planning, 43, 75

S
Schedule
   compression factor, 180
   performance index (SPI), 213
   variance (SV), 213
Scrum
   process, 79
Share
   processes, 216
Software lifecycle, 227
SPICE, 12, 14, 225
Sprint, 11, 77, 80, 81, 140, 151, 234, 236, 239
Staffing plan, 185
Staff line project organization, 207–208
Stakeholder
   -analysis, 168, 169
Standard DIN 69901, 29
Standards, 1–4, 6, 7, 12, 22, 29, 39, 41, 59, 63,
      76, 89, 97, 102, 105, 124, 135, 136,
      148–151, 171, 215, 217, 219,
      223, 247
Start-up workshop, 61, 62
Status Report, 5, 7, 50, 62, 136, 142, 150
Steering committee, 26, 55, 56, 61, 169
Strategy processes, 43
Stress tests, 85, 147

Supporting the team, 234
SWOT analyses, 194–195, 199, 200
System
    -lifecycle, 136
    -test, 2–4, 23, 32–34, 54, 60, 63, 66, 68, 72,
        74, 75, 80, 85, 91, 94, 97, 134, 138,
        143, 144, 150, 151, 153, 155, 156,
        160, 221, 238

T
Targeted approach, 132
Test
    aborts, 115–117, 138, 139
    analyst, 53, 149
    architecture, 33, 74, 96, 116
    automation, 18, 34, 41, 53, 63, 68, 71, 77,
        93, 98, 102, 112, 147, 150, 163, 175,
        187, 188, 204, 216, 239, 243,
        247, 248
    cases, 3, 4, 7, 10–15, 21–26, 31, 32, 34, 38,
        39, 42, 43, 49–54, 59, 60, 63–65, 67,
        68, 70–78, 80, 81, 83–87, 89, 91,
        93–99, 103, 109–117, 122, 124, 125,
        132, 133, 136–139, 142–144,
        147–150, 152–158, 163–166, 171,
        174, 175, 186–188, 216, 219, 224,
        228, 229, 235, 237–239, 241–243,
        246, 248
    case specification, 3, 4, 181
    charter, 239
    clusters, 83
    concepts, 2–3, 10–13, 25–27, 30, 32, 33,
        37–47, 49, 60, 63–65, 68, 73, 75, 78,
        83, 84, 87, 89, 90, 93, 94, 109, 110,
        116, 117, 120, 121, 137, 141, 143,
        147–150, 152, 164, 165, 174, 175,
        182, 203, 204, 239, 245, 247, 248
    cover, 10, 22, 37, 73, 80, 113, 133, 230, 231
    data generators, 132, 133
    data provision, 52
    design specifications, 3, 4
    deviation report, 5
    directive, 40, 105
    documentation, 7, 9, 12, 13, 32, 85, 116,
        135–137, 139–141, 148, 150, 151,
        204, 216, 245, 247
    driven development, 10, 79, 80, 234
    duration, 3, 15, 98, 112, 179–181, 191, 234

    effort, 4, 10–14, 23, 32, 34, 38, 52, 53, 68,
        74, 86, 93, 96, 98, 116, 124, 132,
        140, 185, 187–189, 216, 224, 236,
        246, 247
    effort estimates, 226
    environment, 3, 11, 12, 14, 15, 38, 54, 64,
        70, 73, 75, 80, 81, 91, 94, 96, 101,
        102, 110, 112, 113, 115, 124, 130,
        139, 143, 147–149, 151, 152,
        154–163, 181, 186, 189, 221, 236,
        239, 245, 248
    environment in the cloud, 159–162
    environment management, 156–157, 175
    environment manager, 148
    evaluation report, 5
    expense planning, 96, 116
    factory models, 49
    factory services, 49
    fallback state, 83
    final report, 64
    goal-oriented strategy, 74
    indicator, 25, 141, 188
    interruption, 41, 116
    log, 4, 7, 74, 136–138
    manager, 5, 7, 10, 14, 22, 24, 25, 33, 34, 39,
        40, 42–44, 46, 50–53, 62, 64, 79, 89,
        116, 117, 124, 136, 143, 154, 158,
        164–166, 170, 171, 174, 182, 186,
        192, 207, 215, 216, 220, 221, 230,
        237, 238, 245–247
    maturity matrix, 224
    methods, 33, 39, 67, 72, 74, 78, 86, 95, 96,
        101, 104, 113, 130, 132, 133, 137,
        138, 148, 215–224, 230, 234–237,
        239, 248
    object handover report, 6
    objects, 2, 3, 6, 12, 21, 22, 39, 40, 46, 63,
        67–74, 81, 83, 86, 89, 96, 97, 99,
        110, 115, 132–134, 137, 138, 141,
        143, 148, 149, 155, 157, 186,
        188, 191, 203, 220, 221, 224,
        234, 237
    organization, 7–9, 11, 49–56, 70, 72,
        101–105, 152, 156, 159, 215, 221,
        223, 225, 227–230, 233–239, 248
    personnel, 2, 52–53, 103, 104, 119, 147,
        154, 175–176, 230
    phases, 5, 10, 12, 15, 21, 22, 24, 26, 32, 39,
        46, 52, 61, 63, 67–72, 80, 91, 108,

116, 117, 120, 141, 154, 158, 160,
164, 180–186, 203, 204, 216,
245, 247

plan, 2, 7, 13, 25, 32, 33, 40, 52, 81, 91, 114,
136, 137, 139, 141, 147, 152, 157, 174,
179, 183, 186, 229, 235, 247

planning, 2, 3, 12, 29, 32–34, 51–53, 70, 76,
77, 137, 140, 148, 149, 160, 174,
179, 182–188, 218, 220, 221, 228,
233, 248

points, 6, 12, 25, 39, 40, 42, 50, 51, 53, 74,
75, 98, 102, 104, 109, 116, 138, 148,
157, 158, 187, 219, 226, 236, 239,
243, 246

processes, 2, 3, 5–7, 12, 13, 15, 21, 23, 33, 38,
42, 46, 52, 59–61, 63–65, 68, 77, 79,
81, 84, 89, 91, 94, 98, 101–105, 110,
117, 133, 136, 144, 151, 154, 157, 158,
160–163, 166, 207, 215–231, 233, 234,
236, 239, 242, 243, 245, 247, 248

process improvement (TPI), 216, 224,
225, 231

productivity, 34, 40, 50, 51, 91, 188–190

progress, 5, 6, 24, 25, 40, 51, 75, 115, 141,
144, 148, 150, 164, 182, 220, 221

progress report, 6, 50

reporting, 4–6, 24–27, 34, 60, 124, 143,
225, 231, 237, 247

reports, 4, 5, 7, 26, 50, 136, 137, 141, 143,
148, 170, 171, 203, 204, 218, 220,
221, 237

required, 3–5, 7, 13–15, 23–25, 34, 43,
52–54, 60, 63, 68, 75, 81, 85, 89, 91,
94, 96, 110, 130, 133, 136–138, 140,
143, 147, 148, 153, 155–158, 160,
175, 182, 203, 218, 219, 224, 233

resources, 3, 15, 32, 33, 41, 52, 60, 63, 95,
98, 99, 105, 116, 123, 130, 148, 154,
186, 208, 228, 229, 245

restart, 41, 116–117, 138

risks, 2, 3, 11, 14, 21, 33, 41, 51, 63, 64, 81,
85, 90, 91, 98, 110, 116, 117,
120–127, 149, 154–156, 182, 201,
204, 220, 221, 226, 245, 246

scenarios, 11, 63, 64, 74, 76

scheduling, 3, 52, 54, 157, 183, 185, 238

scope, 2, 3, 10, 12, 13, 27, 29, 33, 47, 49,
60, 63, 75, 76, 93–94, 109, 112, 114,
139, 142, 154, 166, 174, 182, 191,
199, 229, 237

script, 4, 15, 34, 52, 77, 85, 93, 102, 133,
137–139, 147, 152, 157, 163, 239

services, 49, 86, 101–103, 149, 158, 159,
216, 225, 227–230

specifications, 3–4, 7, 12–15, 21, 27, 33, 42,
43, 64, 68, 74, 75, 83, 111, 132, 138,
140, 147, 150, 151, 175, 226, 230,
247, 248

stage profile, 6

stages, 4, 7, 10, 11, 13, 21, 78, 81, 89, 98,
132, 136, 141, 153, 154, 163, 203,
204, 216, 220, 239, 248

strategies, 9–18, 38, 77–80, 151, 216, 218,
220, 221, 229, 247

target, 13, 18, 21, 33, 70, 86, 132–134,
143, 156

tasks, 2, 3, 11, 22, 23, 29, 34, 40, 43, 46, 53,
73, 84, 102, 103, 123, 134, 138, 147,
148, 150, 153, 154, 164, 175, 177,
180, 233, 234, 238, 242

tasks in regression testing, 152–153

tools, 4, 11–15, 27, 31, 32, 34, 39, 50, 52,
78, 81, 83, 85, 101–104, 115, 124,
133–134, 148, 151, 153–154, 157,
182, 221, 228, 229, 241, 242, 248

Test effort, 11, 29, 34, 51, 52, 70–72, 81,
103, 110, 115, 182, 186–188,
221, 226

Testing maturity model (TMMI), 217–218

Test points, 33, 40, 188

Test process improvement (TPI), 219, 225, 227

Testware management, 231

Time deviation, 213

TMap, 216, 219–222

TPI model, 223–225

TPI next, 223–231

Traceability matrix, 65, 141, 204

U
User stories, 10, 79, 80, 111–113, 239

Utility analysis, 197–200

V
VARISC, 173

Versioning, 37, 39, 84

W
White-box
procedure, 72
test, 74, 80, 132

Work breakdown structure (WBS), 30

Work plan, 176, 179–190

Printed in the United States
by Baker & Taylor Publisher Services